Volunteers
and
the Making of
Presidents

VOLUNTEERS AND THE MAKING OF PRESIDENTS

Jane Dick

DODD, MEAD & COMPANY

NEW YORK

Grateful acknowledgment is made to the Oral History Collection of Columbia University for the use of excerpts from the following:

The Reminiscences of Ralph H. Cake, copyright, 1977 by the Trustees of Columbia University in the City of New York.

The Reminiscences of Lucius D. Clay, Sr., copyright, 1977 by the Trustees of Columbia University in the City of New York.

The Reminiscences of Jacqueline Cochran, copyright, 1975 by the Trustees of Columbia University in the City of New York.

The Reminiscences of Arthur Gray, Jr., copyright, 1977 by the Trustees of Columbia University in the City of New York.

The Reminiscences of Mary Pillsbury Lord, copyright, 1980 by the Trustees of Columbia University in the City of New York.

The Reminiscences of Dr. Charles Masterson and Howard K. Pyle, Jr., copyright, 1980 by the Trustees of Columbia University in the City of New York.

The Reminiscences of Stanley M. Rumbough, Jr., copyright, 1977 by the Trustees of Columbia University in the City of New York.

1 2 3 4 5 6 7 8 9 10

Library of Congress Cataloging in Publication Data

Dick, Jane.
Volunteers and the making of Presidents.

Includes index.
1. Presidents—United States—Election.
2. Electioneering—United States. 3. Voluntarism—
United States. 4. United States—Politics and
government—1945. I. Title.
JK524.D52   324.7'2   79–27734
ISBN 0–396–07839–7

To my husband, Eddie,
with gratitude and love.
And in memory of our daughter,
Marnie Dick Last.

Illustrations

Contents

Acknowledgments

There are two friends to whom I owe the most: Lloyd Garrison and Calvin Fentress III. Lloyd's interest, help, and confidence in this book and the many opportunities I had to test my ideas against his well-informed mind have been an inspiration. And without Calvin's earlier diplomatic but insistent prodding, I might never have started to write it.

I am very grateful to many others, who were most generous in giving me extensive interviews. Theodore White was one of the first to encourage me, during a general discussion of my project and of the Stevenson chapters particularly.

For information on the Willkie chapters, I turned to Oren Root, Marcia Davenport, former Governor Harold Stassen of Minnesota, Gardner Cowles, the late James A. Farley, Stefan Lorenz, the late Glen A. Lloyd, and the late David A. Randall, who was Librarian of the Lilly Collection at Indiana University, where the Willkie papers are deposited.

On the Eisenhower chapters, I consulted George A. Poole, Stanley M. Rumbough, Jr., the late Mary Pillsbury Lord, and Louis M. Starr of the Butler Library at Columbia University, who gave me access to the Eisenhower histories in their Oral

History Collection. These are verbatim transcripts of personal interviews with Charles F. Willis, Jr., Stanley M. Rumbough, Jr., General Lucius Clay, Jacqueline Cochran, Arthur Gray, Jr., Ralph H. Cake, Mary Lord, Dr. Charles Masterson, Howard K. Pyle, Jr., and others, which were invaluable to me. I am grateful to all of the foregoing, and to the Eisenhower Library in Abilene, Kansas, for their cooperation.

For recollections used in the Stevenson chapters, in addition to Lloyd Garrison, I am very much indebted to William McC. Blair, Jr., Walter Johnson, Hermon D. Smith, Carl McGowan, Willard Wirtz, Barry Bingham, the late Archibald Alexander, Katie Louchheim, Clayton Fritchey, Mary McGrory, Richard F. Babcock, Porter McKeever, Ralph Martin, former Governor Edmund G. ("Pat") Brown, Sr., of California, Edward D. McDougal, Jr., Judge Hubert Will, Chester Kerr, John Hersey, the late Jack Shea and his wife, Felice, a judge, Edward Costikyan, Stanley Karson, Florence Medow, and Walter Skallerup.

I am grateful, too, to Jane Gunther, Franklin D. Roosevelt, Jr., Marjorie Benton, Gene Pokorny, Curtis Gans, Charles S. Potter, Mary Swander, Ruth Huey, Stuart Forbes, and to Arthur Miller of the Lake Forest College Library for help in various ways. And I particularly want to thank a dear friend, Ellen Garrison, for her interest and encouragement while I was writing this book, and for making her and Lloyd's home a haven for living, working, interviewing, and drawing inspiration when my work so frequently took me to New York. My great indebtedness to my husband and family for their support and patience goes without saying.

I should like to thank Sally Wise and Marianne Larsen for their enthusiastic and helpful research. And there is only one Margaret Wells, who typed this manuscript, quite literally day and night, for months, turning into years, and never said no to an SOS from me. My long-standing gratitude to her remains boundless. Mrs. Herbert Kahn typed the final draft expertly for the publisher, and I want to thank her as well as Elda Orpet,

Sandra Lechner, and Anne Gottschalk who typed various sections of the manuscript from time to time.

Finally, to my superb and patient editor, Allen Klots of Dodd Mead & Company, go my very special thanks for the delightful, educational, and stimulating experience of working with him.

Jane Dick
Lake Forest, Illinois

Introduction

Every fourth year hundreds of thousands of ordinary Americans —men, women, students and, often, quite young children— plunge into the extravaganza of a presidential campaign. The majority of these volunteers are apolitical during three and a half years out of every four. But, when campaign time rolls around, a charismatic candidate, an emotional issue, or a telephone call from a neighbor will rouse them to action.

The experience or know-how of these amateur politicians ranges from zero (a suburban housewife who has responded to her neighbor's call), through fifty percent (the highly motivated college student who has majored in political science), to the old-time volunteer who has already worked in at least one campaign and, by now, rates himself or herself on a par with the pros. What these people have in common is enthusiasm and total dedication for the duration of the campaign.

Surprisingly, in spite of every American's vaunted right to participate politically, it was not until the election of 1940 that amateurs actually organized nationwide to nominate their own presidential candidate. That year the amateur Willkie Clubs dramatically routed the old guard pro-Taft bosses at the Republican National Convention and nominated Wendell Willkie. They then proceeded to become the backbone of his presidential campaign. Twelve years later—in 1952—amateurs supporting both candidates, Dwight Eisenhower and Adlai Stevenson, played key roles in the nominating processes and added their own special fervor to that memorable campaign.

Though Eisenhower was reluctant when he was first urged to seek the nomination (at one point both parties approached him), the popular clamor for him, which organized itself into a national network of citizen groups, finally overcame his doubts. Under this mounting pressure, he resigned as supreme commander of the Allied powers in Europe, charged with organizing the defense forces of the North Atlantic Treaty Organization (NATO), and came home to campaign for the Republican nomination.

The effect of the hero's return was electric, and it was reciprocal. The fervor of his followers mounted almost to a frenzy with every personal or television appearance and the laudatory stories that poured out daily onto the front pages of every morning and evening newspaper. These demonstrations of affection and admiration from his countrymen so moved the General that he responded with unexpected ardor to the crowds and with a new zeal to fulfill their belief in him. Campaigning, which he had rather dreaded as a duty, became an exhilaration, and his famous grin and expansive gestures, in turn, communicated this to his cheering audiences.

Adlai Stevenson was more than reluctant. He did not want to be nominated for the presidency. He wanted to remain as governor of Illinois, and he did everything in his power, up to the very moment of his nomination, to discourage a small but determined group of amateurs from working for his nomination.

They succeeded in spite of his adamant position. When he made his acceptance speech, which was carried over all the major television networks, despite the time (it was nearly two o'clock in the morning), it seemed that almost everyone in the country was listening. His eloquent inspirational message— such an extraordinary departure from the traditional political speech—so moved the country that his admirers, both Democrats and Republicans, had become legion overnight.

He waged his campaign in the same spirit and on the same level. His amateurs immediately coalesced into a nationwide volunteer organization, and the pride that they took in his special brand of campaigning inspired them to selfless devotion and hard work throughout the campaign.

John Mason Brown said of the two 1952 candidates: The General and the Governor were both men whose goodness and modesty were beyond question. They were equally determined to clean up "the mess in Washington." They were equally honest, equally concerned with efficient government, and equally convinced that, to be healthy at the top, it must be healthy at its lowest levels. Each was animated by the same genuine patriotism. Each had the same passion for peace. And both, in their very different abilities, were uncommon men.

Since 1952, neither Republican nor Democratic organizations have dared ignore the amateurs. In fact, if a party's candidate does not personally inspire spontaneous citizen activity, the organization will even recruit a "citizens" or "volunteers" arm, and try to sell this synthetic front organization as the real thing.

But the real thing is quite different. Only on rare occasions does a magnetic leader, speaking to the deep concerns of a large segment of the population, as happened in 1940 and again in 1952, inspire a groundswell of public enthusiasm across the country. Local groups will meet, local clubs will organize spontaneously and independently, lines of communication will develop overnight, and before the politicians are aware of it a grass roots movement, bent on the nomination or election of a popular favorite, usually not the organization's favorite, has been launched.

Prior to the 1940 Willkie campaign, there had been only three in American history that can be compared with it insofar as they inspired ordinary citizens to political activity: the campaigns for the election of Andrew Jackson in 1824, for the nomination of John Charles Frémont in 1856, and for the nomination and election of Abraham Lincoln in 1860. Citizen activity then differed from that of the twentieth century primarily in two respects. First, the amateurs were probably just as enthusiastic, but they all organized locally, never nationally, which greatly diluted their effectiveness. Second, no tradition of continuing citizen activity was sparked by any of these campaigns. But, because of the similarities between them and those of 1940 and 1952, and because of their intrinsic interest, I shall discuss them briefly in the opening chapter.

It was the three colorful candidacies—those of Willkie, Eisenhower, and Stevenson—in this century which aroused such a surge of popular enthusiasm that almost the entire population became involved either as active participants or enthusiastic rooters. Moreover, the interest in and respect for politics that these campaigns engendered did not evaporate with the end of the campaigns. Many of the amateurs, having found the experience so exhilarating, the game so fascinating, and the stakes so important, moved on into local or state party politics and infused new life and ideas into both parties at the all-important grass-roots level.

In the opinion of James Q. Wilson, author of *The Amateur Democrat,* "the principal reward of politics to the amateur is the sense of having satisfied a felt obligation to 'participate,'" and he adds that the greater the aims, the greater the satisfaction. This applies not only to amateurs in politics, but also to citizen volunteers in a variety of other fields. To appreciate their achievements, one has only to consider their tremendous contributions in such important movements as those for civil rights, environmental protection, equal rights for women, Chicanos, Latinos, and American Indians, and the anti-Vietnam

War movement. The volunteers in these various movements have awakened public opinion, influenced legislation, and revealed the power of aroused citizen action. Since this book is about volunteers in electoral politics, however, a discussion of their participation in other areas is beyond its scope.

United Press International Photo

A national party convention is one of the focal points of volunteer political activity. Shown above is Chicago's International Amphitheatre as the 1952 Republican National Convention opened its first ses-

I

Yesterday

In early July 1952, shortly before the Republican National Convention was to open, General Dwight Eisenhower, greatly admired by the American public but no favorite of the professionals who controlled the convention machinery, arrived in Chicago to seek his party's nomination for the presidency. Chicago was well known as "Taft territory." Colonel Robert R. McCormick, powerful publisher of the *Chicago Tribune,* was an ardent Taft supporter. Senator Robert Taft had been defeated twice for the nomination, and the Colonel knew that he could do a great deal in his home territory to right this dreadful injustice. In addition, the dominant wing of the party was solidly behind Taft.

The Illinois Citizens for Eisenhower, an organization which had been working for several months in the face of these formidable obstacles to gain overt support for their candidate, realized that all of the newspapers, newsreel and television cameras from the whole country would be at the station to cover the popular general's arrival. What if a sparse crowd were there to greet him? The group had been valiantly struggling for several months to put together a statewide organization in this isolationist state and pro-Taft city. Now it would have to call on its spotty, scattered, but devoted organization to deliver.

So they put on a telephone blitz; office and home telephones began to hum, importuning the heads of every committee in the greater Chicago area to get their troops to the station to greet the man they wanted for president.

When Eisenhower stepped off his train at eight o'clock that morning, seven thousand fans, shrieking "We want Ike" and waving improvised signs and banners, mobbed the General. The crowd filled Northwestern Station's huge central waiting room and the great train shed. No one who saw the look on Ike's face when he took in the enormity of his welcome will ever forget it.

He slowly made his way, with police assistance, down the platform until he was in the center of the crowd in the train shed. Suddenly, he vaulted onto a flat baggage cart. The crowd went wild and, grinning his famous grin, Ike held up his hand for silence and said, "They told me Illinois is enemy territory. If this is what it is, I want a lot more of it." Pictures and news accounts of his arrival in Chicago were on the front page of every newspaper in the country.

Political amateurs, such as those who organized the Chicago welcome for Ike, are not a recent phenomenon in America. Amateurs have been part of American politics since before there was a United States. Fundamentally, the American Revolution was put together by amateurs: young men like Thomas Jefferson, rabble-rousers like Sam Adams, pamphleteers, farmers, and middle-class merchants. Theodore White, in an interview which he granted me, points out that "all revolutions, all great upheavals, eventually fossilize in structures—the administration, the bureaucracies, professional politicians, professional leaders," but that "every great upheaval in America . . . is presaged by an amateur movement."

Also, since before the founding of the Republic, citizens have organized peacefully to protest unfair or unpopular policies, including unjust taxes, the abridgment of civil rights or military action of which they disapproved. They have led the fights to update our antiquated state constitutions and spearheaded much local reform, and they have frequently joined together to support candidates or issues which aroused them. Alexis de Tocqueville's observation in 1832, that "Americans of all ages, all conditions and all dispositions, constantly form associations," has been true ever since. Over the years there have been countless state or local groups that have organized more or less spontaneously to support candidates with strong citizen appeal.

But the first presidential candidate that aroused a veritable frenzy of nationwide enthusiasm and citizen activity was Andrew Jackson in 1824, eight years before de Tocqueville made his observation. Essentially, this election was a contest between Jackson and John Quincy Adams. It was also the first in which the people really had an opportunity to participate. Though the president was technically elected by the electors, this was the first time that, owing to legislative reform in most states, the popular vote determined how the electors were to vote.

Many Americans are surprised to discover that originally, in the majority of states, the people did not vote for the presidential electors; the state legislatures did. Citizen resentment at having no direct voice in this process forced the gradual abandonment of the system and, by 1824, most states were electing their presidential electors by direct male popular vote.

The reform of the election process also permitted popular participation in the selection of candidates. No longer were they nominated by "King Caucus," a closed committee of the United States Congress, but rather by state legislatures and other bodies. Now the people had an incentive to band together in support of their own candidates. Moreover, that year a people's hero, Andrew Jackson, was one of the four presidential nominees—all running as Democratic-Republicans. If none of the candidates received a majority of the electoral votes, the House of Representatives was empowered to decide between them.

Never had the citizens taken such interest in the choice of their president. "Old Hickory" became a public idol. Meetings were held, resolutions adopted and Hickory Clubs formed. Hickory poles became Jackson's symbol and were soon being raised all over the country. A contemporary western newspaper reported that "the popularity of Jackson rests on the gratitude and confidence of the whole people. He is not an office seeker, he is not a party man, and if elected will owe it to no congressional caucus nor any legislative cabal. . . ."

Unfortunately, the people's choice was not the winner that year. Jackson, though he received the greatest number of electoral votes, did not have a majority. As a result, the decision was thrown into the House of Representatives. Though Jackson had ninety-nine votes to John Quincy Adams's eighty-four, Henry Clay, in what Jackson supporters called "a corrupt bargain," gave his electors, and the election, to Adams.

Four years later, the people had their victory and elected Andrew Jackson over Clay. In 1832, they re-elected him. But by 1828 the country's energies were concentrated on reviving the two-party system. More emphasis was placed on building mass nationwide support for the parties than on electing a popular hero, though it was extremely helpful to have one at the head of a ticket. Jackson's party was now called the Democratic-Republican party or simply the Democratic party and, in the campaigns of 1828 and 1832, the party bigwigs got behind their candidate. The Democratic professionals adopted many of the techniques that Jackson's amateur followers had used in 1824, even going so far as to rechristen many of their local ward committees "Hickory Clubs." The amateurs must have felt complimented. Great numbers of them volunteered to work for their hero with the party organization. But they learned, to their dismay, as the Citizens for Eisenhower did over a century later, that much of the creativity and elan of a volunteer movement is drained from it when it is absorbed by the regular party organization.

William Henry Harrison, when he ran for president on the Whig ticket in 1840, was an exception to the rule that it is the unusual candidate that inspires grand-scale popular enthusiasm and support. The complete antithesis of Jackson, this ordinary man had been only moderately successful both in civilian and (despite two or three legendary exploits) military life. Nonetheless, his backers—professionals with large reinforcements of eager volunteers—conducted such a clever grass-roots campaign, complete with innovative public relations gimmicks, that they created a people's hero. Fantastic crowds turned out at "Tippecanoe" rallies and drank carloads of cider and Log Cabin whiskey; "Tippecanoe and Tyler too" was a slogan that was soon being chanted on every town and village street in the country. No formal independent organization ever developed on Harrison's behalf, as he was the party's choice as well as the people's.

The popular fervor was so great at the end of the campaign that Harrison was elected by an overwhelming majority. Unfortunately, the electorate never knew whether he would have proven to be as great a president as they had believed, for he died in Washington one month after his inauguration.

A bizarre legacy of Harrison's campaign was provided by Philadelphia's E. C. Booz Distillery, which supplied all of the whiskey for the campaign and, in so doing, added a new word to the American language.

The nomination of John Charles Frémont as the Republican presidential candidate in 1856 and the campaign that followed were, in terms of popular demand, the closest historical prototypes of Wendell Willkie's eighty-four years later. One could not imagine two men who arrived on the political stage so differently equipped in background and experience as Frémont, the glamorous young pathfinder, explorer of the West, and Willkie, Wall Street's utility magnate. One characteristic that they had in common, however, was that mysterious quality we now call charisma. And one experience both of them lacked in common was any prior involvement in professional politics.

Tales of Frémont's courage and daring as he explored the

West had made him a public hero. After he married the charming and capable daughter of the influential Senator Thomas Hart Benton of Missouri, the story of their devotion and his reliance on her became legendary.

Both parties offered Frémont the nomination—the Democrats, tentatively, if he would endorse the Fugitive Slave Law and the Kansas-Nebraska Act. The former was designed by the Southern planters, and gave the federal government sweeping powers to catch and return runaway slaves. It provided heavy penalties for officials who did not strictly enforce the law, as well as for citizens who helped in any way in the escape of a slave. The bitterly contested Kansas-Nebraska Act, which had been passed in 1854 when the territories of Kansas and Nebraska were organized, allowed for the extension of slavery into these territories, and presumably into all subsequent ones. Frémont refused to endorse either.

This was the year that the new Republican party was being built around the issue of the compromise with slavery, and long before June 17, when the Republican convention was to meet in Philadelphia, Francis P. Blair, Sr., a distinguished Washington journalist and antislavery leader, called on Frémont. Blair announced, on behalf of a group headed by a galaxy of eminent writers, artists, and newspapermen, that Frémont was their choice for the presidential nomination. Though experienced in their own fields, these men were largely political amateurs. Blair had been close to President Jackson and other officeholders, but had held no political office himself. There were a few professionals among them, but very few. In this category there was one name that stood out, that of Abraham Lincoln, a young member of the Illinois legislature, whose debates with Stephen A. Douglas in Peoria, Illinois, the previous October had made him a national figure overnight. Frémont agreed to let his name be put in nomination at the convention.

These illustrious amateurs did not have an easy time at this first convention of the new Republican party. Much attention has been given by Frémont's biographers to the proponents of various interests who tried to thwart his nomination. Their machinations were as involved as were the anti-Willkie maneuvers years later. And chief among the maneuverers were the tough politicians who, as the historian Stefan Lorant, in an interview, observed, were forced, by popular demand, to accept Frémont's nomination, as their later counterparts at the 1940 Republican convention had to capitulate to the nomination of Wendell Willkie.

The Frémont-Buchanan campaign was as exciting and bitter as the Roosevelt-Willkie contest to come. It involved almost the entire electorate, and masses of volunteers poured into the Fremont Clubs which sprang up with amazing speed and spontaneity all over the country. Irving Stone, too, observed that the phenomenon "was not to be equaled until the advent of the Willkie Clubs in 1940."

Theodore White, in his interview with me, gave the amateurs massive credit for the nomination and election of Abraham Lincoln in 1860:

> There were never more amateurish people in the world than the abolitionists and the free-the-slave people and the good church people of Illinois and New Hampshire and Massachusetts. These were people who knew nothing about politics—nothing whatsoever—and they were ridiculous. But they had organized by 1854, they had put together a frivolous candidacy in 1856, and they had created a president in 1860.

In addition to these earnest abolition-minded amateurs, Lincoln had another broadly based army of volunteers which appeared more or less spontaneously, and was highly visible. The most succinct description of the origin of the "Wide-Awakes" was given, of course, by Lincoln's biographers, Nicolay and Hay:

> Political clubs, for parade and personal campaign work, were no novelty. Now, however, the expedients of a cheap but striking uniform and a half-military organization were tried with marked success. When Lincoln made his New England trip, immediately after

the Cooper Institute speech, a score or two of active Republicans in the city of Hartford appeared in close and orderly ranks, wearing each a cap and large cape of oil cloth [to protect their clothes from the wax dripping from their torches] and bearing over their shoulders a long staff, on the end of which blazed a brilliant torch-light. This first "Wide-Awake Club," as it called itself, marching with soldierly step and military music, escorted Mr. Lincoln on the evening of March 5, from the hall where he addressed the people, to his hotel. The device was so simple and yet so strikingly effective that it immediately became the pattern for other cities. After the campaign opened, there was scarcely a county or village in the North without its organized and drilled association of Wide-Awakes, immensely captivating to the popular eye, and forming everywhere a vigilant corps to spread the fame of, and solicit votes for the Republican Presidential candidate. On several occasions twenty to thirty thousand "Wide-Awakes" met in the larger cities and marched in monster torch-light processions through the principal streets.

A year less a day from the time the Wide-Awakes first escorted Mr. Lincoln through the streets of Hartford he was inaugurated president.

There have been, of course, other candidates who have aroused great popular enthusiasm, such as William Jennings Bryan, Democratic candidate for president against McKinley, whose "Cross of Gold" speech at the 1896 Democratic convention enthralled the electorate. But the party was solidly behind their candidate at this point and his idolatrous followers lent their weight to Bryan's campaign by turning out in vast numbers to cheer his spellbinding oratory.

Teddy Roosevelt was another. But the circumstances surrounding him were unique. Appointed Republican vice president in 1901, he became president that same year when McKinley was assassinated. A colorful and popular president, he was re-elected in 1905 with the strong backing of members—both professional and lay—of his party and many independents. Two of the most powerful forces motivating volunteers are the nonsupport or hostility of the party regulars for their favorite and the slim chance of his being nominated or elected without their help. The popular incumbent President Roosevelt had neither of these handicaps.

It was in 1940 that Wendell Willkie, a self-made captain of industry, electrified the country with his high-minded appeal to political idealism and global commitment, his staunch and reasoned advocacy of private enterprise, and his relentless opposition to the domestic policies of the New Deal, while patriotically supporting his opponent's foreign policy. A nationwide surge of admiration for this forthright man coalesced with amazing speed into the Willkie Clubs.

Wendell L. Willkie, whose astonishing nomination as Republican candidate for President in 1940 was largely attributable to the work of amateurs.

II

The Tycoon

On January 16, 1940, the *New York Sun* revealed that Wendell Willkie, a lifelong liberal and politically-active Democrat, had registered as a Republican. Why?

Could he possibly have dared dream that only five months later—in June of that year—the Republican party, at probably the most extraordinary convention in the history of either party, would have nominated, against their will, this newly-converted political maverick as their candidate for president of the United States? Yet this is precisely what happened.

Surprisingly, Arthur Krock, the *New York Times*'s respected and widely-read columnist, nearly a year before Willkie's official conversion, in his column of February 23, 1939, had first mentioned the name of the dynamic young president of the Commonwealth and Southern Corporation. He called Willkie "the darkest horse in the stable" for the 1940 Republican presidential nomination.

Scant attention was paid at the time to this passing reference, and Oren Root, Jr., who later organized the successful Willkie Clubs, claims that Willkie simply "happened" independently to a number of different people at about the same time.

In August 1939, Willkie "happened" to Russell Davenport, managing editor of *Fortune* magazine. Returning home from a meeting of the *Fortune* Round Table, Davenport announced to his wife, Marcia, "I've met the man who ought to be the next president of the United States."

"Whose idea is it," she asked. "His or yours?"

"It's spontaneous," he said. "You see him and you know it."

"I knew, of course," reports Mrs. Davenport, "that he meant Wendell Willkie." Shortly thereafter Willkie "happened" to influential columnists Dorothy Thompson and Raymond Clapper; then, via the Davenports, to Henry Luce of Time, Inc.; and subsequently to the Cowles brothers, Gardner and John, publishers of *Look* magazine as well as of newspapers in Minneapolis and Des Moines.

This formidable array of media power was to be an undoubted asset to Willkie in his spectacular campaign for the nomination for the presidency. When the ranks were subsequently swelled by the addition of banker Thomas W. Lamont and the bulk of the anti-Roosevelt financial and business community, however, Willkie was to find himself repeatedly charged with being a Wall Street captive and a stooge of big business. His attackers, however, did not take into account two very potent factors—the character of Wendell Willkie himself and the bold idea of a twenty-eight-year-old New York lawyer, Oren Root, Jr.

Willkie's background did not fit the stereotype of an eastern establishment figure. He was the grandson of German immigrants who left Europe following the revolutionary disturbances of 1848. Wendell, the fourth of six children, was born in 1892 into a moderately well-off family in the small town of Elwood, Indiana. Both his father and mother were lawyers, his mother being the first woman admitted to the Indiana bar. An indifferent student in grammar school, Wendell was more partial to outdoor sports and practical jokes than he was to studying. Nonetheless, his wide-ranging curiosity, his huge appetite for reading on those subjects that interested him, and his retentive mind prepared him well for high school. Here he was a popular student who divided his time more evenly between his studies and athletics.

At Indiana University he made a name for himself in various ways. He was independent, liberal, and articulate and outspoken both in private and public debate. His frequent challenges to conservative positions and his advocacy of socialism caused consternation in the faculty. He was, both by inheritance and conviction, a liberal Democrat and was active in the Campus Jackson Club.

To earn his tuition for law school he taught for a year at the high school in Coffeyville, Kansas, where he proved to be an enormously popular and stimulating teacher. This was followed by a summer job in Puerto Rico. Many years later he told Gardner Cowles that seeing the cruel and hopeless misery of the peons who worked the sugar plantations had been the major influence in his "not thinking like a typical American millionaire."

His law school career was brilliant, and its finale typical. He won every scholastic honor during his last year, but was given his degree only after heated debate among the law faculty and at the last moment in the privacy of the administration office. Having been chosen class orator, he had in his address, "The New Freedom," according to Donald Bruce Johnson in his *The Republican Party and Wendell Willkie,* "criticized the Indiana law school and the Indiana constitution before an audience which included a majority of the Supreme Court justices of the State," and he included "an outspoken condemnation of economic domination of the nation by private interests, coupled with eulogies for President Wilson's reforms, and pleas that Indiana follow them."

Willkie's subsequent history conforms more nearly to the establishment stereotype—a few months of law practice, enlistment as a private in the Army during World War I, marriage to an attractive girl, service overseas cut short by the armistice, return as a captain, and a new job.

The road that eventually led to New York, Philadelphia, and almost to Washington started in Akron, Ohio, in the legal department of the Firestone Tire and Rubber Company. Within two years Willkie resigned to join a prominent firm of utility lawyers, who soon made him a junior partner. Meanwhile, he had, with his usual energy, plunged into civic affairs. He was called on more and more frequently as a public speaker and, by the time he left Ohio with his wife and son in 1929 to join the New York law firm of Weadock and Weadock, he was generally recognized as one of Akron's outstanding young citizens.

Weadock and Weadock, representing the gigantic new utility-holding company, Commonwealth and Southern Corporation, now offered young Willkie a challenge commensurate with his talents and ambitions. A hard worker, he shortly became the right-hand man of the president of Commonwealth and Southern and, when the president retired in 1933, he designated Willkie as his successor.

The revolutionary changes that the new president made in the company, together with his tireless salesmanship and flair for public relations, soon produced extraordinary results. In addition to heading it up, Willkie became a one-man public relations department for the huge utility company. His genius was inborn, much of it resulting from his rugged good looks, his self-confidence, his articulateness, and his willingness to challenge the orthodox or conventional, no matter how tough his opposition. But he always argued his sales points, as he later did his political battles, with logic and persuasiveness.

While the sale of light and power utility appliances had decreased alarmingly throughout the United States, Commonwealth and Southern, in six years, doubled the sale of electricity, quadrupled appliance sales, and reduced its rates twenty-seven percent below the average for the entire country. By then Willkie had become a director on the boards of a number of other corporations and his independence, energy, and candor had won him the admiration of the business community.

Though the phenomenal record of Commonwealth and Southern may have recommended him to the eastern establishment, his long and dramatic fight with the government over public versus private ownership of power attracted national attention.

The court battles which began in the fall of 1933, shortly after Roosevelt unveiled his plan to create the Tennessee Valley Authority, were bitterly fought for nearly six years until August 15, 1939, when Willkie, having finally lost, handed over for "fair compensation" Commonwealth and Southern's Tennessee Electric Power Company and all its properties to the T.V.A. His public relations sense was nowhere better demonstrated than when this celebrated case had finally reached the Supreme Court. Willkie, a lawyer himself, made a dramatic appearance before the court with Commonwealth and Southern's attorneys. In this locked-horns battle, despite losing the case, Willkie emerged as an outstanding public figure and, in anti-Roosevelt, anti-New Deal, anti-third-term quarters, as their hero.

The press had made the most of the long drawn-out battle and Willkie, as the central figure and most eloquent spokesman for "free enterprise," had become the New Deal's most articulate and colorful critic. At a Columbia University alumni luncheon that autumn, Willkie disclosed the value he put on the free enterprise system when he defined American liberties as "built upon a tripod—the democratic process, our civil liberties, and free enterprise. If any one of the parts of that tripod falls, all three will fall."

Fate wasted no time in taking a hand in Willkie's subsequent fortunes, and he, of course, characteristically cooperated. The day after the Tennessee properties had been handed over to the government, Arthur Krock's column for the second time brought Willkie's name, now more prominently, into a discussion of possible Republican presidential nominees.

Three days later, the Willkies found themselves weekend guests of Russell Davenport and his wife at their country house in Connecticut. Marcia Davenport reported that here the two men discovered an "intellectual and temperamental affinity like the anvil and the hammer, between which the forged iron takes form"—a relationship which lasted until Willkie's death in 1944. It became a crucial factor in his political fortunes, for Davenport now had the complete confidence of the man he felt "ought to be the next president of the United States." He became Willkie's personal confidante and advisor, and Davenport's role as his speech editor—and later his speech writer—gave him a position of peculiar influence in the unfolding Willkie drama.

That spring and summer, ominous events in Europe had made it increasingly apparent that Adolf Hitler was preparing for war. In March he had seized Czechoslovakia. President Roosevelt continued his fruitless attempts to awaken America and his myopic Congress. He appealed directly to the American people to strengthen his hand with Congress, asked for a commitment from Hitler not to attack the weak countries (and received the scathing response that the führer would solemnly promise not to invade the United States), and kept stepping up his campaign to induce Congress at least to vote for repeal of the Neutrality Act, which was effectively preventing us from giving any real help to the Allies. But the country remained divided and the Congress adamant.

On August 20, during the Willkies' weekend with the Davenports, Hitler made his next imperious move by demanding Danzig. The following day, Germany and the Soviet Union announced their non-aggression pact. Talk turned from Willkie's personal future to the catastrophic developments in Europe and what could be done to forestall the worst, for they all viewed the recent events with as much consternation as the President did.

Less than two weeks later, on September 1, Europe's—and

the world's—troubled peace was shattered. Hitler marched his troops into Poland. Two days after that, Britain and France declared war on Germany, and World War II began. Not being involved in or consulted on matters of government policy, Willkie heard of these cataclysmic events over his radio at home.

It is important to remember that Willkie, though a stern critic of the New Deal at home, had been a consistent supporter of Roosevelt's foreign policy. While all too many members of Congress had appeared blind to what Germany and Italy had been up to that summer, Willkie had watched with alarm as Hitler, having rebuffed Roosevelt's every peace effort, gobbled up Czechoslovakia and signed a military pact with Mussolini, while Italy invaded Albania and Japan continued her outward expansion. Willkie had spoken out in support of Roosevelt's plea to Congress for revision of the Neutrality Act to enable the United States to give aid to the democracies under attack. Both men had been dismayed by the defeat of the measure in July 1939, and Willkie no doubt was as relieved as Roosevelt when the controversial act was finally revised in November.

In January 1938, Willkie had appeared in a debate on the popular radio program, "America's Town Meeting of the Air" (it claimed two million listeners for its weekly programs). His opposite number was Assistant Attorney General Robert H. Jackson, and the topic was "How Can Government and Business Work Together?" Regardless of the listeners' political or economic orientations, it was generally conceded that Willkie, in his spirited defense of private enterprise, had proved to be the far better debater and came through to the listening audience as a responsible, progressive, sound businessman—the kind that every American could be proud of.

In April 1940, an editorial about Willkie, written for *Fortune* by its managing editor, Russell Davenport, and an article in the same issue entitled "We the People," written by Willkie with some editorial help from Davenport, roused widespread inter-

est and an enormously favorable response. It was these articles
—together with "Mr. Willkie's Petition," a short eloquent sum-
mation of "We the People" which appeared in the same issue
—that inspired a young Princeton graduate, Oren Root, Jr., by
then a New York lawyer, to what proved to be extraordinary
action. Root says that for some time before the issue of *Fortune*
came out, he had been hearing a great deal of talk about
Willkie. Also he had read Arthur Krock. He just had a "gut
feeling" that Willkie was the man who should be president. Of
the three front-running candidates for the Republican nomination, Taft and Vandenberg were "strong isolationists" and
Dewey was "wobbly." With "all the things that were going on
in Europe," it was essential to have a candidate with the sort of
world view that Willkie had.

Root says that he liked Willkie, "a couple of his friends" liked
him, and he was sure there were many more if they would only
"declare themselves." So he drew up and sent out a sample
mailing of a "Declaration" embodying "Mr. Willkie's Petition,"
as it had appeared in *Fortune*, asking nothing more of the ad-
dressee than that he or she "declare" for Willkie.

Though relatively unknown at the time, Root is one of the
few people still living who played a key role—it is probably not
an overstatement to say *the* key role—in the nomination of
Willkie. A brief picture of him as he is today, and of his activities
along the way, may shed some light on why he was the person
who saw the challenge and the opportunities in Willkie's candidacy—long shot as it was—and decided to do something about
it.

Oren Root is a tall, handsome, gray-haired man with a dark
complexion. He is a great-nephew of Elihu Root and his mother,
the former Mercedes d'Acosta of New York, was not only a
famous beauty, but was the founder of the Lighthouse for the
Blind.

Root is a somewhat liberal "Rockefeller Republican" and is an
independent thinker and a scholar. He can be a spellbinder,

with a fine sense of oratory and his use of gestures and a rich flexible voice to make his point. On one occasion he so inspired his audience that they rose, with thunderous applause, just a few moments after he started speaking.

Although somewhat aloof and retiring, he is a loyal friend, a devoted husband and father, and has strong convictions and a brilliant legal mind. In World War II, he had the spirit to forego a safe berth in the Navy in Washington; through connections, he arranged to be assigned to Admiral Kirk's staff as an Intelligence officer for the amphibious landing in Normandy in June 1944. He received Admiral Kirk's personal permission to leave the flagship, which was standing off Omaha beach shortly after D-Day, to survey conditions on Utah beach and, in particular, the Navy's participation and report back to the Admiral.

Root had the initiative, following the war, to go it alone in New York and to found the successful law firm of Hatch, Barrett & Root, of which he is today of counsel.

Mr. Root's original idea in 1940, of mailing out the Declaration was so simple that it has been described as almost childlike. He selected, as test groups, the members of Yale's class of 1924 and Princeton's class of 1925—hardly a cross section of American society, but nonetheless groups probably widely dispersed geographically and throughout the business and professional worlds. In those days it would not have occurred to a young man in a hurry (the convention was barely two months off) that he should have at least polled some women and perhaps a sampling of labor. Blacks, of course, were, for the most part, still in the South, Puerto Ricans in Puerto Rico, and the under twenty-one sector of the electorate did not have the vote yet!

To his test groups, at the cost of 150 dollars, Root sent copies of his Declaration embodying "Willkie's Petition," as it had appeared in *Fortune.* It began with the words, "We, the undersigned people of the United States, believe that Wendell Willkie should be elected President of the United States." and included enough spaces for fifteen signatures.

He hoped that those who received it might be motivated to have it duplicated at their own expense and sent to other groups. Root did not presume to make this suggestion in his mailing, but he included the printer's name and address "as a hint." The results were flabbergasting. Four days after the Declarations went out, Root had to have twenty thousand more printed and, by the time the convention opened in the end of June, the Pandick Press, which printed the originals, had printed over 277,000, and twenty other presses had also gotten into the business. In a September 1977 letter from Root, he said that it was probably sometime in April or May 1940 that he put one three-line fundraising advertisement in the *New York Herald Tribune.* The immediate result of his modest beginnings was an astounding avalanche of telephone calls, letters, petitions, contributions, and offers of help. The deluge threatened to swamp him and his law firm. Taking a leave of absence, he rented a "hole in the wall" as headquarters. Thus was born the phenomenal pell-mell organization, grandly called the Associated Willkie Clubs of America.

On the same day, April 9, that Root was mailing out his Declaration, two other significant events took place. Hitler invaded Denmark and Norway, and Willkie appeared as a guest on the enormously popular radio program, "Information Please," with a listening audience in the millions. Willkie conducted himself so brilliantly, tempering his knowledgable answers on a wide range of subjects with wit and humor and projecting himself once again as a sound businessman with intellect and a social conscience, that his popular following was greatly increased across the country.

It was at about this time that General Hugh S. Johnson mentioned Willkie for the first time in his widely syndicated column, saying that he would make a powerful candidate if nominated and a great president if elected. When asked for his reaction, Willkie replied, "If the government keeps on taking my business away at its present rate, I'll soon be out of work and looking for a job. Johnson's offer is the best I've had yet." This offhand retort was given more weight than it probably deserved at the time.

Meanwhile, Oren Root had sent a copy of his Declaration to Willkie, explaining that he had not consulted him about the public mailing beforehand in the belief that any advance contact with Willkie might give rise to charges of collusion, with Willkie trying to promote his own candidacy.

The very next day, Root got a call from Davenport asking for an immediate meeting at which he told Root that Willkie urgently hoped he would cut out his operation, at least for the time being. At this time Willkie and Davenport still only envisaged Willkie as "the darkest horse in the stable," available in case of a deadlock. Premature exposure and an active campaign, they felt, might hurt his chances. Root finally persuaded Davenport to take him to see Willkie. Root's logic and persuasive powers overcame their objections, but Willkie firmly told Root that he would not associate himself in any way with Root's activities. Root returned, unfettered, to his office to try to catch up with his escalating organization.

Russell Davenport, though Willkie's closest adviser, was not his only one at this point. Starting in the autumn of 1939, a small group had coalesced around him, their objective being quietly to prepare the ground for Willkie to take advantage of a possibly deadlocked convention. Among the group were Charlton McVeagh, a talented writer with wide-ranging connections in the Republican party; Sinclair Weeks, a Boston banker; Harold E. Talbott, a prominent financier from Dayton, Ohio; and Harold J. Gallagher, an able New York lawyer with a reputation as a good organizer. McVeagh was admiringly regarded by the rest of the group as a pro because, though he had never held public office, he had more than once been a delegate to a Republican National Convention. Almost all of the others were complete neophytes. The chief activity of this group, aside from thrashing out the substance of a Willkie program, was to give him as much exposure as possible, without at that time showing any interest in him as a presidential candidate. This meant, among other things, arranging as many speaking dates for him as possible.

Much of this activity took place in the Davenports' spacious New York apartment. In an interview at her apartment on July 28, 1972, Mrs. Davenport made a few comments on this operation:

There was only one professional politician that was in at the very early stages because none of us knew any more about the mechanics of a political convention than we knew how to fly to the moon. He's dead now, but he was a really completely professional politician. His name was Charlton McVeagh. He was, of course, a Republican, but he was prepared to be a maverick, and there just had to be somebody that knew all the pols in all of the prospective state delegations that was going to start being in touch with them all, and Charlton McVeagh did it from this apartment. And that went on the whole winter of 1939 and 1940. This began in the autumn of 1939; whoever was preparing to do something was here and they would put their heads together. Very early in the thing nobody had the thinnest idea how you organized the votes of delegates or how you reached delegates in a political convention. I don't remember who it was that came up with Charlton McVeagh because he had been a delegate to the Republican conventions and knew all these Republicans. . . .

He was a private individual. He was not a member of Congress and by profession he must have been a lawyer. Those people always were. And that's what happened. He came up to this apartment. The telephones began to multiply like flies on a hot day. Charlton would sit surrounded by telephones, telephoning all over the country to the key people in these various states. . . . He was trying to get people on our side who would be active in organizing the choosing of the delegations that would go to the Philadelphia convention. The convention took place in June and Charlton was at this the whole six months before. And now that I think of it I wonder who paid those telephone bills. I wouldn't be surprised if I did although they must have been monstrous. But we didn't have any money involved—I mean in the sense that today, for example, look what it costs somebody just to run for a nomination. Of course there was no television in those days and there were no great expenses.

It is impossible to evaluate the impact of McVeagh's costly telephone campaign. He was not trying to get delegates committed to supporting Willkie's candidacy; such an ambition would have seemed very farfetched at the time. His purpose was simply to get the name of Wendell Willkie known so that he might be turned to by delegates in case of a deadlock.

Mrs. Davenport also recalled Willkie's visits to their apartment:

Wendell used to come up here, and of course Russell was very close to him and that made Russell a little vain, and the ideas out of which the whole concept of what Wendell would be as a candidate—there always must be somebody with whom the thing goes back and forth, and Russell was very much that, and Wendell used to come up here to the big room. If Wendell had come into a little room like this, of course, the walls would have burst; but there is a big drawing room there which is shut so it just doesn't have to be coped with in the summer, and he used to come into that room and fall into a big armchair and start to talk, and I wouldn't like to indicate how he sat but he would sit in an armchair and the first thing he would do would be throw one leg over the arm of the chair and presently the shoe on that foot would start to go and eventually that foot wouldn't have a shoe on it. Then the necktie would first be loosened like this and by degrees the necktie was not all the way off, but just untied and one end hanging this way and his collar open, and his hair was terribly rumply all over the place and he was a constant smoker and he made the most unholy mess when he smoked. We used to keep him surrounded with barrages of ashtrays and it made absolutely no difference. The ashes were all down his front, on the rug, on the furniture—he was so concentrating on what he was thinking about and he was like a bull in a china shop anyway. He was bored by all kinds of amenity and order and of course he loved the girls. There is nothing the matter with that—so did Lincoln and so did other people. He was very attractive to women who didn't even know him. He had a great deal of masculine charm. He was a very masculine man.

Mrs. Davenport's account of Willkie confirms many other less lively descriptions. An impression of "bigness" runs through them all—a big man physically, with big ideas, big plans, big aspirations, big hopes. He seemed to fill a room when he came into it. His overwhelming masculinity is referred to approvingly, time after time, by both men and women. His tousled appearance apparently had great appeal. (He is never referred to as "unkempt"—always "tousled," "rumpled," or by some other indulgent adjective.) His dynamic personality, his energy, his decency, his broad engaging smile, his direct blue eyes, his fine compelling speaking voice (which unfortunately gave out from overuse during the campaign), and his profound belief in the American dream are all cited as reasons for his powerful appeal.

For many years Willkie had an extremely devoted relationship with Irita Van Doren. He had met her in New York when she was book review editor for the *Herald Tribune.* She was no beauty, no femme fatale. Tall, statuesque, intellectual, she was not the stereotype of a woman who would attract a politician.

But she was intelligent and wonderfully articulate. She knew all of the literary people in New York, and she brought Willkie in contact with a whole new world of people and ideas, a far cry from his old business associates and his newer political circle.

Willkie's wife Edith had been his high school sweetheart. Since leaving Elwood, he had grown but she had not. He was, however, devoted to Edith in his way and determined not to hurt her. He was also very clearsighted and realized that, in those days, if he was going to run for president there could be no family dissension. The close friends who knew about Irita kept as silent as he on the subject.

It was a shock to two of his intimate friends, therefore, when he announced to them, "I've had a request from some New York reporters for a press conference. I've decided to tell them to meet me at Irita's house." His friends' silence must have made him sense their unstated query and their concern over the wisdom of his decision.

He continued, "Everyone knows about us—all the newspapermen in New York. If somebody should come along to threaten or embarrass me about Irita, I would say, 'Go right ahead. There is not a reporter in New York who doesn't know about her.' " He told his friends that Irita would not be present during the conference, and there the matter was dropped.

Willkie might be described as a womanizer. And he liked variety. Women of all ages, interests, and tastes attracted him. But his many brief flings or passing affairs did not affect his relationship with Irita or, apparently, his marriage.

As a private person it was said of him,

> He likes to earn the stuff [money] and he likes to spend it, though his ways of spending it are not the orthodox ways of pleasure. His personal expenditures are small and his personal habits simple. But a close friend admits that he "must have sent at least fifty boys and girls through college."

Those who knew him well felt that the good Indiana earth gave him his special strength.

In mid-April, with the convention deadline little more than eight weeks away, Willkie's two bands of amateurs were still plotting strategy in the Davenports' living room and only just beginning to mobilize nationwide grass-roots support from Oren Root's "hole in the wall." Meanwhile, the avowed candidates had long been going about the serious business of speaking at rallies, entering primaries, and negotiating for delegates —getting pledges of support from the only people who really counted, those who would cast their votes on the convention floor in June.

Thomas Dewey, New York's thirty-eight-year-old district attorney, had the support of most of New York's enormous delegation, and he had taken the Wisconsin, Nebraska, and Illinois primaries by impressive margins. The Gallup poll of May 3 showed him to have sixty-seven percent of the vote-getting strength and the best chance of anyone to beat Roosevelt. Other polls gave approximately the same estimates. His well-disciplined supporters duly contacted every one of the thousand convention delegates with this information. His only apparent weaknesses—very minimal—were the defection of a few delegates in the otherwise solid New York delegation and the defeat of an unauthorized delegation pledged to him in Massachusetts. He was far and away the frontrunner.

Next to him—but considerably behind—came Senator Robert Taft of Ohio, of whom it had been said that "both his strength and his weakness came from the fact that he looked like all sixteen million Republicans rolled into one." He was thought to represent the Republican philosophy of 1940 more accurately than any of the other would-be candidates. He was a professional with well organized support and solid conservative backing in the National Committee, and he was popular in the South. He entered no primaries, preferring to attend to his Senate duties and negotiate for his delegates. He could prove to be a formidable contender.

The bandwagon of an earlier frontrunner, Senator Arthur Vandenberg of Michigan, had lost some of its steam. Nevertheless, he had powerful supporters in Senators Gerald Nye of North Dakota, Arthur Capper of Kansas, and Charles McNary of Oregon, a solid Michigan delegation, and a scattering of other support around the country. He could well be a compromise candidate in a deadlock, as could a considerable number of favorite sons who were waiting in the wings.

Willkie's own bandwagon was rolling merrily along. The political innocence of his enthusiastic supporters was one of his most powerful assets, as it kept them from recognizing the almost insuperable odds against them and fortified them with largely unjustified optimism. Arthur Krock had prophesied that Wendell Willkie's nomination would take a miracle and "miracles don't happen anymore"; but Willkie's amateurs, believing almost blindly in the power of "we the people," did not doubt that this miracle could and would happen.

Willkie had already given his destiny a considerable nudge in January when he had changed his political registration from Democratic to Republican. Apparently, this switch was at the suggestion of Mrs. Willkie, who felt that consistency demanded it of the New Deal's most forceful critic. In February, he scored a great success during an evening of informal discussion at Yale's Saybrook College. At the end of the scheduled program, students plied him with questions for two or more hours. His supporters were delighted with the response of the young to their man's dynamic appeal.

In March, Willkie demonstrated his characteristically independent thinking in an article that appeared in the *New Republic* on the eighteenth. In an eloquent plea for the protection of our civil liberties, he argued that the views and rights of communists and of Nazi sympathizers were entitled protection equal to those of any other American citizen. That same month, in Taft's home state of Ohio, in a speech to the Toledo Rotary Club, he accused "businessmen drunk with power, and a public drunk with money" of having broken down "the safeguards protecting individual liberties." He then scolded Wall Street and the big corporations for their power-hungry, money-hungry irresponsibility and questionable practices in the 1920s. It must have stunned his audience when this foremost advocate of private enterprise said that many of the regulations and laws enacted by the current administration were "sound in principle and most will never be removed from our statute books." These positions could hardly have recommended him to Republican conservatives—either politicians or businessmen.

Yet, as later events would prove, there must have been many young businessmen in that audience, and all across the country —"the Junior Chamber of Commerce type," as Gardner Cowles called them in an interview on June 20, 1972, who listened and were enormously attracted by Willkie's fair-mindedness, his forthrightness, and his liberal views. Perhaps above all, they were attracted by his deeply-rooted faith in America and its limitless potential. As Cowles has described them, "They weren't the disillusioned ones or the cynical ones. They were the people who wanted to hear somebody say that America had a great future and that if they worked hard they were going to make a great success and fortune and so on."

Willkie, despite or perhaps in conformity with his zeal to eradicate abuses, "was preaching an optimistic philosophy that in their eyes contrasted with what they considered the negative philosophy of Roosevelt and the New Deal."

Years later, when Mrs. Davenport was asked to describe a typical Willkie volunteer, she immediately cited Oren Root. "He was the brains and the core of the volunteer movement." But there were thousands like him all over the country, similarly motivated, who gave of their time, work, and substance—often at considerable sacrifice—for the man and the cause in which they so deeply believed.

As Mrs. Davenport said:

> The thousands of people who signed the round robin letters and formed the Willkie Clubs were reacting to the New Deal and too much Franklin Roosevelt. They were obviously intelligent and world-minded, or they would have been simply routine Republicans for Taft or Dewey. They were against a third term for Roosevelt. They were not afraid of the chance the United States would get involved in the war. They were independents, most of them completely innocent of the real inside workings of party politics. They were typified by Oren Root. He was just smarter and more articulate than the masses.

It was these young men and women—small businessmen, insurance people, bank employees, white-collar workers, housewives, doctors, lawyers, teachers, members of the press, in general, the lay leadership of towns, especially small towns all over the country—who not only were captivated by Willkie's personality, but electrified by his call to action. They became the heart and core of the pre-convention Willkie Club movement.

Marcia Davenport saw the majority of them as

> thoughtful, responsible American people who were instinctively mistrustful of the man [Roosevelt] and opposed, not so much to what he did or aimed to do, as the way he did it. This definition rules out the rich and privileged, the angry who called him a traitor to his class, the diehard Republicans to whom he would anyway have been anathema, the reactionaries who viewed all social change or reform as communism or the next thing to it. These people who were inherently opposed to Roosevelt [other than the blind opposition I have defined] were moderate—moderate of means and in social ideas, open-minded, independent in their occupations and in their capacity and desire to think for themselves. . . . They were alarmed at the imminence of a third term for Roosevelt, already too deeply entrenched for the good of the democratic process, even while they approved his foreign policy.

Careful sifting of the Willkie Club records and correspondence and the recollections of observers and participants of that period bear out Mrs. Davenport's view of the great majority of the members.

In April, the month that Oren Root first sent out his Declaration, Willkie made two important speeches: the first at the newspaper correspondents' annual Gridiron Club dinner in Washington, to which the capital's top politicians are invited; the second in New York at the Waldorf Astoria before the American Newspaper Publishers Association's Bureau of Advertising. The choice of these two forums, which gave him maximum exposure to the newspaper world, was clear evidence (if it had not become evident before) of Willkie's ambition. His felicitous speech in Washington roused great interest in him among the correspondents, and his Waldorf speech (urging a return to Jeffersonian liberalism through defeat of the

New Deal) won him some powerful new adherents: Mr. and Mrs. Ogden Reid of the *New York Herald Tribune,* Roy Howard of the Scripps Howard chain, and John and Gardner Cowles, who had met Willkie for the first time two nights before at the Davenports' apartment.

Meanwhile, Oren Root was trying to bring some order out of the chaotic fervor which was organizing itself into Willkie Clubs, now starting to proliferate all over the country both with and without encouragement. Root, in a conversation on August 8, 1972, said that the statistics that were given out from time to time about the clubs and their membership were largely guesswork, as it was impossible to keep track of their numbers. Many organized themselves locally, and later affiliated with the Associated Willkie Clubs of America. Many never affiliated at all, either before the convention or during the general campaign, but they called themselves Willkie Clubs and worked as hard as the others.

The methods used by the Associated Willkie Club headquarters, in addition to the continual mailing out of Declarations and filling bulk orders for them, were most informal and could not, of course, have worked if Willkie had not been a man who ignited such enthusiasm. The function of the Associated Clubs at this point was to create as much publicity as possible for their hero, to try to rouse zeal for him in the areas where he had not yet been heard of or caught hold, and—even more importantly —to channel the mounting national enthusiasm through the clubs for one concerted purpose: the nomination of Wendell Willkie at the Republican convention.

Oren Root and those around him went about these tasks in the same uncomplicated way that they had at the beginning— relying on the direct approach and its multiplying effect. Root reasoned that everyone who had responded to his original Declaration (by May 1 he had received 200,000 signatures) was a potential Willkie Club organizer—the prompter the reply, the greater the potential. At the outset, Root answered every letter himself and made hundreds of personal contacts and telephone calls to those who had shown interest or promise. The immediate results were as spectacular as those of the mailings.

One of Root's earliest enlistees was Donald J. Smith, a fraternity brother of Willkie at Indiana University, who was then living in New Jersey. Smith's job as president of a sizable corporation took him to many parts of the country; on his trips he never missed an opportunity to talk about Willkie. No group at any meeting, luncheon, fraternity get-together, or any other business or social gathering went away without having been apprised of Willkie's extraordinary qualifications to be president of the United States. By the latter part of May, Smith not only had activated a strong Willkie Club movement in New Jersey, but as a direct result of his contacts clubs had been organized in Oregon, Los Angeles, San Francisco, San Antonio, St. Louis, and Atlanta. One of the first acts of the Los Angeles Club was to have ten thousand Declarations printed at its own expense, signed, and sent on to Root. Smith himself sent Declarations enclosed in his personal letters to several hundred friends and acquaintances, offering to make free—or, in large quantities, at cost—copies of the Declaration available to all who would send them out. Almost immediately, he received several thousand requests.

In New Jersey, the clubs organized a write-in drive for Willkie in the state's May 21 preferential primary for convention delegates. Dewey's was the only name on the ballot, and he received 340,744 votes. But the three-day campaign on Willkie's behalf produced 24,240 write-in votes for him. In view of the fact that the campaign for their fledgling candidate was put together at the last minute, Willkie's supporters were heartened by this result.

Other early Willkie Club leaders were equally active. The founder of the Maryland chapter also organized in North Carolina, starting clubs in Charlotte, Winston-Salem, and Greensboro. In Pennsylvania, on Thursday, May 9, a vice president of Philadelphia's Baldwin Locomotive works heard a suggestion that he organize a club. By Monday, he had rented an office, put together an organization, and mailed out invitations to forty Philadelphians to join the club. He had also sent letters to friends throughout the state, asking them to organize clubs or to suggest people who might. By Wednesday, the fifteenth, Pennsylvania was operational. Time was of the essence for the convention was now less than six weeks off.

Club activity became increasingly feverish. By mid-May the Knox County, Maine, Willkie Club, not content with just organizing locally, had already mailed two hundred Declarations throughout the country. On May 16, two offices were opened in Boston.

Connecticut started early and was extraordinarily active. By the middle of May they had Willkie Clubs in 129 towns, and the Hartford headquarters had collected over a hundred thousand signatures in the city alone. Though the club movement had started in the Northeast, the rest of the country was rapidly catching up. Three weeks after Oren Root's original mailing had gone out, the Pandick Press had printed seventy thousand more Declarations, and other states and individuals were printing them themselves.

Unsolicited contributions had been received from forty-two states. Willkie's hometown, Elwood, had begun to organize, getting signatures on petitions. And on May 15, in Alf Landon's Kansas, citizens of Independence organized for Willkie. Willkie himself, by now encouraging rather than opposing Root's activities, opened a Willkie for President Club in Chicago at about the same time. And reports of lively activity came from such various states as Massachusetts, Missouri, Iowa, and West Virginia. There was even considerable activity among conservative Democrats in the deep South.

Meanwhile, Willkie was making more and more speeches, and captivating the crowds.

To liberal and conservative audiences alike he consistently propounded his theory of liberalism.

In the pre-war [World War I] years we fought against the domination of the people by Big Business. We now face the domination of the people by Big Government. The liberal who fought against one kind of domination thirty-five years ago should find himself fighting against this new kind of domination today.

Willkie, a liberal Jeffersonian, was so strongly opposed to the transformation of the Democratic party by Roosevelt that he genuinely believed that it was undermining democracy. He was convinced that democracy could only be preserved by throwing out "the New Deal party." He hoped to achieve this by way of a liberalized Republican party.

Many of Willkie's younger adherents had no doubt inherited their Republicanism. Others lived or worked in Republican environments. But most of them knew a good deal more about the rest of the world than their parents did and were far more internationally minded and liberally oriented. Willkie appealed to everything they believed in. Furthermore, young people, who tend to be more idealistic than their elders, are strongly attracted by fearless outspokenness and philosophical arguments coupled with vigorous action. They flocked to the Willkie Clubs.

By June 12, nearly 500 of these clubs were hard at work. They had already distributed 150,000 copies of Willkie's principles and over 350,000 Willkie buttons. Only twelve days later, when the convention opened in Philadelphia, Willkie Club headquarters claimed a membership of 750 affiliated clubs with 50,000 working volunteers who had sent out more than 750,000 pieces of literature including thousands of handy Willkie kits for canvassers. How many unaffiliated clubs and volunteers were working, and the amount of material that had been printed and distributed by these independent groups, no one could guess.

Oren Root announced that, altogether, about four and a half million people had signed the Willkie petitions. Root's faith in the multiplier method had succeeded beyond his most extravagant expectations.

The results of Willkie's skyrocketing popularity and of the gospel being spread by his growing army of volunteers were showing in the opinion polls. Less than seven weeks before the convention opened, the Gallup poll of May 8, sampling Republican voters' preferences for their party's nominee, mentioned Willkie's name for the first time, giving him a three percent rating. Dewey, however, who had rated fifty-three percent in March, had risen to sixty-seven percent, with Vandenberg and Taft next in popularity. Nine days later, May 17, Gallup gave Willkie five percent and drew attention to the "Willkie boom" that had "started almost overnight." A month later, just over a week before the convention opened, Dewey, though still ahead, had dropped considerably, and Willkie, now in second place, had jumped to seventeen percent.

Within the next week, Willkie made another spectacular jump. Just before the convention opened, Gallup's figures showed that, while Dewey had dropped again and now had a forty-seven percent rating, Willkie had gained twelve percentage points and was currently preferred by twenty-nine percent of those polled, with Taft and Vandenberg trailing far behind. Harold Ickes, Roosevelt's secretary of the interior, called the Willkie boom "one of the most remarkable phenomena I have ever seen in American politics."

As convention time approached, the Willkie Clubs devoted increasing attention to the care and influencing of delegates. Because most of the clubs were not organized until it was too late to affect the selection of delegates, they concentrated their efforts on persuading and trying to convert those already picked. Parmet and Hecht concluded that the clubs "had conducted an amazingly effective mail campaign." They had assembled lists with the names and addresses, often including

pertinent background material, of every delegate and alternate, all or whom had been sent packets of Willkie material.
They had contacted key people in almost all of the states, concentrating their strongest pressures on important political
figures and influential newspapers, urging them to come out for
Willkie. Their theme was: "He's going to win the nomination.
He has the best chance of winning the election. You'd be smart
to support him now."

In April, the Davenport group had organized the "Voluntary
Mailing Committee for Distributing Willkie's Speeches." Gossip attributed its organization to jealousy over Root's sudden
prominence. But there is no evidence of this and certainly there
was more than enough for both to do. In any case, with the
approach of the convention, the Davenport-McVeagh-Gal-
lagher group and the Willkie Clubs developed a spirit of cooperation, and the coordination of their work in Philadelphia
proved most effective.

Convention officials and delegates began arriving in Philadelphia several days before the June 24 opening. And so did
Dewey, Taft, Vandenberg, Willkie, and all of the favorite sons
and the dark horses whom Willkie had now left at the post.
When reporters questioned him about his plans Willkie replied:

> I have no campaign manager, no campaign fund, no campaign head-
> quarters. All the headquarters I have are under my hat. I have no
> ghost writers. I've entered into no deals or understanding with any
> political leaders or anybody else. If I accidentally am nominated and
> elected President of the United States, I shall go in completely free
> of any obligations of any kind.

At another time he said, "I'm not running for anything, and I'm
not running away from anything. But I would be a liar if I said
I wouldn't like to be President or wouldn't accept a nomination."

Supporters of the various candidates by this time were

thronging the streets and the hotel lobbies trying to buttonhole delegates, cheering their favorites, or just gaping. Philadelphia was a bedlam, made worse by the stifling heat that lasted all that week—well before the days of airconditioning.

It soon became apparent that a great number of the convention "visitors" wore Willkie buttons, were mostly young, and were determined to talk to all the delegates they could corner. Root had not overlooked a detail. Almost ten days before the opening of the convention he had sent a letter to Willkie Clubs across the country, pointing out that a strong show of popular support and enthusiasm at the convention should impress the delegates. The response, once again, was unexpected and overwhelming. At their own expense or sent by their clubs, thousands of supporters flooded into Philadelphia for the final push.

Some observers felt that the immense pressure the amateurs put on in Philadelphia, including the chanting from the galleries during the nominating proceedings, became irritating to many of the delegates and was actually counter-productive. This is hard to evaluate. What was unmistakable, however, was the genuineness and spontaneity of the unplanned, unsubsidized descent of Willkie's amateurs on Philadelphia. How many of them were influenced by Mr. Root's letter, how many came compulsively, without solicitation, determined to make the final push for their man, how many were carried there by the bandwagon psychology that was sweeping the country, it is impossible to say. What seems clear is that this was no "conspiracy" engineered by an elite group in New York, but plain, largely middle-class American citizens bent on having a voice in the nomination of their party's candidate.

The opening session of the 1940 Republican National Convention was brought to order just before noon on June 24, with three sessions scheduled for each day. But for the first two days the most important business was being transacted outside of Convention Hall. All the would-be candidates had established personal headquarters in their hotel suites from which they and their staffs were energetically pursuing delegate support. At Willkie's headquarters in the Benjamin Franklin Hotel, his amateurs handled the visiting delegates with skill and dispatch. Though his suite was small and unostentatious—this lowkey background having been considered the most appropriate for a utility magnate accused of being financed by Wall Street—the Associated Willkie Clubs had two large and bustling headquarters, and the Voluntary Mailing Committee for Distributing Willkie's Speeches had its own office. From Monday the twenty-fourth through the twenty-seventh, Willkie worked, from nine each morning until two the following morning, at persuading, convincing, and charming delegates and potential supporters alike. Many of the delegates called on him spontaneously. Others were brought by already-converted delegates, party leaders, or amateur enthusiasts. The pace was frenetic, tension grew, as did interest in Willkie and pledges of support. Willkie estimated that he had personally talked to over six hundred of the thousand convention delegates by Thursday, June 27.

Meanwhile, pressure on the delegates was not all coming from Philadelphia. It came from every part of the country with growing intensity. Floods of telegrams, petitions, letters, and postcards from their home states were inundating delegations and individual delegates. On June 26, the *New York Herald Tribune* estimated that nearly a million messages had been received between Saturday and Tuesday nights. When these delegates returned to their hotels, they found packets of material from the Voluntary Mailing Committee awaiting them.

No doubt some overenthusiastic or unscrupulous Willkie partisans added to the nationwide deluge by sending duplicate or faked letters or telegrams. And probably a great number of the legitimate ones were sent at the urging of the Willkie Clubs and their leaders who, despite warnings that too much pressure on the delegates might boomerang, nonetheless felt it was their last available card and they must play it. But the genuineness of the Willkie fervor as demonstrated by the milling throngs on the streets of Philadelphia, by the magnitude of the outpouring of messages from every area in the country, and by the fact that so many people cared so much that, whether prompted or not, they took the trouble to communicate appears to be incontrovertible evidence of the widespread popular enthusiasm for Willkie. In fact, in July 1940, when the Senate Campaign Expenditures Committee was asked to investigate alleged improprieties in the phenomenon of the telegrams, the chairman of the committee, Senator Guy Gillette, reported that the members were in unanimous agreement that they had not, at that time, been given sufficient evidence to warrant an investigation, a statement which was reiterated the following February in the committee's final report.

Meanwhile, inside Convention Hall the opening day, June 24, had been taken up by the usual business—the welcoming speeches; the referral of the temporary roll of delegates to the credentials committee; the election of the temporary chairman, Governor Harold Stassen of Minnesota; and the inevitable number of patriotic and party-loyalty speeches. Stassen had become known as the "Boy Wonder," having been elected two years before as the youngest (thirty-one years old) governor in Minnesota's history and was energetically pursuing reforms. So his keynote speech was the highlight of the evening session, with the delegates all appraising him as another possible dark horse.

During the second morning, the delegates approved the nomination of Representative Joseph W. Martin of Massachusetts, Republican minority leader of the House and a thoroughgoing party man, as permanent chairman. In the evening, former President Hoover addressed the convention, receiving an enthusiastic fifteen-minute ovation, which produced agonizing worry in the Willkie camp. Hoover presented a threat in his own right if he should decide to make another try for the nomination, or he could use his influence and prestige to avoid the deadlock which Willkie's supporters still regarded as his real hope for the nomination.

Outside Convention Hall, there were a number of encouraging developments that day. Rumors were circulating that some of Dewey's support was eroding—that Willkie was picking up most of it—and people were even beginning to say that Willkie was now the man to beat. Wall Street betting commissioners were now quoting even odds on Willkie. And that afternoon, Stassen, now free of his duties as temporary chairman, called a press conference and announced his support of Willkie, saying he was going to vote for him on the *first* ballot. As most of Willkie's sparse delegate strength was on later ballots, after individual delegates had carried out their prior commitments, this was a powerful assist.

Willkie promptly asked the governor of Minnesota to be his floor manager. Nothing more clearly testifies to the genuine amateur standing of both Willkie and his close advisors than the "fascinating anecdote" Stassen told in this connection, during an interview on July 27, 1972.

> When the news flashed that I had told my delegation I was going to vote for Willkie on the first ballot—and at that time he, of course, had very little known support—well when that news flashed out, he phoned me and said he would like to see me; so, with a few other members of our delegation that were also going to vote for him, we went over to his rooms and he thanked me and then said:
> "I would like you to be my floor manager."
> I said, "Well, Wendell, you shouldn't change floor managers right in the middle of the convention."
> He said, "I don't have a floor manager."
> I said, "You're kidding."
> He said, "No, I haven't reached that stage yet."
> This was the second night of the convention!

By this time, however, Willkie's entourage did boast of a few real pros: Raymond Baldwin, governor of Connecticut; Congressman Charles A. Halleck of Willkie's home state of Indiana; Senator Styles Bridges of New Hampshire; Governor Ralph Carr of Colorado; Governor William Vanderbilt of Rhode Island; Sinclair Weeks, national committeeman from Massachusetts; Samuel Pryor, national committeeman from Connecticut; and Walter Hallaran of West Virginia. These advisors had urged the belated choice of Stassen and, when the amazed governor accepted, they agreed to serve under him as floor leaders. Later additions to the group which worked for Willkie on the floor of the convention were a number of his amateurs: the nucleus of the Davenport group including Davenport, Gardner Cowles, as well as Willkie Club leaders Oren Root and James H. Douglas, Jr., of Illinois.

Among the earliest of the professionals to put his political future on the line for this recent convert to Republicanism was his fellow Hoosier, Charlie Halleck, who had announced his support on June 12. Two weeks later, it was Halleck who placed Willkie's name in nomination at the convention.

Most of the others had only announced their support in the last few days before the convention opened. Sam Pryor, though a Willkie believer for several months, publicly supported him for the first time on June 20—four days before the opening session. Governor Baldwin of Connecticut (thanks to diligent cultivating by Pryor) not only came out for Willkie on June 23, the day before the convention opened, but "delivered" the sixteen votes of the Connecticut delegation to him at the same time. This crucial support remained the only solid bloc of votes pledged to Willkie on the first ballot.

The Resolutions Committee, which recommended the party platform, had the immensely difficult task of drafting the foreign policy plank under the critical world conditions. It had to be general enough to be reasonably acceptable to both wings of the widely split party and not embarrassing to the eventual nominee, whatever his ideological position on aid to the Allies. It wasn't until the afternoon of Wednesday, June 26, that the committee's work was accomplished—so successfully, in fact, that the platform, containing its all-things-to-all-delegates foreign policy plank, was adopted unanimously immediately after the opening of the session.

The real drama began on the twenty-sixth when the roll calls of the states started. The preliminary roll call was simply to ascertain which states were planning to put names in nomination and the order in which these nominations would be made. With Alabama and Arizona each in turn yielding to New York, that state's delegation announced that it would place two names in nomination, those of Thomas Dewey and Frank Gannett. Arkansas then yielded to Ohio, whose delegation claimed the honor of nominating Senator Robert Taft.

There was alarm in the Willkie camp when Indiana's name was called and the delegation passed. But when at the end of the roll call Indiana "reconsidered" and announced that Willkie's state would put his name in nomination, the galleries erupted in shouts of "We want Willkie," which drowned out the proceedings of the convention for a long time.

When this was stilled and the preliminary roll call had come to an end, the serious business of the actual nominations began. Dewey, "a lifelong Republican," was the first to be nominated by John Lord O'Brian of New York. After a twenty-five-minute demonstration on the floor and cheering from the galleries, four seconding speeches were made.

Representative James A. Wadsworth of New York then placed in nomination the name of Frank E. Gannett, a newspaper publisher from Rochester. Unhappily for him, this elicited only two minutes of applause.

The third nomination was made by Grove Patterson of the *Toledo Blade,* who extolled the unique qualifications for leadership of Senator Robert Taft of Ohio. In particular, he emphasized Taft's experience in government and his proven ability as a vote getter. (The Dewey and Taft nominations had both stressed qualifications to which Willkie could make no claim.) The demonstration for Taft was louder, longer, and better prepared than Dewey's.

Everyone knew, by this time, that Willkie's name was to come next. From the moment that Representative Charles Halleck of Indiana reached the rostrum in order to nominate him, the chant from the galleries that had already become the theme song of the convention, "We want Willkie," mounted from a rumble to a roar. At the same time, a chorus of hisses and boos erupted from the delegates. When Chairman Martin tried to restore order by reminding the visitors in the balconies that they were guests, a voice shouted back: "Guests, hell! We're the people!"

It was almost impossible to calm the galleries. Every time Willkie's name was mentioned or someone started to cry "We want Willkie," the spectators, now completely out of control, joined in more loudly and insistently than ever. The chairman, at long last and with great difficulty, managed to quiet the hubbub sufficiently to recognize Halleck. At the first mention of Willkie's name, however, the uproar began all over again—boos and catcalls from the delegates and a deafening crescendo of "We want Willkie" from the galleries. Finally, the courageous young Indiana Congressman managed to place the name of Wendell Willkie, a former Democrat, in nomination as the Republican candidate for president of the United States. This was the moment everyone had been waiting for, so as Halleck carried on, the din finally subsided in order to hear his words.

Halleck pictured Willkie as the American dream incarnate—small town boy from good but simple home achieves fame and fortune through hard work and native intelligence. When Halleck asked, "Are we to understand . . . that any man is barred from our deliberations who has been an American success?" the galleries roared back, "No!"

The demonstration that virtually exploded at the end of Halleck's short effective speech was this time, surprisingly, not confined to the shrieking galleries. Though some delegates just sat and watched, and the boos of others were drowned in the general chaos, the Indiana delegation started marching around the aisles. After a fight among several New York delegates for the privilege of carrying the state's standard, the mayor of Syracuse finally rushed it triumphantly to the head of the march, as other states and individual delegates fell in behind. For excitement, enthusiasm, duration, and obvious spontaneity the demonstration for Willkie totally eclipsed those that had gone before. When order was at last sufficiently restored, three seconding speeches were made and the long session adjourned.

At 11:00 P.M., the delegates walked out onto streets in pandemonium. Dense excited crowds jammed the sidewalks. Hundreds of marching Willkie Club members and other volunteers roaring "We want Willkie" paraded with banners flying, brass bands blaring. As the galleries emptied onto the steaming streets, mixing with the crowds and adding to the excitement, the impression created was overwhelming: Though the Republican convention might not want Willkie, America did—an impression strongly reinforced by the stacks of telegrams and the packets from the Voluntary Mailing Committee that greeted each weary delegate as he or she arrived at his hotel.

The next morning, the twenty-seventh, the *New York Herald Tribune* came out for Willkie. Its editorial endorsement, carried in a box on the front page, urged the convention to nominate Willkie, saying, "Such timing of the man and the hour does not come often in his day. We doubt if it ever comes twice to a political party." (Despite these doubts, "the hour" came again twelve years later—or so it appeared to the *Herald Tribune*— when another front-page editorial used the same words in endorsing General Eisenhower.) On the same day of the *Herald Tribune* endorsement, the balloting began.

Anyone who has been to or watched a national party convention on television (impossible in 1940) knows of the suspense and excitement generated by the balloting when there is a real contest and the outcome is in serious question. As the balloting proceeds and candidates gain or lose votes, the tension grows almost unbearable. Though there have been conventions at which it was necessary to take many more ballots, there have been few where interest and emotions ran higher and friction was greater than in 1940. With the isolationists bitterly opposed to the aid-to-the-Allies wing of the party, the oldtime pros and the hyperactive amateurs at daggers drawn, and "the man to beat" a registered Democrat only five months before, it was no wonder that tempers were growing increasingly short as the time for balloting approached.

Furthermore, that afternoon, June 27, Convention Hall was an inferno. Day after day the blazing outdoor temperatures and the body heat of the delegates and spectators had built up temperature records inside the auditorium. By this fourth day the thermometers in the hall registered well over a hundred degrees even before it filled up and the huge hot lights necessary for the newsreel cameras were turned on. Marcia Davenport remembers Convention Hall as "a hell of sealed-in heat" and the night sessions ones of "torture because of the blazing illumination."

After convening the afternoon session at 4:30 P.M., the chairman announced that he was moving at once to the first ballot. "Alabama," he called, and the voting started. And so did the "We want Willkie" chant from the galleries. As the roll call proceeded, each time Willkie picked up some votes the galleries clapped and chanted some more. The chairman kept admonishing them—to no avail. The rhythmic chant seemed to have no end and no beginning, only greater or lesser intensity.

At the end of the first ballot, Dewey had 360 votes, Taft 189, and Willkie a surprising 105. As the Dewey forces had counted on between 400 and 450, and Willkie hadn't hoped for more than about 75, Willkie's supporters were elated. Surprising, too, was the poor showing of Senator Vandenberg, with only 76. The remaining votes were scattered among the nine other serious candidates and favorite sons, including 17 for Hoover.

Tension was high as the second ballot began, and mounted as votes started shifting. The galleries went wild with each switch to Willkie. When the votes were tabulated Willkie and Taft had each made substantial gains—Taft now had 203 votes, Willkie 171—but Dewey had slipped to 338, a bad sign for him.

The session was then recessed from 6:45 to 8:30, and it was during that period that Stassen managed a secret meeting in a freight elevator backstage to try to persuade Alf Landon to swing the votes of the Kansas delegation to Willkie.

On the third ballot, Willkie moved out ahead of Taft into second place. As the result of some very major breaks in the delegations of New York, Massachusetts, and Delaware, Willkie ended with 259. Dewey, though still ahead, had dropped to 315, while Taft's small gain put him at only 212.

The galleries were uncontrollable when the fourth ballot put Willkie in the lead. A big gain of 47 votes brought his total to 306. Dewey's slide continued—down to 250, while Taft, with 43 new votes jumped to 254.

It was apparent at the start of the fifth ballot that the contest was now between Willkie and Taft. The critical question was which one would pick up more of the Dewey votes. As the tension and the temperature in the jammed auditorium both soared to record highs, the race whipsawed back and forth. When the Kansas delegation gave all of its votes to Willkie, the galleries exploded. But Pennsylvania's crucial 51 votes were once again cast for Governor James, their favorite son. At the end of the roll call, Willkie and Taft had picked up the identical number of additional votes—123 for each, bringing Willkie to 429 and Taft 377. Willkie needed only 72 more to win the nomination.

By this time it was past midnight and Taft's leaders hurriedly decided to ask for an adjournment until morning so that they could organize a last minute stop-Willkie drive. But Joe Martin, whether perfunctorily or deliberately (he had been an impartial chairman, but was known to favor Willkie), had been quicker than they and had called for the sixth ballot before they had time to make their motion.

The first break for Willkie came when Senator Vandenberg released all of the Michigan delegation which, until then, had voted solidly for him. Thirty-five of the 38 votes went to Willkie amid ecstatic cheers from the balconies. This news reached the

Pennsylvania delegation in the midst of a caucus called to decide on their next move. Pennsylvania passed. Michigan's switch, however, appeared to have started a bandwagon. State after state gave additional votes to Willkie until Virginia's 16 put him over the top with 502 votes.

Willkie's supporters were now deliriously excited, their ranks swollen by hundreds more who were throwing away their Taft and Dewey buttons and were donning Willkie's. The galleries and the floor outdid each other in their unrestrained jubilation. No one could possibly hear Governor John Bricker's motion to make the nomination unanimous, nor any of the traditional good-loser speeches made on behalf of the defeated candidates. It was a very long time before Governor Stassen could be heard to thank the convention for its fairness and move for adjournment.

The next morning, the convention reconvened and nominated Senator Charles L. McNary for vice president. The final session met at 4:30 P.M. to hear Willkie accept the nomination. He arrived with Mrs. Willkie, both soaking wet from a sudden rainstorm, and walked to the rostrum through a mass of cheering, flag-waving delegates.

Willkie's speech was short, moving, and apparently impromptu. People who were at the convention remember it that way, and it is said that no copy of the speech exists today. Perhaps its spontaneity was its greatest asset, for his evident sincerity rang through every word. Standing there before the convention delegates, a large impressive figure, unmindful of his drenched appearance, he spoke so eloquently of his gratitude to the party for nominating him and of what they could do together for the country that he won the hearts of many new adherents and the support of all. He spoke as a winner.

There was only one bad moment in his off-the-cuff speech. As he concluded, he made a gigantic Freudian slip. He called on *"you* Republicans" to join him and help him. He ignored it, as the delegates evidently did, and went on to the end, to a burst of enthusiastic applause and renewed demonstrations. He was the darling of the convention that night—not only in the galleries, but on the floor. For the moment, the Republicans appeared to have united behind the man most likely to beat Roosevelt.

The next day they all dispersed—the candidate to New York to wind up his Commonwealth and Southern affairs, the delegates to their home states, and Oren Root and his Willkie Club members, heady with victory, back to their various headquarters to try to figure out their role in the upcoming presidential campaign.

Two questions—in addition to that of the provenance of the mail and telegram blitz—that have been argued since the closing of the 1940 convention are: "Were the galleries packed?" and "Was it really the amateurs that nominated Willkie?"

The charge that Samuel Pryor, chairman of the convention's Committee on Arrangements, had packed the galleries for Willkie arose at the convention itself, as soon as the pro-Willkie sentiment in the galleries became evident. The national committeeman from Texas, Colonel R. B. Creager, a Taft supporter and a member of the Committee on Arrangements, made the accusation.

To the charge that seats had been allocated unfairly Pryor answered that the great majority of seats had been assigned well in advance, as is customary, to the individual states, which had in turn distributed them through ordinary party channels. With most of the delegations then committed to other candidates or favorite sons, the packing charge did not seem credible. To the other accusation—that, during the convention, Pryor had issued thousands of standing-room-only passes to Willkie supporters, Pryor replied that he had issued as many of these tickets as the fire marshal allowed to anyone who asked for them. "Apparently," he commented, "there were more Willkie supporters in Philadelphia than those of other candidates."

On the day the balloting began, Creager arranged for extra security guards at the gates to the hall and to the balconies in order to screen illegal ticketholders. However, "We want Willkie" continued to thunder from the galleries, and the excitement and enthusiasm mounted to the end. When Oren

Root, who checked the galleries from time to time, was asked his opinion of the charge about the standing-room-only passes being deliberately allocated to Willkie supporters, he said that he was convinced it was untrue. Then he added, in an interview, "But I wouldn't have put it past Sam to have tried it."

The widely-held conviction that the amateurs had been the decisive factor in Willkie's nomination was, of course, immediately attacked by the professionals. They conveniently forgot that it was not until almost the eleventh hour that Willkie won the support of a handful of pros, without whose skillful management at the convention his nomination would certainly have been in doubt.

But it was the amateurs who, in an incredibly short time, made Willkie known around the country, who both generated and captured the widespread enthusiasm for him, and then turned this powerful force on the delegates at Philadelphia. Professionals want to win, and without this strong demand from the grass roots it is impossible to imagine that the very small band of professionals who finally spearheaded the Willkie drive for delegates would have undertaken it, and inconceivable that they could have "blitzed" the convention as the amateurs did.

The charge that this popular uprising was created by Wall Street and "the Power Trust"—that it was, in fact, a Wall Street "conspiracy"—was made immediately by hardcore Willkie opponents such as Senator George Norris, Representative Luther Patrick of Alabama, and John Elliott Rankin of Mississippi.

Senator Styles Bridges countered these charges in the Senate by pointing out that, far from conspiring for his nomination, the utilities industry was scared to death of becoming "a political football" in a Willkie campaign, and many of his associates urgently tried to dissuade him from his course.

There is no question about Wall Street and the news media being helpful to Willkie. Though, compared to today, the techniques of selling a president via the media (newspapers, magazines, and radio) were in their infancy, Wall Street did have powerful connections around the country and certainly used them. But no conspiracy between them can possibly account for the frenzy for Willkie that swept the country between April and November.

Marcia Davenport says:

> I was at the nerve-centre of the Willkie pre-nomination and Presidential campaigns, working with my husband. . . . I saw something rather more genuine and spontaneous than these collective pressures. For that matter, every Presidential nomination and campaign since 1940 has been increasingly a phenomenon of pressures, in recent years particularly, by advertising experts and the hypertensive techniques of television broadcasting, and bankers have not been idle bystanders either. It is demonstrably mistaken to assume that support by newspaper publishers and their editorial staff will get a candidate nominated or elected.

And Governor Harold Stassen, the professional who guided Willkie's fortunes through the convention, in discussing the relative importance of the role of the amateurs vis-à-vis that of the pros, stated emphatically:

> Certainly in modern times, certainly in degree and in impact, the Willkie volunteer movement was outstanding because of one thing. There is no doubt whatsoever in my mind that if it hadn't been for the volunteer movement, the Republican Party never would have nominated Willkie whereas it was the volunteer movement that made the difference for nomination. And, secondly, that it was a kind of turning point in [Republican] policy at that time, which the volunteers did a lot toward.

In his exhaustive work on Willkie's relations with the party, Donald Bruce Johnson sums up the general consensus in one short sentence:

> The party of Harding, Coolidge, and Hoover, over the objection of its congressional wing and many local bosses, accepted a former Democrat, a corporation president, and political maverick as the result of a popular uprising of the nonpolitical components of the party's rank and file assisted by a relatively small band of floor leaders.

This crowd of Willkie enthusiasts, more than ten thousand unable to enter the already jammed Buffalo Memorial Auditorium to hear their candidate speak, reflects the success of the volunteer Willkie Clubs.

III

"Win with Willkie"

The amateurs' conviction that they were responsible for Willkie's nomination gave enormous impetus to the Willkie Clubs in the ensuing presidential campaign. It also exacerbated the usual difficulties between the professionals and the amateurs. The second and last chapter of the great 1940 crusade was just as exciting, but fraught with many more problems than the first.

Willkie's first move was to try to effect his personal reconciliation with the old guard without tarnishing his independent image or losing the confidence of his more liberal supporters. At his request the National Committee appointed a body representing all the elements in the party to try to unite the badly split Republicans. When the candidate's next suggestion of a troika—consisting of the chairman of the Republican National Committee, a personal representative of Willkie, and his campaign manager as chairman—to run his campaign was turned down, Willkie appointed his own largely professional advisory committee. Unfortunately, neither committee proved to be very active, so most of the crucial decisions were eventually made by Willkie himself, with the advice of the small coterie of predominantly amateur advisors who had been with him from the start.

His dismissal of John Hamilton as chairman of the National Committee and replacement with House Leader Joe Martin was a logical but controversial move. Although Hamilton had been friendly to Willkie and helpful to his aspirations at the convention, he represented the old regime in the eyes of the voters. A candidate with new ideas and more progressive policies was entitled to select a chairman whose views were more in accord with his own. Nevertheless, Hamilton was very popular with the regular organization, which Willkie would need, and even though Willkie kept him on as executive director of the committee, Hamilton's demotion angered many. On the other hand, Martin, a respected and popular congressional leader, soon discovered that it was impossible for him to do justice to both jobs, and both eventually suffered.

From Willkie's retreat in Colorado Springs, where he went for "a rest" following his nomination and the winding up of his business affairs, plans were announced for the campaign. Two campaign headquarters were to be established—one in New York for the East, one in Chicago for the rest of the country. The Willkie Clubs were to continue under Oren Root, and were to be entirely independent of the campaign organization and the National Committee and responsible only to Willkie. Root immediately announced plans to reorganize and expand the clubs on a state-by-state basis and said that they would "cooperate with the Republican state organizations."

By the middle of July, 560 official clubs, geared to the new requirements of the presidential campaign, had been authorized. How many unaffiliated clubs there were then or later was never ascertained. The Willkie Clubs were planned to be self-supporting and, in an effort to obtain maximum grass-roots participation, charged only twenty-five cents for membership. Another independent volunteer organization, responsible only to Willkie, was Democrats-for-Willkie, which did not get under way until August 12. Their members were so determined to maintain their Democratic identity that they even refused affiliation with the Willkie Clubs. This top-heavy plan of organization, with the candidate himself the only coordinator, was inefficient and created many problems.

Although Democrats-for-Willkie had the strong leadership of Lewis W. Douglas and John W. Hanes, two prominent former New Dealers, as well as Alan Valentine, president of the University of Rochester, and raised a good deal of money, the anticipated widespread revolt of Democrats against the third term never materialized. Heartened by the support of such leading Democrats as Al Smith, former governor of New York, Senator Edward R. Burke of Nebraska, Harry B. Coffee, a Democratic Congressman from Willkie's home state, and a number of other prominent professional and lay Democrats, Willkie had confidently anticipated that the grass roots would follow suit.

But tremendous numbers of people all over the country: the poor, the disadvantaged, the underprivileged—those whom "the party of the people" claimed as their own—had profited greatly from Roosevelt's New Deal. Immediately after he became president in 1932, he took decisive measures to combat the "Hoover depression," give help to its victims, and restore the economy to health. Many of these measures, such as those designed to ease the financing and construction of new homes, helped industrial recovery as well as the individuals hardest hit by the depression. For the New Deal reforms were not solely concerned with helping the poor and unemployed. Industrial and agricultural recovery were equally important, in fact basic to enabling the President to carry out his other goals. He began consciously to employ fiscal policy as an aid to recovery, and government regulation of business increased from then on.

For the hard-pressed farmers, by acts of Congress and executive decrees, he tried to guarantee a fair return for their labor and restore their purchasing power.

Needless to say, many of Roosevelt's moves were controversial. Excessive government "meddling" with the economy was attacked, and some programs worked better than others.

But it was a stupendous record of action, designed to help everyone—business, labor, the farmer, the homeowner, the consumer, and the disadvantaged. No one could deny that the average citizen was a lot better off than when Hoover left office. Despite grumbling in many quarters, generally speaking, despair had given way to hope.

It was on this record that Franklin Roosevelt was running for a third term. And the regular Democrats across the country were citing this record of accomplishment, warning of the danger of a Republican administration turning the clock back and reminding the people—now heart and soul with the Allies in their grim battle for survival—of Roosevelt's early and continued efforts to give them all possible aid while keeping us out of war. After all, "no third term" was only a tradition, and traditions are not legally binding. The warning "Don't change horses in the middle of a stream" began to worry many people as much as the third-term issue.

In spite of all of this, Willkie never lost confidence that his philosophy was the right one, and that his being an ex-Democrat would make it easier for those within the party who believed as he did to rally to him. But this attitude had a seriously adverse effect within his new party. To ease this step for the disaffected Democrats, he became increasingly reluctant to tie himself too closely to the regular Republican organization. This embittered many of the pros and generated a necessarily heavy dependence on his amateur advisers and workers. Accusations along these lines started as early as during his so-called vacation at Colorado Springs when many professionals complained that they were unable to get appointments with him while, according to Sam Pryor, his amateur staff allowed "all the screwballs in the United States" to visit him. Pryor added that Willkie was "completely out of touch with the real party leaders" during that time. Whether these statements were accurate or not, the impression that was created was one that persisted and became accentuated throughout the campaign.

The country at large, however, seized with a Willkie frenzy difficult to exaggerate, was for the most part unaware of this developing friction. The Willkie Clubs were proliferating at a rapid rate in spite of a high-level decision to confine them to skeleton operations during the remainder of the summer, using the interval to reorganize and lay plans for the Labor Day opening of the campaign. The purpose of the clubs would now be to carry Willkie's vision for America to a much wider audience, and to provide a home base and active work for Independents and Democrats inspired either by anti-third-term sentiments, Willkie's personal magnetism, or his optimistic confidence in America—the so-called "higher-purpose appeal."

The key to winning, according to the best calculations, would be the Independent vote, which had been increasing at every recent election. With the third-term issue thought to be a potentially major factor, unhappy Democrats needed a place to go. Many preferred the Willkie Clubs to the more ideologically rigid Democrats-for-Willkie because the clubs were available, lively, and had already demonstrated their effectiveness.

The national Willkie Clubs' new plan of organization divided the United States into a number of regions to each of which coordinators were sent. Their assignment was to work out plans with the already existing clubs and, using the simple but successful chain-reaction technique developed in the spring, to establish as many new ones as possible before the September launching of the official campaign.

Root, himself, was fully aware, and had been warned by Joe Martin, of the importance of clearing club activities with the regular organization in every state and locality. In July, he called a meeting of the Willkie Club state leaders and stressed this point with specific instructions about procedure. Also to allay the professionals' suspicions of the clubs as a threat to the regular organization, Root announced that his organization would disband immediately after the election. Nonetheless, it was a tightrope to walk then—as it has been in every campaign since—to appeal to Independents and dissident members of the opposite party while clearing plans with the regular party organization, which is sometimes tolerant, occasionally cooperative, but all-too-often actively hostile to the amateurs.

In spite of the precautions Root had taken, trouble between the two groups soon developed and mounted throughout the campaign. Added to the discord between the clubs and the regular organization were growing difficulties with the established Young Republican National Federation, which felt it was "playing second fiddle" to the Willkie Clubs. The fact that the federation was responsible to the Republican National Committee while the clubs reported directly to the candidate added to this impression. The Young Republicans shared the professionals' contempt for the unorthodox and often naïve methods of the amateurs, as well as the regular organization's jealousy of the amateurs' success and—despite Root's assurances—a deep-seated fear that the clubs would try to take over. The amateurs, on the other hand, were not fully under the control of their leaders. Flushed with their victory over the old guard at the convention, impatient with the old politics and local party politicking, cocksure about their own innovations, they often plunged brashly ahead with organizing and planning, giving scant regard to the local party or the Young Republicans. Just as often, the state or local organizations tried to thwart the amateurs, frequently for their own private ends.

In Pennsylvania, old guardsman Joseph N. Pew, who had belatedly delivered Pennsylvania's delegation to Willkie at the convention, was intent on building his own political machine and was openly hostile to the expansion of the Willkie Clubs there. Professional help had to be rushed to the clubs' chairman to avoid a donnybrook.

There was three-way trouble in Baltimore between two Republican factions and the campaign finance chairman, all apparently more interested in obtaining control of the collection and expenditure of campaign funds than in the election itself. For a while the Willkie Clubs appeared to be the only groups working for the candidate in Maryland.

The original organizer of the Kansas Willkie Clubs, Jay Scovel, a small-town lawyer, was actually dropped as chairman after the convention. The party regulars, headed by Alf Landon, wanted complete control of the Kansas campaign, and a protest went to Joe Martin, who passed on the organization's edict to Root. Root had to swallow it, but it was a bitter pill for him and Scovel.

Yet the official campaign had not even begun. Willkie had not yet met "the Champ," as he referred to Roosevelt.

Willkie chose his home town of Elwood as the place to receive the official notification of the party's nomination and give his formal acceptance speech.

August 17, the day Wendell and Edith Willkie arrived in Elwood, was a typical August day in Indiana. The temperature has been variously recorded as 102 to 112 in the shade, and the prairie sun was blazing. But every street through which they were driven had been brilliantly decked out in flags and "We want Willkie" pennants and posters. There were so many people cheering them along the way that the Willkies feared there might be a sparse gathering to greet them and hear his speech in Calloway Park.

They were mistaken. A big crowd of hometown folk was swelled to a mass meeting of gigantic proportions by enthusiastic supporters who had poured into little Elwood from all over the country. In spite of the burning heat, the biting insects, inadequate facilities, and the din and confusion, people had been gathered there for hours patiently waiting for the moment of Willkie's arrival.

As their car drove into the park, a tremendous cheer went up and, despite their police escorts, it took a long time for the Willkies to get to the flag-draped rostrum that had been erected for him, and even longer to calm the crowd.

The Republican candidate's formal acceptance speech was delivered before an audience of over two hundred thousand people. Determined that his first statement should be an accurate reflection of his own beliefs, whether it pleased the Republicans or not, he gave them "an outline of the political philosophy that is in my heart." Unfortunately, his delivery was far more subdued than usual, and the speech had a mixed reception at the time, and in the press the following day.

People accused Davenport of having written an essay rather than a rousing speech for the candidate. Furthermore, woven into the text was unequivocal support both for Roosevelt's foreign and domestic policies. Willkie actually quoted Roosevelt in supporting the President's determination to extend to the "opponents of force the material resources of this nation." He emphasized the necessity of regulating the "force of free enterprise" and endorsed point by point practically all of the domestic reforms of the New Deal, including collective bargaining; the establishment of wage and hour standards; the regulation of utilities, securities, and banking; unemployment and old age insurance; and federal aid to farmers. Norman Thomas, the Socialist presidential candidate, remarked, "He agreed with Mr. Roosevelt's entire program of social reform and said it was leading to disaster."

Nevertheless, there must have been great numbers of people throughout the country who recognized that this speech embodied the honest convictions of an honest man, and who applauded it. The newspapers, whose publishers were almost all Republican-oriented, were practically unanimous in approving it. But far more important, the polls, reflecting the national clamor for him, showed Willkie's popularity at an all-time high. Gallup reported that, in Ohio, "a good barometer of national political sentiment," Willkie would receive fifty-three percent of the vote.

Two weeks later, on Labor Day, the campaign opened formally and auspiciously for Willkie. One of his first steps was to meet with twenty-one regular Republican leaders from the eastern and midwestern states. In response to their stressing the importance of rousing the enthusiasm of the party organization, the candidate said that, though he supported the work of the Willkie Clubs and would continue to do so, the party leaders could rest assured that any interference with the regular organization would not be tolerated. He also relieved their anxieties about patronage, promising that it would continue to go to them and not to the Willkie clubs or the Davenport group. When Root was questioned during a later interview about the reaction of the Willkie Club members to this pledge, he replied crisply, "They weren't looking for patronage. They didn't want plums."

The day after this meeting, Oren Root made his first speech under the auspices of the Republican county committee at Binghamton, New York. It proved to be a successful attempt to improve relations between the two groups, but it was but one of a few drops in a very large bucket.

In the twelve months since Germany's invasion of Poland and England and France's declaration of war, the world situation had gone from bad to very much worse. During a curious period of German inactivity, the British set up a naval blockade of Germany, and the British and French troops whiled away their time behind the Maginot line. Then on April 9, the Germans launched a surprise attack on Norway and Denmark. In May, they overran Luxembourg and invaded Holland and Belgium. On the thirteenth, they outflanked the Maginot line, raced to the English channel, and the desperate but heroic evacuation from Dunkirk followed. On June 22, two days before the opening of the Republican convention, France signed an armistice with Germany, and the Vichy government was set up under Marshal Pétain.

Meanwhile, the President, with the unofficial but loyal support of Wendell Willkie, the man who was now his opponent, had been doing all within his power to stem the tide. He continued to speak out against aggression and international greed, to awaken America to what was at stake for us and the rest of the world. After the fighting started, he speeded up his effort to build United States strength and make America "an arsenal of democracy."

Then on July 10, the Nazis sent their first armada of bombers across England and the Battle of Britain was on. At first, the Luftwaffe concentrated on industrial targets and on shipping. But on August 13, the all-out blitz began, with London and other populous centers on the daily bombing schedule.

Willkie's campaign officially opened when the London blitz was at its terrifying height.

He spent most of September whistle-stopping by train across the western United States. Until the advent of the airplane in sufficient numbers and with sufficient routes, campaigning across the vast continent of America was of necessity done by whistle-stop for three or four months. The Willkie campaign was probably the last one that had to rely on this method. Although Truman in 1948 and Eisenhower and Stevenson in 1952 all included some whistle-stopping in their campaigns, it was no longer indispensable, but was more a matter of creating a nostalgic impact and newsworthiness.

Traditionally, a whistle-stop train consisted of a varying number of cars carrying the candidate, his family, his campaign staff, his research people, secretaries and typists, and—very importantly—members of the press, who were to send eyewitness accounts back to their papers of the doings aboard the train and the candidate's speeches at the stops. And, of course, there were dining cars.

There were compartment cars for the more important members of the entourage, and cars with upper and lower berths for lesser lights. The candidate, with his family, occupied the rear car, so that he could easily step out onto the observation platforms to woo the crowds at the short stops when there was not enough time to parade into town to address them in the city square or a local auditorium.

Basically, this was the setup of the Willkie train when it left New York on September 12. It did not start under auspicious circumstances, as the Gallup and Roper polls had both just shown a sharp decline in Willkie's popularity following his meteoric rise—perhaps because he had been out of circulation too long.

The friction, which Marcia Davenport later described as "bitter warfare" between "our sworn enemies," the professionals, and the "wild-eyed amateurs," began on the campaign train. Because it was more convenient to have his friend, idea man, and speech writer, Russell Davenport, close at hand, and because many of his friends with whom he felt most at home had been among his leading amateur supporters, they were all assigned to the Willkies' car or the one adjoining. Among them were Raymond Buell, a well-known economist, the man who had invited Willkie to the *Fortune* Round Table meeting at which he had introduced him to Davenport; Elliott Buell, a financial expert; Pierce Butler, Jr., of Minneapolis, a prominent Democrat for Willkie; Bartley Crum, a San Francisco lawyer; and, from time to time, Oren Root. There was only one person among them considered by the professionals to be "a real Republican"—John B. Hollister of Cincinnati, who was a law partner of Senator Taft, and active in his Ohio organization.

This, of course, created jealousy among the professionals. The much larger number of top Republican officials aboard strongly resented the amateurs' influence and the disproportionate amount of time Willkie spent with them. This gave rise to the accusation that Willkie's volunteer workers, Russell Davenport especially, were making it impossible for them to see the candidate.

Davenport, though a fine writer, was a disorganized man. Constant confusion was the result, and the press carried almost daily accounts of the chaos and anarchy aboard the train, and the professionals' complaints about the naive and high-handed methods of the amateurs.

But this time the dissatisfaction with the candidate was not confined to the professionals. Now some of Willkie's rank-and-file supporters were becoming worried. The war was in the forefront of everyone's mind and, if Willkie approved so whole-heartedly of Roosevelt's handling of America's role, was it sensible to try to jettison the seasoned leader under such critical world conditions?

As early as 1935, President Roosevelt had become increasingly concerned about international developments. That year, in a letter to Bernard Baruch, the influential New York financier who was his trusted friend and advisor, Roosevelt confided, "I still worry about world affairs more than domestic problems, which include the election." He had watched Japan's invasion of Manchuria and Germany's rearmament with growing concern, but the overwhelming isolationism of this country tied his hands as far as taking strong measures was concerned. With great reluctance he signed new neutrality acts and resolutions which the Congress, reflecting its constituencies, had passed.

By December 1937, the Japanese army had crossed into China and was well on its way to taking it over, with Nanking about to fall. The American gunboat, the U.S.S. *Panay,* lying at anchor on the Yangtze River, not far from Nanking, was in the process of evacuating, on the advice of the Chinese foreign office, American citizens—largely embassy staff, American businessmen, and newspaper correspondents. Two Japanese warplanes, with no provocation, suddenly flew over her, bombed her, and sank her. The Yangtze, by treaty, was an international waterway and Joseph Grew, the United States ambassador to China, expected an immediate declaration of war by the United States. Instead, the Japanese apologies for their "mistake" were accepted in Washington. The crisis subsided and soon became merely the *Panay* "incident," and did little to change the public's mood of isolationism.

Again the President was frustrated by his inability to move public opinion, as he had discovered when, shortly before, he had dedicated a bridge in Chicago. In his speech, he had suggested that the time had come "to quarantine the aggressors." This phrase aroused a storm of protest, accusing him of being a warmonger, and worse. He had to wait for another opportunity.

Then in September 1938, came Munich and the signing of the pact in which France and Britain ceded, under the leadership of Neville Chamberlain, the Sudentenland, a good portion of Czechoslovakia, to Hitler. In the spring of 1939, the führer seized the rest. The fate of Czechoslovakia at last awakened America—or a large part of it—when people began to realize that, as one of the bulwarks of the free world, our own interests and safety were at stake. Shortly afterward, the President recalled our ambassador from Berlin in protest against the atrocities against the Jews in Germany.

He summoned the congressional leaders to the White House, and there he laid before them all the evidence he had from his intelligence people. From the evidence, there was only one conclusion to be drawn: Hitler was on the march, and the Allies had only an even chance—if that—of holding their own. The President asked for a revision of the Neutrality Act to enable the United States to help the beleaguered Allies. William Borah, the powerful isolationist senator from Idaho, refused. No one supported the President.

In his January 1939 message to Congress, the President explained that the part of the Neutrality Act to which he strenuously objected was the blanket arms embargo section. It actually aided the aggressors by forcing the United States to withhold arms from the Allies as well as from Germany. Though he would prefer repeal of the entire act, the President asked for executive authority to limit the embargo to aggressors only, with the President empowered to make individual decisions. In July, an attempt was made in Congress to enact this measure. It failed.

In September, four days after the country was rocked by the news that Germany had invaded Poland on the first, Congress acted. They formally proclaimed United States neutrality.

Roosevelt, determined to get around the difficulties caused by the arms embargo, proposed a plan which became known as "cash and carry." Our shipping would remain restricted, but nations could come in their own ships and pay as they picked up what they needed. This, of course, favored the strategically-located Allies of western Europe. After delicate presidential negotiations and heated congressional debate, the Neutrality Act itself was finally repealed, as the President had hopefully predicted to Prime Minister Chamberlain a month earlier.

Then in June, when Italy joined Germany and declared war on France, the president gave the British fifty overage destroyers. In return, he got ninety-nine-year leases for the United States on all the British air and naval bases in the Western Hemisphere.

Meanwhile, public opinion in the United States had polarized into two camps: the isolationists and the so-called interventionists. The term *interventionist* included everyone from out-and-out warmongers to those who felt the most likely way of avoiding America's getting involved in the war was by giving all possible aid to those who were fighting our cause for us—the hard-pressed Allies.

Within days of the announcement of the overage-destroyer deal, a Yale law student, Robert D. Stuart, Jr., son of R. Douglas Stuart, a prominent Republican and president of the Quaker Oats Company, announced the formation of the Committee to Defend America First. Young Stuart got General Robert E. Wood, another well-known and respected Republican, and chairman of the board of Sears Roebuck and Company, to head it. Charles Lindbergh was one of its early members. Its stated objective was to be ready to fight for the United States—but *not* Britain. "America First" soon became, and remained, the most influential antiwar organization in the country.

In response to America First, William Allen White, editor of the *Emporia Gazette* (Kansas), organized the Committee to Defend America by Aiding the Allies. Because of its long name, which embodied its objectives, it was usually referred to as the William Allen White Committee. Among its leaders were Robert Sherwood, the playwright; John J. McCloy; and Mrs. Dwight Morrow, Lindbergh's mother-in-law. This committee had immediate widespread support, including almost all of the major newspapers in the country except the *Chicago Tribune* and the *Washington Times-Herald.* In isolationist Chicago, the home of Colonel McCormick, General Wood, and the Stuarts, and the national headquarters of America First, the courageous young lawyer who accepted its chairmanship was named Adlai Stevenson.

The President's destroyer deal in June, and his continuing efforts to inform the American people and help the Allies, won the approval of more and more of the public, and, of course, the strong support of the White committee. This focusing of attention on Roosevelt's every move diverted the public's attention from the Republican candidate, now out of the limelight, planning his campaign and issuing occasional statements from his temporary headquarters in Denver.

The organizer of the Maine Willkie Clubs reported that members of the Committee to Defend America by Aiding the Allies (whose membership frequently overlapped with that of the clubs) were becoming somewhat disenchanted. When, on September 27, the news broke that Japan had joined the German-Italian alliance, the case was strengthened for keeping the experienced incumbent.

Nonetheless, Willkie campaigned through the West with his usual vigor. He believed profoundly that the New Deal was undermining America's traditional bulwarks: the democratic process, our civil liberties, and the free enterprise system. Shouting and gesticulating from the rear platform of his train he hammered home these themes a dozen times a day at whistle-stops, meetings, and rallies all across the western states. And he became more and more sure of himself. At the railroad station in Topeka he cried out, "I'm the cockiest fellow you ever saw. If you want to vote for me, fine. If you don't, go jump in the lake and I'm still for you."

In Lincoln, Nebraska, he went on the offensive, defending business as the American way of life. He said that he was a businessman and proud of it. And he challenged people who had any reservations about his qualifications on that account to vote against him.

Just before he had left New York, at a chance meeting in the Waldorf Hotel barber shop, Jim Farley, who was strongly anti-third-term, advised Willkie that there was only *one* issue that would get votes this year—the question of a third term. But Willkie, convinced that his mission was to make people understand all that was at stake in the election, made surprisingly little use of the third-term issue. He earnestly exhorted his audiences to preserve our traditional freedoms against all comers—big government and big business alike. And he would cry out, in a voice growing hoarser at every stop, "only the strong can be free and only the productive can be strong," a phrase he first used in his Elwood acceptance speech. Finally, his voice gave out and a throat specialist had to be called; he stayed with Willkie until the end of the campaign, but Willkie's voice never regained its fine dynamic quality.

Although Willkie had some cool receptions and the Democrats kept talking about a "slump" in his fortunes, the campaign picked up momentum and, by the end of his western tour, his supporters counted it a great success. The polls were mixed—some indicating another slide in his rating (his adherents felt these samplings were not up to date and did not reflect the recent upturn), while others showed another surge in popularity and Gallup gave Willkie a twenty-five percent stronger rating with the independent voters than Landon had in 1936.

Another indication of renewed enthusiasm was the rapidity

with which the Willkie Clubs were proliferating, a process that continued to accelerate until election day. A report of the Associated Willkie Clubs of Illinois to their national headquarters for the week of October 21–25, for example, shows that forty-eight new clubs affiliated with the state clubs on the twenty-first, thirty-five on the twenty-second, forty-five on the twenty-third, and thirty on the twenty-fourth. Unfortunately, the report for the twenty-fifth is missing. These reports include only clubs outside of metropolitan Chicago and indicate they were active groups and were forming in virtually every county. Chicago was organized on a precinct basis and reported separately. Though there were probably some "paper" organizations among them, the Chicago clubs were for the most part lively and hardworking. James H. Douglas, Jr., vice chairman of the Illinois Willkie Clubs, stated in his final report that there were 2200 affiliated clubs in Illinois, that "more than half of that number were in Chicago, and a large number of the Chicago clubs were organized as precinct clubs."

On October 22, the *Willkie Club News,* mimeographed "house organ" of the Peoria, Illinois, club, reported that their "Volunteer Worker's Organization" consisted of a chairman, 10 ward chairmen, 132 precinct chairmen, and 660 volunteer workers. Estimating that there were at that time in the neighborhood of 20,000 independent voters in Peoria, the *News* asserted:

> This organization can and will yield a tremendous influence on them. This is a Crusade for Freedom and Democracy. Democrats, Republicans and Independents are working together to preserve the type of government our forefathers established. All races and creeds are represented.
>
> Peoria has never experienced such a movement. Every precinct in the city will be covered by workers who are voluntarily giving their time to help out in a great cause.

There follows a report of the ward meetings already held and the others scheduled, where workers' kits containing supplies and instructions were distributed and reports given. This section ends: "We must reach every man and woman in every walk of life . . . in every type of employment . . . of every political belief. There is little time left, *JUST THIRTEEN DAYS MORE!*"

Following an impressive list of "Reports and News Items," the final paragraph tells the "hundreds of Peorians—eager to join this Crusade" how they can help and where they can enlist.

An example of advance planning was contained in volume one, number two of the *Idaho Willkie Club News,* which had been mimeographed for distribution by the end of September, and was sent to each club in Idaho as it organized. It reproduced the "plan of organization" which had been successfully used by the local Boise club. It included advice on precinct work, business house work, and how to organize committees and meetings. It quoted the *New York Times* editorial supporting Willkie ("the first time it has supported a Republican presidential candidate since 1908"), outlined a "plan of the independent campaign," and then listed "suggested salient points," with brief arguments for each:

Labor and Industry
Farmer
Third Term
Roosevelt's Hypocrisy
Democrat (FDR "not a Democrat but a New Dealer")
Warning
War Situation
Willkie's Attitude Toward Business

The Willkie Club files in the Lilly Library at Indiana University are filled with largely improvised plans and reports from every state on the activities of the loosely associated clubs. These documents apparently had been sent to national headquarters more as a matter of information and for distribution to other clubs, if desired, than because of any formal requirement to submit them.

Today's emphasis on politics and political education in

schools and colleges, together with the advent of television, has vastly increased the know-how of political activists. To them the methods of the Willkie Club amateurs may seem crude and to have left much to chance. The miracle is that, with no professional or educational background in politics, faced in many areas with obstructionism from the party organization, and with so little time, they fashioned a relatively effective—if spotty—campaign. And their enthusiasm sparked a movement about which Roosevelt said at the end, it "almost broke the Democratic line of defense."

In the final crucial month, Willkie and his supporters pulled out every stop. The tired candidate, barnstorming the country, began answering Democratic "smears" with increasingly irresponsible statements of his own. Exhaustion, scurrilous personal attacks from the opposition, and a fierce desire to win distort anyone's perspective, and unworthy charges flew back and forth with mounting intensity until the end of the campaign.

As Willkie carried his attack into some of the most diehard Democratic areas, and as the Willkie Clubs doubled and redoubled their efforts and their numbers, other groups joined in the allout drive. National No Third Term Day, October 23, was jointly celebrated by the regular Republican organizations, the Willkie Clubs, the Young Republicans, and other national and local groups. Meanwhile, a host of other voluntary organizations had sprung up, including the Citizens Information Committee, largely a fundraising organization which did some fairly effective precinct work toward the end, and such specialized groups as the Women Workers for Willkie, the Garment Workers for Willkie, the American Writers for Willkie, the Willkie War Veterans, First Voters League, We the People, the Committee of Ten Million Businessmen, Professionals and Farmers, and many more.

The October 27 Gallup poll showed that Willkie's electoral count, which had fallen to a low of thirty-two in late September, had dramatically risen, was accelerating, and had now reached 117. Gallup even predicted that it would be the undecided vote that would determine the outcome of the election. An alarmed President at last took to the hustings and made six major speeches in New York in the few remaining days.

The voter turnout on November 5 was the largest in American history—over forty-nine million people flocked to the polls. Not only the Willkie Club members, but many of the professionals had grown increasingly confident. One proper suburban volunteer, covered with Willkie buttons as she bravely paraded near the polls in one of Chicago's most unsavory Democratic wards, reported that she was swept into the embrace of the Republican precinct captain shouting, "God damn it, baby, we've got the bastards on the run." But such hopes were to be shattered, Roosevelt received 27,244,160 votes and Willkie 22,-305,198—more popular votes than any previous Republican presidential candidate. The electoral vote disparity was far greater: 449 for Roosevelt, 82 for Willkie. The campaign which the *Journal of Politics* called "one of the most exciting and bitter . . . in American history" had ended.

Volumes have been written about why Willkie lost. Most of the reasons given are bound to be speculative. There is only one on which almost everyone agrees, and it was clearly the over-riding one—the war in Europe. Roosevelt himself had predicted that, if the war were over before election day, Willkie would win. Ironically, the very issue that contributed so substantially to his nomination was undoubtedly the decisive factor in Willkie's defeat. Foreseeing, in the spring of 1940, the inevitability of war, he had been the champion of aid to the Allies and of United States preparedness while Taft and Dewey were campaigning on isolationist platforms. By the time Willkie launched his presidential campaign, however, Europe was in flames and he found himself up against the Commander-in-Chief, who not only had been first to advocate the policies of which Willkie and now the majority of the country approved, but had courageously carried them out. The electorate was faced with a clear-cut choice: whether to exchange an experienced leader for an inexperienced one in the middle of a violently turbulent stream.

As happens at the end of every campaign, postmortems attribute all sorts of wisdom to the strategy of the winner, while the loser—by hindsight—has made incredible mistakes. One of the charges made against Willkie's conduct of the campaign was that he lost because he largely ignored the Republican professionals—from the National Committee down to the grass roots —while favoring the amateurs. Hence, the regular organization, by and large, "sat on its hands."

If there actually was sufficient apathy or obstructionism on the part of the old guard Republicans to have made the difference in the outcome, then the party, not Willkie, was the loser. Thanks to the "Willkie Crusade," inspired by his personal magnetism and his advocacy of ideals in which so much of the country believed, and which his nationwide network of Willkie Clubs carried to the grass roots, the defeated candidate found himself a popular hero.

In spite of bickering and conservative opposition, Willkie and his amateurs had reoriented the party. From 1940 until the Goldwater debacle in 1964, the liberal wing continued to be the dominant wing of the Republican party nationally, both in respect to domestic and foreign policy. Even Dewey, in his two subsequent campaigns, reflected this change in ideology.

Furthermore, Willkie's vision of "one world," was later eloquently expressed in his influential book of that title and in his countless impassioned speeches, both at home and abroad. It was a pioneering version of Adlai Stevenson's concept of "spaceship earth"—which, four decades after Willkie, has become so clear to us all.

The 1940 Republican candidate died four years after his defeat, in August 1944, at age fifty-two.

It was Willkie's army of amateurs, whose faith, enthusiasm, and dedicated work played such a large part in his extraordinary career, who blazed the way that subsequent armies of volunteers have followed or imitated. Their story is an important segment of our unique political history.

United Press Photos

General Dwight D. Eisenhower in 1952. Volunteers persuaded him to become Republican candidate for President that year and then, as Citizens for Eisenhower, were vital to his nomination and election.

IV

The General

The Republican party desperately needed to win in 1952 after twenty years of unbroken Democratic administrations. The number of Democrats and Independents who, in 1940, had been troubled by the specter of a third term was now vastly swollen as people realized that another Democratic victory would mean one-party government for nearly a quarter of a century.

After their unsuccessful 1940 experiment with Wendell Willkie, a political neophyte, the Republicans in 1944 had put up Thomas Dewey, an established big-name politician, as their presidential candidate. When he lost they renominated him in 1948, and that year the party achieved the well-nigh impossible by pulling defeat out of the very jaws of victory. By 1952 they knew, and the country knew too, that to have a chance of winning, the minority Republican party needed a hero at the top of its ticket; and, since World War II, General Dwight D. Eisenhower had been America's most universally respected top-ranking hero.

Charles F. Willis, Jr. and Stanley Rumbough, Jr., cofounders of the organization that was to become the Citizens for Eisenhower, were therefore clearly reflecting the needs of the party and the desires of a large part of the population when they decided, in June 1951—over a year before the Republican convention—to create "a citizens movement which would ask the General who was still then in NATO, to become a candidate." There had been a time when their organization might have been called the Citizens for MacArthur. Willis, in a later discussion of why they decided to support General Eisenhower, commented, "We thought either he or General MacArthur would make a fine president of the United States." When Willis was asked if this was because they knew how to get things done, he answered, "Yes, and their integrity; without checking with either one of them, we decided that Eisenhower was much more politically saleable, and would capture the imagination of the people faster, and we could get further with it."

"And," Willis's interrogator commented, "he was already established as a national hero."

Rumbough explained that they felt Eisenhower was more saleable "because of his personality. People identified with his humanity and humility. We felt that MacArthur was brilliant, but austere and dictatorial and, therefore, not necessarily in touch with the desires of the electorate."

Rumbough, thirty-one, and Willis, thirty-three, both from Long Island, but whose businesses were in New Jersey, had originally met through their wives, roommates in school. Willis and Rumbough had a common bond through the fact that they were both multidecorated fliers in World War II, Willis in the Navy and Rumbough in the Marines, and had an entrepreneurial approach to business. Together, they had helped form an aviation business in which Willis was still working; Rumbough had left because of the needs of a family business. They lived near one another and, though inexperienced politically, often found themselves discussing what Willis described as "the concern about the Korean War and the mess in Washington as it was called at that time." Rumbough said that they did not like "the caliber of the men that were running the government." He commented that he and Willis were "completely idealistic." Whatever spurred them to action, it was when they confronted each other with the age-old rallying cry of the amateur, "let's stop talking and do something about it," that things began to happen.

Rumbough and Willis rented a loft in Hoboken for their headquarters because they were advised by professional politicians "that New York was a dirty word, as far as the rest of the country was concerned," and, with a handful of other eager neophytes, blithely set about organizing nationwide support for the General's candidacy. Willis has emphasized that this was before any political movements for Eisenhower had started.

Although no organized political body may have been at work, an unofficial presidential campaign on Eisenhower's behalf had been going on for years. Eisenhower is on record as saying that the first suggestion that was seriously made to him about the presidency was in 1943. At that time, a discussion of the subject initiated by an American newspaperman, Virgil Pinkley, was closed when the General commented, "Virgil, you have been standing out in the sun too long." That same year, the World War Tank Corps Association passed a resolution expressing confidence in Eisenhower's fitness for the presidency, and in 1944 the General had to discourage Senator Arthur Capper of Kansas from putting his name in nomination at the Republican convention that summer.

In 1945 in Berlin, at their first meeting following victory in Europe, President Truman virtually offered Eisenhower the Democratic nomination when he said, "General, there is nothing that you may want that I won't try to help you get. That definitely and specifically includes the Presidency in 1948." At this time Eisenhower had given no indication of his party preference, the President apparently was not then considering running again, and evidently the leading Democrat was as well aware as the Republicans of the value of having a living legend heading the party's ticket. But the astonished General chose to treat it as a joke and replied laughingly that he could assure the President that he would not be his "opponent" in 1948. It was the summer of 1945, too, that speculation about Eisenhower and the presidency was heightened, following an ecstatic home-town reception in Abilene for the conquering hero on his triumphant return from the war.

In December 1945, the President ordered General Eisenhower back to the United States to become chief of staff of the Army. This post in Washington, by its nature, kept him highly visible and easily accessible henceforth. In December 1947, a single newspaper advertisement for Eisenhower in the *Westporter-Herald* stimulated the formation of thirty-five Eisenhower Clubs in Connecticut alone. The interest and inquiries about his possible candidacy never subsided and, as he said after his return to Washington, "began to complicate" his life. When, in January 1948, the General received a letter from a New Hampshire newspaper publisher asking him to allow his name to be entered in the state's Republican primary, he took decisive action by sending a reply which included the following:

> ... my decision to remove myself completely from the political scene is definite and positive. I know you will not object to my making this letter public to inform all interested persons that I could not accept nomination even under the remote circumstances that it were tendered me.

This momentarily quieted speculation about his candidacy. But when, after resigning as chief of staff, he accepted in the spring of 1948 the presidency of Columbia University, a post traditionally held by a civilian, his action seemed to the general public to negate all of the reasons he had given in January for his nonavailability for political office.

His letter to the New Hampshire publisher had also included a statement of his conviction that "the necessary and wise subordination of the military to civil power will be best sustained and our people will have greater confidence that it is sustained, when lifelong professional soldiers, in the absence of some obvious and over-riding reasons, abstain from seeking high political office. . . ." The fact that the new president of Columbia was still a general of the Army, theoretically on active duty for life, either was unknown to many or, as the General has suggested, "conveniently overlooked." Cynics, in fact, concluded that a man of such superb qualifications and experience in a field vital to our country could move into a lesser job, for which he had no credentials or expertise, for only one reason: to give him a civilian launching pad for the 1948 presidential nomination.

The fact that many of the powerful political amateurs who were later in the forefront of his 1952 presidential drive were among those who secured the Columbia appointment for him may be only coincidental. Eisenhower firmly denied the charge of ulterior motivation. He was not a devious man, and he was clearly on record at that time as not wanting the presidency. There is no evidence to support the cynics' theory. But, whatever his motives, Eisenhower's new post appeared to eliminate the problem of his military background while keeping its aura, and it gave him an ideal nonpartisan platform from which to keep the public informed of his views.

His continued denials of interest in the nomination of either party (he repeatedly said that he was neither a Republican nor a Democrat) finally dampened the hopes of his supporters and, in 1948, Dewey and Truman were, fairly predictably, nominated by their respective parties.

Dewey was the odds-on favorite to win. Sixteen years of continuous Democratic leadership had begun to concern many people. And Truman, whose presidency will probably be given a pretty favorable rating in history books, was not a popular president. The election turned out to be one of the closest presidential contests in American politics. On election night, as the returns came in, it became a horse race, seesawing back and forth all night. At one point, the favorite had such a big lead that the *Chicago Tribune* brought out its famous special edition with the banner headline "DEWEY DEFEATS TRUMAN." At the end, however, when the final votes were counted, the incumbent president had won by a slim margin.

During that spring and in the course of the two nominating conventions that summer, Eisenhower received over twenty thousand pieces of mail and telegrams, which were subsequently analyzed by Columbia's Bureau of Applied Social Research. The findings revealed the leading role that the Independents were already playing in the Eisenhower boom. The bulk of the letters came from political Independents, with only eleven percent indicating any party affiliation or preference. Even more surprising, only eleven percent were interested in or cared about his views on important matters of policy. They were attracted by the personal qualities of this man and eighty percent would support him on whichever ticket he ran.

Almost as soon as the astonishing returns of 1948 were in, a Republican drive started for Eisenhower in '52. It was a disorganized effort at first, born of frustration and despair about the party, rather than a sustained and organized endeavor to persuade the General to rescue it. It was not until 1951 that the latent Eisenhower forces began to move again seriously—first here and there, and later in a coalescing of all of his old support, reinforced by an inrush of new enthusiasts. It was becoming increasingly apparent to many that Eisenhower's nomination was the one hope for the Republicans to end twenty years of an entrenched Democratic bureaucracy and an administration which even many Democrats had come to distrust.

Meanwhile, in December 1950, President Truman had asked Eisenhower, at the unanimous request of the member countries of NATO, to assume the military command of the NATO forces. As Eisenhower reports it: "Since I was still an officer in the Army, I replied that if the President as Commander-in-Chief felt that I could undertake the assignment with a better chance of success than any other soldier of his choice, my affirmative answer was inevitable." So the "soldier" resigned from Columbia, put on his uniform again, and in February 1951 returned to Europe as supreme commander of the Allied powers in Europe.

Strangely enough, his new and exalted post did not long deter important American visitors of both political parties from beating a path to his headquarters to discuss the presidential nomination. He took time to see a great many of these callers, "with politics almost the single subject on their minds." For the most part, they were political leaders and personal friends, and his answer continued to be "I'm not interested" or, to intimates, an elaboration of the substance of his January 1948 letter to the New Hampshire publisher.

It was that June of 1951 that Charles Willis, an Independent, and Stanley Rumbough, "basically a Republican," with no access to the supreme commander and no political prestige or know-how, determined, nonetheless, to launch their citizens' movement to impress Eisenhower that his support was much wider and deeper than that of a few party leaders and his personal friends—that the American people wanted him too.

Like Oren Root in 1940, Willis and Rumbough started with some simple practical steps. But, unlike lawyer Root's approach, these businessmen viewed their job as a gigantic public relations campaign. "We decided," said Willis, "that, knowing nothing about politics, we would use our sales approach." Their immediate task, as Rumbough saw it, "was simply . . . to organize the scattered public opinion so that it would have more impact on Eisenhower and he would agree to run."

Because Representative Hugh Scott of Pennsylvania was one of the few influential professionals who had openly declared himself for Eisenhower, and because it was he who had astutely advised them to open their headquarters in Hoboken, New Jersey, rather than New York City, he was the only politician to whom they now turned for advice. Willis reports that he "gave us encouragement, but I think he thought we were a little balmy—knowing nothing even about how delegates are selected to go to a convention." They decided that the way to begin "was to start Eisenhower Clubs in all the major cities in the country." Using the techniques they knew best, they got a copy of *General Foods Sales Manual,* which told "about how to set up stores and sell products; we adapted that to how to set up Eisenhower clubs and sell other people on the idea of becoming members of the clubs."

They then went about trying to find a chairman in every state who would, in turn, do in his own state exactly what Rumbough and Willis were trying to do nationally. The state chairmen were to locate county chairmen who would then recruit city chairmen. They would then try to find people willing to organize clubs. The original state leaders were people that one of the two national leaders knew personally or knew about. Willis commented, "We didn't just pick a name out of the phone book." As both were members of the national Young Presidents Club, their contacts were plentiful at that level. As soon as leadership was found, a sample of the Eisenhower Club manual was sent to the state chairmen, who were then to buy at cost as many as they needed, at least one for each club. The adaptation of *General Foods Sales Manual* bore the following headings:

General Information and Purposes
Organization
Membership
Basic Needs
Membership Acquisition and Enlargement
Conduct of Meetings
Special Projects (including how to organize rallies and how to put out
    publicity releases)
General Projects (listing all available campaign items such as
    banners and buttons, where they could be bought and for how
    much; special pamphlets and promotional gimmicks from "I
    like Ike" records to matchboxes and T-shirts)

Joint Projects (samples of petitions, programs, advertisements with
instructions how to get them placed as well as how to utilize the
local newspapers, how to put on round-table discussions, etc.)

The manual included instructions on how to organize parades
and public events and carried reprints of "Where Ike Stands"
from the *Readers Digest* and "Where Eisenhower Stands on
National and World Issues" from the *Christian Science Monitor,*
as well as quotations from a number of prominent political
figures. Doorbell ringing, if discussed at all, was evidently given
a very low priority.

The state and local leaders were almost all amateurs, but their
national chairmen did not leave them unequipped to move
directly into action. When Mr. Rumbough was asked about his
and Mr. Willis's background in the field of public relations, he
said, "We didn't have that experience but we researched this
field and discussed our project with various individuals. We took
their knowledge and put it in printed form, and tried to encourage the clubs to use this knowledge."

An unusual feature of this operation was that, with the exception of the contribution of some office furniture, contributed by
Mr. Jack Straus, president of R. H. Macy, it was financed, from
June 1951 until early 1952 (when it became part of the overall
campaign for Eisenhower), entirely by Willis and Rumbough,
who each put in four or five thousand dollars apiece. As Rumbough put it, "It was a pretty difficult thing for two young men
to support."

This comment might seem misleading in view of the fact that
Rumbough was a member of the Colgate family and was mar-
ried at that time to Nedenia Hutton (now the actress Dina
Merrill). As his wife was the daughter of Marjorie Merriweather
Post, heiress to the Postum Cereal Company fortune, and E. F.
Hutton, the financial resources he might have tapped were
enormous. But he and Willis were independent self-reliant
young men, determined not to be subsidized by their families

in their risky venture. They themselves, and other Americans who cared deeply enough, would have to support their idealistic gamble to success or failure. Fortunately for them, they had only one paid worker, a secretary. The rest of the staff were enthusiastic and loyal volunteers. Mrs. Dolly Hirshon has the distinction of being the first. Many worked full time. Those who had jobs that they could not afford to leave volunteered evenings and on Saturdays and Sundays. The two chairmen themselves, who originally tried to run their organization by working full time at their businesses and "overtime in politics," soon took leaves of absence until after the convention. Willis just told his associates to run his business, and "for almost six months neither of us were doing anything but checking by telephone how the business was progressing." Meanwhile, from their small headquarters they kept in touch with the leaders of the increasing number of Ike clubs by telephone, telegraph, and letter, sending out almost daily bulletins telling them what to do and how to do it.

From the standpoint of getting the nomination, Eisenhower was more fortunate than Willkie had been, in that Eisenhower, in addition to his dauntless amateurs, had a group of very influential Republicans working on his behalf long before the opening of the convention. General Lucius Clay, former deputy to Eisenhower and his successor, in 1947, as commander-in-chief of the United States forces in Europe, recounts that in the fall of 1951 he received a telephone call from Thomas Dewey inviting him to a meeting at Dewey's apartment at the Roosevelt Hotel in New York. There he found Herbert Brownell, a prominent New York lawyer, and Russell Sprague, former Republican national committeeman from New York, who headed Dewey's 1940 drive for the nomination, with his host. The four discussed the possibility of Eisenhower's candidacy. The consensus was that he could get the nomination if he would agree to run for it, and that he would be the only Republican nominee sure to win. Clay felt that, to persuade Eisenhower to say he would accept the nomination if it were offered to him, he would need some indication that there was a real possibility of it happening. The group was in agreement that, if Eisenhower were approached "cold" with this proposition, "with no organization and no demand," he would reject it. So, while the amateurs, largely ignored by the pros, were at work mobilizing the popular demand, these party leaders determined to put together a small group of tough professionals to support Eisenhower's candidacy.

Already under way that fall was a similar small but not very active movement of party stalwarts, among whose leaders were Senator Frank Carlson of Kansas and Senator James Duff of Pennsylvania. It was decided to combine the two groups into a single organization. Henry Cabot Lodge, senator from Massachusetts, agreed to head it.

The leaders then started communicating with Eisenhower. Clay describes the result of this dialogue as follows:

> And while he did not say whether he would run or would not run, he did say to us that if we went ahead, he would not disown us. . . . The implication was that if we announced he would run as a candidate, while he might not say he would accept, he would not make a positive refusal. This he promised us.

Clay reports that he went over to Europe at least twice during this period to discuss the progress of the campaign with the General. Still, the General had steadfastly refused to give any indication of his party affiliation. Sherman Adams, governor of New Hampshire as well as chairman of the state's Eisenhower for President Committee, and the other Eisenhower professionals were determined to enter Eisenhower's name in the New Hampshire Republican primary in the spring of 1952. But they knew that, under state law, this was impossible unless they had evidence that he was a Republican. In December 1951, Adams had inquired whether the pollbook at Eisenhower's county seat listed him as having any party affiliation. He had promptly received the following colorful reply from the county clerk:

> Mr. Eisenhower has never voted in this county as far as I know, the Primary laws first put into operation in the year 1928 and he has never voted since then, I have been county clerk since January 14th, 1927, Dwight has never been in the city as far as I know of until after war No. 2 at least he has never voted or I would have known it as the party filiation's books are still here ever since the primary or branding law was passed in the spring of 1927 and never went into effect until the Primary Election of 1928.
>
> Dwights father was a republican and always voted the republican ticket up until his death, however, that has nothing to do with the son as many differ from their fathers of which I am sorry to see, the multitude believes in going into debt and see how much they can spend, it has become a habit and will sink the nation into bankruptcy. I don't think he has any politics.

With no help from this quarter, Adams turned to Henry Cabot Lodge, who flew to Paris to discuss the matter with the General. On his return, Lodge made an almost disastrous public statement. Five days before the January 11 deadline for entering the New Hampshire primary, he called a press conference, announced that Eisenhower had assured him he was a Republican (thus forestalling his being entered as a Democrat), that he would be entered in the Republican primary, and that he would accept a nomination. This last statement—a gamble on Lodge's part—had so infuriated Eisenhower that he had very nearly issued a withdrawal statement. Instead, the following day, he put out a statement saying that Lodge's announcement "gives an accurate account of the general tenor of my political beliefs and of my Republican voting record." In the same statement, however, he included the following:

> Under no circumstances will I ask for relief from this assignment in order to seek nomination to political office and I shall not participate

in the preconvention activities of others who may have such an intention with respect to me.

Of course there is no question of the right of American citizens to organize in pursuit of their common convictions. . . .

Senator Lodge and his associates had a right to attempt to place before me next July a duty that would transcend my present responsibilities. In the absence, however, of a clear-cut call to political duty I shall continue to devote my full attention and energies to the performance of the vital task to which I am assigned.

Paying scant attention to the latter part of this statement, Governor Adams later commented succinctly and with prophetic hindsight that, when Eisenhower backed up Lodge's statement that he was a Republican, "our problem was solved, and the Democrats, then and there as it turned out, lost the election."

It was a long way from January to November and, beyond Eisenhower's personal intentions, which were not to be disclosed for another month, lay the hurdles of the primaries, the convention, and the general election. His supporters were greatly heartened, but far from sanguine about the outcome. What encouragement they felt prompted them not to relax, but to multiply their efforts.

In December, the Rumbough-Willis volunteers had received a request to help fill Madison Square Garden for an Ike rally in early February. They do not claim credit for having conceived this bold idea but, along with a number of other amateurs, they deserve a great deal of credit for its chaotic success.

Jacqueline Cochran, one of the first women licensed pilots and a renowned aviatrix, but politically a complete neophyte, was brought in to chair the rally. She reports that the Garden officials warned her that there had never been a successful political rally in Madison Square Garden even for an incumbent president. Wendell Willkie, who filled the hall in 1940, had been the one exception. But Eisenhower's supporters were going to try to fill it for a noncandidate who wouldn't even be there. Ike was still in Europe, and still publicly committed to remain with NATO until his task was completed.

Cochran discovered that a big prizefight was scheduled in the Garden for the evening of February 8. Reasoning that the stadium would be packed for the event, she decided that the best hope would be to rent it immediately following the fight and then hold part of the crowd and fill the vacated seats with Eisenhower supporters.

Leaving nothing to chance, she looked up the man who had accurately forecast the weather for D-Day and got him to make a prediction for February 8. Dr. Irving Krick made one of the most unusual political contributions in history when he waived his usual five thousand dollar fee and, again with accuracy, forecast mild pleasant weather with no wind for February 8.

Then Cochran, the Rumbough-Willis group, and other volunteers set about filling those seats which they estimated would be vacated by midnight in the Garden. Cochran's self-assigned task was to travel around the country and encourage attendance from as many states as possible. After three weeks, she realized that she needed a co-chairman. Tex McCrary and his wife, Jinx Falkenberg, formerly one of California's top-ranking women tennis players, were recruited. Cochran told these popular and talented radio and television entertainers, "I'll get the people, you put on the show." Rumbough's description of his organization's part in the rally is that they helped with enthusiasm because it "tied right in with what we'd been trying to do —give visibility to the Eisenhower groundswell." He reported that all of the resources of his far-flung volunteers were called upon to help fill the Garden.

Jacqueline Cochran's travels, including visiting between seventy and one hundred factories and organizing "Captains of Flying 50s" (each member pledged to bring forty-nine other people to the rally), the hard work of the Rumbough-Willis "Ike Clubs," and the attraction of Tex McCrary and Jinx Falkenberg and a host of other popular entertainers, combined with enthusiasm for Eisenhower to produce complete pandemonium around midnight of February 8. Trains had rolled in to New York from Pennsylvania, Maryland, and as far away as Texas. Many of the Texans had brought their horses with saddlebags full of silver dollars—"Holler up the Dollar" having been another slogan thought up by Cochran. From trains, buses, cars, and taxis, on foot and on horseback, hordes of Eisenhower enthusiasts converged on the Garden. The fight fans, however, in possession of the seats and knowing what was to come, refused to leave. No one knew how to get them out, and those who held tickets for midnight and had come great distances were determined to get in. Everyone was screaming "We Want Ike." Matters were well out of hand by the time the police and fire departments had rushed every available man to the scene. Cochran, completely stunned, said later, "We couldn't get rid of the people inside the Garden; we couldn't get the people that we had brought here inside the Garden. Oh, it was really a mess. It went on till five o'clock in the morning. I've never seen so many people."

There are as many opinions as there are accounts of the event itself, as to who should get the major credit for the tumultuous success of the rally. But there are two points on which most observers agree: the rally, frenzied as it was, was an undreamed of psychological success, and it was a one hundred percent amateur effort. Arthur Gray, Jr., who, after the convention, became the chairman of special events for the Citizens for Eisenhower-Nixon, but whose first volunteer effort was the Madison Square Garden rally, has commented that its organization "was such an incredibly difficult task that no politician wished to be actively involved." Only one politician even attended—Governor Sherman Adams of New Hampshire.

Jacqueline Cochran was trying to catch up on some overdue sleep the morning following the rally when she was awakened by a telephone call telling her that it had been decided that she should fly to Paris with the film of the entire rally to show to

General Eisenhower. Cochran had met the General a number of times in the past and it was thought that she would be the most appropriate emissary. An appointment had already been made for her for the following day. Of course, she responded. Flying her plane solo across the Atlantic, she arrived on time.

Eisenhower's own words best describe Cochran's visit and its effect on him:

On February 10 Miss Jacqueline Cochran arrived on a special mission. Two days earlier there had been a mass meeting at midnight in New York's Madison Square Garden, arranged by supporters who were hoping by this means to add weight to their argument that I should become a candidate. The entire proceedings were put on film. As soon as the film was processed, Miss Cochran flew the Atlantic and brought it immediately to Paris. Her second task was to get me to sit still long enough to view it. By the time she reached our home, she had gone thirty-five hours without sleep.

As we conferred, Miss Cochran told me about the opposition of the so-called pros in politics, who, although part of the Eisenhower group, believed that no meeting of this kind, held after the completion of a Garden fight that same evening, could possibly draw a crowd at midnight. They felt that a poor turnout would slow up the Eisenhower movement which they thought was then gaining momentum. Miss Cochran asked that my wife be with me when we viewed the film. It was shown in our living room at Villa St. Pierre in Marnes-la-Coquette.

Fifteen thousand people had assembled in Madison Square Garden. It was a moving experience to witness the obvious unanimity of such a huge crowd—to realize that everyone present was enthusiastically supporting me for the highest office in the land. As the film went on, Mamie and I were profoundly affected. The incident impressed me more than had all the arguments presented by the individuals who had been plaguing me with political questions for many months. When our guests departed, I think we both suspected, although we did not say so, that our lives were to be once more uprooted.

Cochran recounts that, following the film showing, and after others had left, the General invited her to have a drink. When it was handed to her she raised her glass with the toast: "To the President?" She says that she was the first person ever to say this to him and he burst into tears. "Tears were just running out of his eyes, he was so overwhelmed and so overcome by the public demonstration that he had had of his value and the love the American people have and had, thank God both." She told him that from all that she had gathered he would have to go back to the states and work for the nomination. He would not be drafted in Paris, she said.

After further discussion Eisenhower said to her:

> I want you to go and see General Clay and tell him to come over and see me. . . . You can go tell Bill Robinson that I'm going to run. . . . You can go talk to Bill Robinson, and you can tell Bill Robinson, Clay and Jock Whitney, but, he said, "not another single person can be told under any circumstances."

Cochran flew back to New York and promptly imparted her momentous secret to Robinson and Whitney, but found it almost impossible to get an appointment with General Clay who was by then chairman of the board of Continental Can Company. She finally managed to make an unpublicized appointment with him in front of Grand Central Station, and it was there that arrangements were made for Clay to meet Eisenhower on February 16 in London. The two Generals met at the home of Brigadier Sir James Gault, Eisenhower's British military assistant during World War II. Two of Eisenhower's American friends, George Allen and Sid Richardson, were also present.

Clay reports that at this meeting he told Eisenhower

> that the time had come when he had to cast the die, that we could only be assured of success from then on if we knew and the public knew that we actually had a candidate, and we had to know: (1) that he would run if nominated; (2) that he would run for the nomination; and (3) that he would come home before the convention.

With considerable discussion and with some reluctance, he finally said he would do all three . . .

Eisenhower's recollection is somewhat different from Clay's. He has written:

At this meeting I tentatively agreed that I would return home to the United States as soon as I could complete my duties in Europe, and if nominated at the convention, would campaign for the Presidency. I was committed in my own mind to run if nominated, but not to seek the nomination.

Although Eisenhower had described a visit of Henry Cabot Lodge in September 1951 as having been "to me, significant," Cochran's arrival with the film of the phenomenal Madison Square Garden rally, a one hundred percent amateur production masterminded and carried out largely by Citizens for Eisenhower, appears to have been the turning point in his own thinking about his possible candidacy. Jacqueline Cochran had given him visual proof that his support was both broader and more enthusiastic than Lodge had indicated or than Eisenhower had dreamed. At the February 16 meeting, Clay got the commitment that all of the General's backers felt essential.

The activities of Clay, Lodge, and the purely professional preconvention group may not seem relevant to an account of the work of the amateurs for Eisenhower, but it is of utmost importance that the latter be viewed in perspective. The Citizens for Eisenhower cannot claim, nor do they claim, to have secured the nomination for their man. Without professional intervention and leadership, it is doubtful if the campaigners for Eisenhower could have prevailed over Taft's organization.

What the amateurs did, and did most effectively, was what Rumbough and Willis had envisaged from the start: They gave "visibility to the Eisenhower groundswell" and consolidated the support of ordinary citizens into a force which was surely one of the critical factors in Eisenhower's decision to run, as well as an important influence on the selection and attitude of the convention delegates.

A very interesting memo, dated January 28, 1952, gives clear evidence of the importance that the professionals were by now attaching to the work of the amateurs. It is on stationery of the *New York Herald Tribune.*

There is no indication as to its authorship, but it was more than likely from Jock Whitney or from Walter Thayer, a lawyer at that time working with Whitney. It is headed: "Memorandum following discussion with Lodge, Vandenberg, Larmon and Brownell."

It says, in part:

Although all involved seem confident of an Eisenhower nomination, I am personally very much concerned about the outcome unless heroic measures are taken to sustain and enhance public opinion in favor of the General.

It is now crystal-clear that two-thirds of the professional politicians who will control delegates not only want Taft but are becoming a little more convinced every day that he can not only become nominated but elected. The drive of the Lodge committee on the political side has been slowed down perceptibly due to the fact that their most effective argument (that is, that Taft cannot win the election) is losing its potency. The other argument in their persuasion kit—to the effect that the rank and file of the Republican party want Eisenhower as the nominee—will begin to fade also unless an organization is developed at once. There should be two major prongs to the public preference organization:

A) Work with the Eisenhower Clubs. A task force should be built in the New York headquarters made up primarily of field workers and a public relations expert, headed by Arthur Vandenberg. An immediate analysis should be made of the club organization, state by state, to determine the weak and the strong spots of these volunteer groups. The methods and personnel of the strong areas should be analyzed and should serve as models for building up the weak situations. A routine of work and planned effort should be developed for this. A constant flow of propaganda material must be developed and sent to these organizations periodically. Plans and schemes for their own money-raising campaigns should be outlined to these organizations so that they can be self-sustaining. An ultimate target should be conceived so that the full force of their work may come to a climax at a given date just before the convention, so that evidences of public preference for Eisenhower can be crystallized and dramatized to the delegates at the local level before they leave for the convention.

The politicians, who originally did not know of the organized work of the amateurs, then took it very lightly, were now proposing to take it over.

It was at about this time that Willis and Rumbough got a call from Henry Cabot Lodge, who was in the process of setting up national preconvention headquarters in New York. He said he wanted to talk to them about their organization. They went to see him, described their operation, gave him a list of thirty-eight state chairmen and over eight hundred active clubs which they had organized, and said, "Look, this is too big for us, and it's something which should tie into your campaign." Lodge immediately agreed and asked Rumbough and Willis to become assistants to the yet-to-be-chosen chairman of the organization they had founded. As Willis has commented:

> It was either get us to come with them or start another one. Of course, this thing was already functioning, and well organized, we thought. So we said "fine." We didn't know anything about politics, but "surround us with politicians and we'll do the organization and management work." So that's exactly what happened.

Willis and Rumbough gave up their Hoboken loft and moved into headquarters in New York's Marguery Hotel. There were plans to tear down the hotel, so it was vacant at that time. The owner was an Eisenhower man and provided the headquarters at a very low rental. Their group was then officially christened "Citizens for Eisenhower" and its thirty-eight chairmen and eight hundred clubs became the nucleus of Eisenhower's very effective preconvention volunteer organization.

At the outset, Lodge appointed Arthur Vandenburg, Jr., as chairman and John Hay Whitney as finance chairman. The original cofounders, Rumbough and Willis, were in charge of the day-to-day operation. Willis reports that he and Rumbough divided the United States in half, each taking charge of the operation of one-half. Arthur Vandenburg, while a delightful individual, was not an inspirational leader, and Willis and Rumbough suggested to Lodge that perhaps more powerful leadership could be found. Luckily, the original state chairmen, who were generally amateurs, continued to function as they had from the beginning. Lodge, following the suggestion of Rumbough and Willis, found a method of moving Vandenburg out of the organization by giving him the title of personal assistant to General Eisenhower.

Walter Williams, former Republican state chairman of Seattle, Washington, was appointed chairman; Paul Hoffman, chairman of the Advisory Committee, and Mrs. Oswald Lord of New York, who had done outstanding work with women during the war, was made cochairman. Sidney Weinburg became treasurer, and Jock Whitney remained as chairman of the Finance Committee.

As it worked out, it appears that the Citizens for Eisenhower retained almost complete political autonomy, while becoming the beneficiaries of keen political analysis and advice and "a constant flow of propaganda material." Their new status also attracted, as volunteers, a great many very high-powered professionals from the public relations, advertising, and entertainment fields. Thus they benefited from both worlds.

As soon as it became known that Eisenhower would accept the Republican nomination if offered to him, the Citizens' emphasis changed from trying to persuade the General that he should be a candidate to trying to convince the delegates to the Republican convention that they should nominate him.

The Campaign Committee, headed by Lodge, Clay, and others, worked with the regular Republican organization. The Citizens' job was to rouse the ordinarily nonpolitical elements in the party and the Independents to active participation. Republicans were encouraged either to run as Eisenhower convention delegates or to persuade others to do so. And all were urged to put pressure on delegates already selected. In some states, the primary vote was binding on the delegates. In others, such as New York, the leader of the state Republican party could virtually dictate the way the delegation was to vote. In many states, delegates were elected on their own, uncommitted to any candidate, and many of these had not made up their minds between the contenders. The Citizens were confronted with a formidable and unfamiliar challenge, but one which gave them great scope.

One day Rumbough had an unexpected caller. The receptionist came into his office and said, "There's a lady in the reception room who would like to volunteer. Her name is Kay Summersby." Rumbough was amazed. She had been Ike's driver during the war and Rumbough was well aware of the widespread unfavorable gossip about their relationship. He told the receptionist to bring her in. When an attractive young woman with reddish brown hair appeared, Rumbough in answer to her offer to volunteer said, "Miss Summersby, the most helpful activity you could undertake would be to stay out of sight." He explained that her presence would, very likely, start all the gossip up again. "To the lady's credit," says Rumbough, "she followed my advice and remained away from the press during the entire campaign."

The Citizens continued to organize along the lines established by Rumbough and Willis, setting up or strengthening already existing Citizens for Eisenhower leadership in every state. Recognizing the importance of the women's vote, and believing that Eisenhower would have a strong appeal for women, they worked with the leadership of a great many women's groups—the Business and Professional Women, National Council of Women, Zonta, women lawyers and doctors, as well as farmers' groups and labor unions. These leaders were, in turn, responsible for communicating with their own members. Through her war work and civic activities in New York, Mary Lord had contacts with a variety of national women's groups. WAC and WAVE committees were easy to organize for "General Ike," but such diversified bodies as the Civil Defense League, the National War Fund, the Junior League, and the Smith College Alumnae were all appealed to for help. Even "women talking to their husbands" was then regarded as a respectable political technique, having not yet been superseded by more militant theories of persuasion. Some later proudly reported that a number of Taft delegates were "stolen" or switched as a result of this conjugal proselytizing. And national and local women leaders were enlisted to speak or make statements in support of Eisenhower.

The women, of course, were not alone in these activities. The men worked equally hard at delegate contacts and at the distasteful and arduous task of major fundraising and the other necessary preconvention activities. But women, with more leisure time and often a greater emotional commitment to the issues or the candidate, are, as Theodore White has pointed out, the strong backbone of any campaign. National volunteer campaign headquarters ordinarily tend to encourage their state and local branches to organize their own men's, women's, youth, and other special groups on a local basis, with suggested activities and guidance supplied by headquarters. The Citizens' technique was closer to that of the National Committees of the two major parties who plan their women's programs from Washington. The Citizens were fortunate in having sufficient preconvention lead time to use this technique, which they did most effectively.

The Citizens had one built-in problem, however. House-to-house canvassing and pressure on delegates were both of major importance in the preconvention fight, but neither would be effective without evidence that the candidate had strong public support. This could best be demonstrated by large turnouts at meetings and rallies. With the New Hampshire primary rapidly approaching, the Citizens' attention was focused on that state, where Taft was campaigning actively and drawing good crowds while Eisenhower was still in Europe.

They tried sending Senator Lodge or Paul Hoffman to speak for the candidate, but neither was a sufficiently strong crowd-getter. "So what we did," recalls Arthur Gray, Jr.,

> was put on a show. Tex [McCrary] would line up the people like Fred Waring [a popular band and choral leader]. Fred Waring is a very good one, as a matter of fact. He traveled all through those early days with a volunteer group of his own chorus or choral group. They put on a show. Jinx [Falkenburg] was batting tennis balls into the crowd. There was a dancer, Beatrice Krafft, who did that Oriental dancing. She was very helpful. And two or three comedians. . . . We'd give about a half-hour, forty-five minute show.

Part of the act was Marty Snyder, Eisenhower's mess sergeant during the war, who distributed Eisenhower's recipes for onion soup and other favorites to the crowd. Then the speaker would be brought on. Mr. Gray summed up a bizarre aspect of American politics when he observed, "We had to build up that sort of carnival atmosphere in order to get the same kind of a crowd that Taft was getting. . . ." Gray unconsciously epitomized the spirit of the amateurs when he commented, "Our candidate was not there. That made it difficult. But not impossible." Based on the success of these attention and crowd-getting techniques in New Hampshire, the Citizens later developed them in other states throughout the primary period.

When Mr. Gray was asked if the effectiveness of the amateurs did not breed hostility among the professionals, he answered philosophically, "Yes, it was natural at that time that they would be antagonistic, because we were both after the same job. We were after it for Ike and they were after it for Taft."

On March 11, on a cold sleety day, a record number of New Hampshire voters went to the polls. Eisenhower "received fifty percent of the total Republican vote and won all fourteen of the state's delegates. Taft came in second with thirty-eight percent." Stassen was an also-ran with only seven percent of the vote and there were about two thousand write-ins for General MacArthur. One week later, on March 18, Minnesotans voted in their primary. Only the name of their former governor, Harold Stassen, was on the Republican ballot. Yet 108,696 people wrote in the name of General Eisenhower to 129,076 who put a cross in front of ex-Governor Stassen's. It has been said that the word *Eisenhower* was spelled almost as many different ways as the number of people who wrote it.

The impact of these primaries on Eisenhower was overwhelming. Only the day before the New Hampshire primary, in answer to a letter from nineteen Republican Congressmen, he had reiterated the essence of his statement of January 7—that he would not ask to be relieved of his present command in order to seek political office, nor would he engage in any pre-convention activities. This time, however, it was noted that "under no circumstances" had been reworded to read "for the immediate future."

The enthusiasm for Eisenhower's candidacy, which had been so dramatically demonstrated at the Madison Square Garden rally and confirmed by two primaries in New England and the Midwest, proved to be irresistible. The General's defenses finally crumbled and, two days after the Minnesota primary, the news was out that he was resigning his command and coming home to campaign for the Republican nomination.

On April 11, the White House confirmed Eisenhower's resignation as supreme commander of NATO, as well as his commission as general of the Army, and that very day Paul Hoffman announced that the candidate would start personally campaigning with a major speech in Abilene on June 4. This would give him a month to help corral delegates and whip up added citizen support before the convention opened on July 7. Eisenhower workers—both professional and amateur—greeted the news with jubilation and relief. This was a preconvention bonus they had not dared hope for. Meanwhile, there was a great deal of spadework to be done in the nearly two months between the official announcement of their hero's return and his actual arrival at the end of May. But having an announced candidate to work for was a keen spur to his followers.

In states where there were active amateur organizations for Eisenhower already functioning, the Citizens simply tried to coordinate with them. "We weren't interested in competition by appointing another state chairman," said Stanley Rumbough.

> So in California we had Bill Hewitt [William Alexander Hewitt] who is now head of the Deere Company [Moline, Illinois], and Roger Lapham, Jr. Those two were previously underway as the heads in California. In New York State, we tied in with Youth for Eisenhower, which was already organized in New York State. Frankly, I can't remember who some of the individuals were at the time, but John Lindsay [later, congressman and mayor of New York] and Rod Perkins were two of them. I remember in Georgia we had a man named Killian Townsend who, I believe, is now a state senator.

By the time of Eisenhower's triumphal return to his homeland, local Citizens groups were multiplying rapidly and "We want Ike" was a refrain heard from coast to coast. After that, his popularity soared with his every public appearance.

Toward the end of May, the Citizens began to consider the focus of their work at the convention. The candidate race had essentially boiled down to the two frontrunners—Taft and Eisenhower—and the intricate political maneuvering, both preconvention and during the week starting July 7, was not for amateurs; it would have to be in the hands of the most skilled professionals.

But there was a tremendous amount the Citizens for Eisenhower groups could do until then. An advance guard was sent to Chicago six weeks before the convention was to open, and lived there until it was over, devising a variety of public relations stunts and gimmicks that, though not very different from those used in William Henry Harrison's day and earlier, were carried off with such enthusiasm and flair that they attracted widespread attention. One of their most original ideas was the use of barrage balloons. This idea was first suggested by Langhorne Washburn, who had been a naval aviator in blimps during World War II. He worked with Stanley Hiller, Jr., the inventor of the Hiller helicopter, in charge of public relations for Hiller. They had helped organize Young Businessmen for Ike, and Washburn was on a leave of absence from Hiller's company to help at the convention.

The barrage balloons were enormous helium-filled balloons on which the name *IKE* was painted in gigantic letters. The balloons were let out on very long cables and floated high above the city, where they could be seen for blocks—often miles—around. Few people were unaware that Ike was in town when the balloons were flying. One day, they hoisted one opposite the Tribune Tower in Chicago and what they hoped was the office window of the newspaper's pro-Taft publisher, Colonel R. R. McCormick. Some Taft enthusiast peppered it with shots and managed to bring it down. It fell in a heap in the street, blocking traffic, and the infuriated police demanded that the Citizens remove it immediately. Instead, they spent the night mending the holes, refilled it with helium, and had it flying again the next morning. The "spontaneous" floor demonstrations that they planned during the six weeks prior to the convention's opening were so skillfully arranged, and the enthusiasm of the demonstrators so obviously genuine that, when they occurred, few questioned their spontaneity.

At about the same time as the public relations group moved to Chicago, so did Arthur Gray, Jr., another Citizen whom Rumbough and Willis had suggested as a key man to help change the

Chicago anti-Ike atmosphere. Chicago was the heart of Taft-McCormick country. Mr. Gray later claimed that people were actually afraid to wear Eisenhower buttons there, that their bankers would call them up and threaten to cancel their loans. Such stories usually become greatly exaggerated in the emotionalism of a campaign and gain credibility with sufficient repetition. There may have been cases of intimidation, but there was a flourishing Citizens for Eisenhower movement in Illinois at that time, headed by Bill Poole (George A. Poole, Jr.) and Marion Hodgkins. Nonetheless, the atmosphere, on the whole, was not a friendly one.

Mr. Gray used the usual amateur network of friends and friends of friends to establish his Chicago contacts. He discovered an "oasis" in the Ambassador East Hotel where the entire management was "very openly" for Eisenhower. They would put him in contact with businessmen that they had heard were for the General. Through one of these contacts, a public relations man who "had been brought up by [Democratic] Mayor Kelly with Mayor Kelly's sons," he learned a lot about the "ins and outs of Chicago politics." This man also introduced him to a key contact, Andy Frain, whose organization was to run the usher service at both national conventions. Frain proved invaluable to the Eisenhower people.

They were being "frozen out" by the Taft-controlled National Committee and were getting "absolutely clobbered" as far as getting their fair share of convention tickets and the invaluable sergeant-at-arms badges. Citizens for Eisenhower were not allowed any seats at the convention. The only reason that Bill Poole, the director and finance chairman of the Illinois Citizens, got into the amphitheatre, even as a spectator, was because his sister was a friend of Arthur Krock, the *New York Times* columnist, who gave him a seat in his box. But when Poole asked his sister if he could use the seat one day and give it on other days to people who had worked as long and desperately hard as he had, the answer was a firm "No." He remembers, too, that John Stuart, an Eisenhower supporter and ordinarily a very good-tempered gentleman, was "mad as hell" at his brother "Doug" (R. Douglas Stuart), chairman of the board of the Quaker Oats Company and chairman of the Republican Finance Committee, when he refused to give John a convention ticket. The powers that be, with the *Chicago Tribune*'s Colonel McCormick masterminding the strategy, were determined that there should be no repetition of the 1940 Willkie blitz.

The rank-and-file Citizen's most useful ally was Andy Frain, who simply arranged for a special door to be left open into the amphitheatre during the sessions, through which the Eisenhower people could be brought in, at will, without tickets and, of course, without seats. The "spontaneous" rallies and demonstrations would have been impossible without this cooperation. Mr. Gray and the other advance group of Citizens in Chicago managed to get donations "quietly" from a considerable number of businessmen and put on rallies in many outlying areas. Gray felt that, by the time the convention opened, the atmosphere in Chicago had moderated considerably.

The Citizens for Eisenhower were convinced that nationwide, the people—Republicans, Independents, and many Democrats—had shown their desire for Ike as the Republican nominee. But Senator Taft, long the darling of the right wing, was a phenomenon in his own way, as he had none of the superficial attributes of a politician. Politically speaking, he was born to the purple in Ohio. His father, William Howard Taft, had been dean of the Yale Law School, chief justice of the United States Supreme Court, and president of the United States.

In basic qualities, young Robert was a worthy son of his illustrious father. He was conscientious, intelligent, and industrious. And he was one of the handful of top-level national politicians who was invariably forthright and honest in any statement he ever made to the American people. Once he was asked by reporters if a statement he had made, which contradicted one on the same subject made a year or so earlier, had been misquoted or taken out of context. He did not use the escape hatch the reporters had offered him. He simply replied, "I have learned something since I made that statement. Now I realize that I was wrong."

All of these qualities made him a respected senator. But in other important ways he was his father's opposite. William Howard Taft had a wonderful sense of humor, a very quick and delightful turn of mind, and was naturally warm and gracious to everyone. Robert inherited none of these attractive and endearing qualities. In addition, having twice been denied the presidential nomination by his party, he had become embittered and more aloof than ever.

It was not easy for the Citizens, who had done so much to make Eisenhower the people's candidate, to bow out at the crucial moment. And it was especially hard to commit their candidate's fate into the hands of the professionals, some of whom had been Johnny-come-latelies to his cause. And jealousy of the Citizens' success bred real hostility on the part of the Taft delegates.

But, as Rumbough commented later, the Citizens did not get into the "political backroom infighting. . . . the Texas Steal had nothing to do with them." So, while the Citizens' quiet work with delegates continued unabated until the rolls were called, some were given the job of creating what Rumbough has called the convention "hoopla."

While the barrage balloons floated over the city, and huge crowds of people who could not get into the convention demonstrated for Ike at the gates of the amphitheatre, the Eisenhower Bandwagon (a spectacular traveling sideshow) roamed the streets, attracting crowds as always, and Jinx Falkenberg batted out tennis balls now seated on the top of an elephant. Inside the convention hall, the Citizens tried to keep their "spontaneous" marches up and down the aisles orderly, so as not to disrupt the proceedings. But this was sometimes difficult. As it had during the primaries, the hoopla proved so successful that many of its features became an important part of Eisenhower's presidential campaign.

The Citizens had now done all in their power to organize the people's will for Eisenhower. The time had come for those professionals who were for him to see that the Republican convention nominated him.

The convention opened on Monday, July 7, with the Taft forces determined to frustrate the ambitions of the Eisenhower people, and nominate, at long last, the choice of the old guard and of the Taft-controlled Republican organization, Robert Alphonso Taft. Even Eisenhower's staunchest supporters were forced to admit that the prospects looked bleak for their candidate.

Guy Gabrielson, the chairman of the National Committee, opened the session with a plea for unity. The temporary roll call was then presented, and the temporary chairman approved. Then a normally routine motion to adopt the rules of the previous convention as the temporary rules destroyed even the facade of harmony which Gabrielson had tried to erect. It was this motion that precipitated the bitter fight, dubbed the "Texas Steal" by the Eisenhower forces, for its adoption would almost certainly assure Taft's nomination. The fight lasted until late Wednesday night, and its outcome proved to be the turning point in the General's nomination. It is essential to understand the background of the steal because it started long before the convention, at the grass-roots level, and was spearheaded by the Citizens and other nonprofessional Eisenhower supporters.

The previous spring, when the Texas Republicans had held their precinct and county caucuses to select delegates to the state convention, people flocked into these ordinarily small, almost private gatherings in unprecedented numbers, and the Taft-controlled party was stunned and infuriated to discover that in almost every caucus Eisenhower candidates had won over those pledged to Taft. Such was the party's low regard for Eisenhower that they charged that most of the Eisenhower votes had been cast by people who weren't even Republicans. At the state convention, where the final selection of national convention delegates is made, the Eisenhower delegates were barred from the hall. So they held their own rival convention. They elected a delegation consisting of thirty-three delegates instructed for Eisenhower and five for Taft, and sent them to the national convention.

Though the organization Democrats of Texas had been the leading offenders in these preconvention, anti-Eisenhower machinations, two smaller delegations, Georgia with seventeen delegates and Louisiana with eleven, had both been guilty of similar tactics and there was a scattering of others under challenge. So the Eisenhower forces were appalled when, on July 2, five days before the convention was to open, the first of these three cases to come before the National Committee's hearings on disputes over seating was Georgia. Predictably, Georgia's one hundred percent Taft delegation was provisionally seated instead of the rival slate of thirteen Eisenhower and four Taft delegates.

By sheer coincidence, the annual conference of state governors was taking place in Houston, Texas, simultaneously with the National Committee hearings. Fortunately for General Eisenhower, he had very strong support among the Republican governors, and Sherman Adams determined to mobilize it in connection with these hearings. The temporary rule that had been adopted at the 1948 convention, to which the Eisenhower forces so strenuously objected, and which had precipitated the battle with the Taft people was Rule Number Four. This permitted the Credentials Committee to exclude from its deliberations delegations or individual delegates whose seats were in dispute if the controversy had been already decided by their state's convention or committee. This would have the effect of allowing a representative of the now provisionally accredited pro-Taft Georgia delegation to sit among the judges when the Eisenhower people raised challenges. If the National Committee should also seat the big pro-Taft Texas delegation, the Mississippi delegation, and the other scattering of contested Taft delegates, then their representatives, too, would sit on the Credentials Committee with the Eisenhower challengers excluded. In that case Taft's nomination would be virtually certain.

In Houston, Governor Adams called a meeting of the nineteen pro-Eisenhower governors present and explained the convention dilemma, and out of this and other hastily-convened conferences came agreement to send a manifesto by telegram to Guy Gabrielson, urging him to support "a ruling that no contested delegate may vote to determine the outcome of any contest." Twenty-three Republican governors signed the manifesto, including several Taftites who had been "persuaded" by a series of intricate maneuvers and one outright ruse. It was then released at a packed press conference before it was sent to Gabrielson, a clever move which made the chairman extremely angry, but insured front-page newspaper coverage from coast to coast.

At the convention, Henry Cabot Lodge and other Eisenhower leaders—Dewey, Adams, and Brownell—decided to take the fight directly to the floor. The year 1952 was the first year that both conventions were covered by that revolutionary new invention, television, and Lodge determined to wage his battle in front of the American people. So the public watched, fascinated, while Taft offered a compromise on the Texas question (offering to split his solid delegation to sixteen seats for Eisenhower and twenty-two for himself), and Lodge haughtily turned it down. Meanwhile the National Committee had proceeded to seat the Taft delegations from both Mississippi and Louisiana, thus giving Taft sixteen additional delegates, and they had voted to accept officially Taft's proposal of a 16–22 split in the Texas delegation committed to him, while refusing any seats to the rival pro-Eisenhower delegation. This was the opportunity Lodge had been looking for and he announced that he was going to appeal to the delegates to overrule the National Committee, citing the Houston manifesto in support of his action.

The plan that Eisenhower leaders had agreed on was to offer an amendment to the controversial convention rule Number Four. The amendment, to be introduced by Governor Langlie of Washington, would simply embody the content of the Houston manifesto, softened by a provision that if eighty percent of the National Committee approved the seating of a delegate or delegation they could be seated. It seemed a reasonable and easily understood proposal. In fact, Lodge was afraid that the Taft people might accept it, thus depriving him of bringing the whole issue into the open and enlisting sympathy for his candidate. Foolishly, the Taft forces fought the amendment, and Lodge had his opportunity.

Rushing dramatically back and forth between the floor and the podium, his every move followed by national television, Lodge's indignant cries of "foul," as against "fair play," won the support of both a great majority of the delegates and the enthralled television public for the adoption of what he cleverly called the "Fair Play" amendment. Hours of acrimonious debate and attempted parliamentary maneuvers on the part of the Taft people ended when one of their amendments to the main amendment, designed in effect to vitiate it, was voted down 658–548, and the Langlie or "Fair Play" amendment was adopted by acclamation.

The final battle took place when the Credentials Committee presented its report to the convention. The committee had considered the appeals of delegates who had not been seated or who had been unseated by the National Committee. As a result of the adoption of Governor Langlie's amendment, the committeemen of Georgia and Texas had been excluded from the credentials deliberations. The committee presented both a majority and minority report. The majority report endorsed the temporary roll call as presented by the National Committee except for a part of the Louisiana delegation and the delegation of Puerto Rico. Then the roll of the contested states was called, the minority report presented, and it was determined that each challenge should be acted on individually.

The roll call proceeded smoothly until it came to Georgia. Then a full-scale debate started. When it ended, the Eisenhower forces, relying on their success in getting the "Fair Play" amendment accepted, demanded a roll call on the question of whether the majority or minority report should be adopted. With the provisionally seated Georgia, Texas, and the contested part of the Louisiana not voting, the minority report was adopted 607 to 531.

The balance of the contests, including reversing the Louisiana seating, went routinely. Then Texas was called. Though there was lengthy and sometimes heated debate, surprisingly, neither side asked for a roll call. The minority report substituting permanently the predominately pro-Eisenhower Texas delegation, as well as those of Georgia and Louisiana, was, at long last, approved by voice vote.

By this time, Eisenhower's bandwagon had gone into high gear. Delegate after delegate who had earlier been undecided or even pro-Taft, incensed by the ruthless tactics being used by the Taft forces and the extreme bitterness they had engendered, went over to Eisenhower. Many knowledgeable analysts of this convention and many of Eisenhower's own people believe that, if Taft had taken the lead in gracefully accepting the Langlie amendment, he might well have been the nominee. Even without the votes of his challenged delegates, he appeared to be sufficiently in the lead to beat Eisenhower until the defection of so many over the bitter issue of the amendment. Many feel he did not condone the rough tactics of his supporters. But he could not have been unaware that they were being used on his behalf. Being associated with them did him great harm, as did the impression that he was against fair play. How can one be against fair play any more than against home and mother?

It was not until Thursday evening that the roll call for nominations began. Though Eisenhower's position was now infinitely stronger, neither candidate could count on victory. The atmosphere was tense when Alabama was called and yielded to Illinois, whose delegation everyone knew was going to nominate Taft, thus putting him first on the list. Senator Everett Dirksen nominated him as "Mr. Republican, Mr. Integrity, Mr. American." Eisenhower's name was put in nomination by Governor Theodore McKeldin of Maryland, who identified his name with victory, and said he was a man behind whom all Republicans, all Americans and all non-Communists could unite. Warren of California and Stassen of Minnesota were nominated by their respective states, and General MacArthur by Oklahoma.

The next morning, the balloting began. There were only two viable candidates, and the suspense grew with every state called:

"Alabama!"

"The great state of Alabama gives 5 votes to General Eisenhower and 9 votes to Senator Taft."

The roll proceeded alphabetically down the list of states:

ARIZONA	4 for Eisenhower, 10 for Taft
ARKANSAS	4 for Eisenhower, 6 for Taft
CALIFORNIA	(70 for its favorite son, Governor Earl Warren)
COLORADO	15 for Eisenhower, 2 for Taft
CONNECTICUT	21 for Eisenhower, 1 for Taft
DELAWARE	7 for Eisenhower, 5 for Taft
FLORIDA	6 for Eisenhower, 12 for Taft
GEORGIA	14 for Eisenhower, 2 for Taft
IDAHO	0 for Eisenhower, 14 for Taft
ILLINOIS	1 for Eisenhower, 59 for Taft

through Louisiana's 13 for Eisenhower and 2 for Taft and Texas' 33 for Eisenhower and 5 for Taft. And so it went, down to Puerto Rico giving its 3 votes to Taft and the Virgin Islands their 1 vote to Eisenhower.

At the end, Taft had 500 and Eisenhower 595, only 9 votes short of the necessary majority. It was then that the Eisenhower supporters went wild while, amidst the uproar, the Minnesota delegates leaped to their feet and in ringing tones their chairman announced that their 19 votes for their favorite son, Harold Stassen, were changing to 19 for General Dwight D. Eisenhower. The usual bandwagon move followed amidst veritable pandemonium and, at the end, Eisenhower had 845 votes, Taft 280, Warren 77, and MacArthur 4. Representatives of Taft and Warren then moved to make it unanimous. The General had won on the first ballot.

Soon after, the new Republican candidate strode onto the podium, raised his arms in an all-embracing gesture, and thanked the convention for honoring him with their nomination.

The story of the Texas Steal and the Fair Play amendment dramatically illustrates the value of professionalism when the going gets rough. But the amateurs were uniquely effective in mobilizing public opinion and in the selection and influencing of delegates. And without these volunteers' all-important role in persuading Eisenhower to run, and their effective work before the convention, there is every likelihood that his "tough professionals" would never have had Eisenhower as a candidate.

In his acceptance speech to the convention, the new nominee paid special tribute to two idealistic young men from New Jersey (who had met him for the first time that week), when he said from the podium, "I would not have been here as a candidate if it had not been for Charlie Willis and Stan Rumbough who started the Citizens for Eisenhower."

Ralph Cake, a thoroughgoing professional, describes the preconvention Citizens as being "a perfect organization, though not very large." Nonetheless, he said that he felt it

> probably had had as much to do with securing the delegates . . . than any one group. I think it was the Citizens who went right down into the precincts and got people working down there, that took away from Mr. Taft delegates from states that they would never have gotten if they had not been in the picture. . . . It was a great organization. They interested people that hadn't been interested in politics before. . . . I really fully believe that it was their efforts that made it possible for Mr. Eisenhower to get the nomination.

This was high praise from a professional. It was also praise that had been earned. For the hard work of the enthusiastic Citizens, who organized early and dovetailed their myriad activities with those of the professional leadership of the General's campaign, was undoubtedly a potent factor in the nomination of Eisenhower for president in 1952.

United Press Photos

Eisenhower (*seated fourth from left*), with state delegates of the Citizens for Eisenhower, of which Charles F. Willis, Jr. (*far left*) and Stanley Rumbough, Jr. (*far right*) were co-founders.

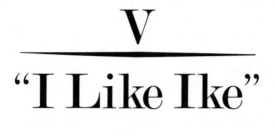

V

"I Like Ike"

Who was this man whom the Republicans had just nominated? Why had he so captivated the American public that large sectors of it—even before they knew to which party he belonged and what his views on important matters of policy were— wanted him for their president? Every American knew that Eisenhower was a war hero. Most Americans knew that he was also a man of peace, a conviction that had recently been strengthened by his diplomatic handling of his NATO command.

Three weeks after the Republican convention, he was watching on television as the Democrats nominated another "uncommon man," Adlai Stevenson, governor of Illinois. A measure of the respect Eisenhower had for Stevenson was revealed in his spontaneous reaction, "If I had known the Democrats were going to nominate a man of Stevenson's caliber, I would have stayed in Paris."

This regard was mutual for, in January of that year, Stevenson had been summoned by President Truman to a private meeting with him in Washington. The President had astounded Stevenson by telling him that he was not going to run again, that he felt that Stevenson was the best qualified for the office, and asked him to run for the nomination in the President's stead. But what amazed Stevenson as much as anything was one of the reasons President Truman gave. With shocked disbelief, Stevenson told a friend later that evening, "I've just had the most incredible experience. I've just come from Blair House, and the President wants me to save the world from Dwight Eisenhower!"

Many Americans, by now, had become aware that Eisenhower had grown up in Abilene, Kansas, in the part of town which its citizens called "the wrong side of the tracks." Like Willkie, he had come from fine German immigrant stock, though the Eisenhowers reached Pennsylvania in the middle of the eighteenth century, nearly a century before the Willkies' arrival in America. Like Willkie, he came from a God-fearing, religiously oriented family. His father had had serious financial troubles from which he never recovered, so his children grew up in very straightened circumstances. Their hard-working mother was the family's real head. Dwight, who was the third of seven sons, one of whom died in infancy, had to work from the time he was a small boy to help support the family and to contribute to his own and his brothers' education. It was said that one of the reasons he wanted to go to Annapolis, and finally went to West Point, was to relieve his family of the burden of his college tuition. What was it about this man that, in 1952, elicited an insistent chorus of "We want Ike" the moment he appeared anywhere? Politics aside, everyone liked Ike. Everyone respected him.

When he started campaigning, crowds came as much to see the wartime hero as to hear what he had to say. They felt honored to have him in their midst. What they saw they liked. For Ike's "electric grin" and upstretched arms (which eventually became his trademark) exuded enormous good will and confidence that encompassed an entire crowd. Furthermore, both physically and psychologically, he gave the impression of strength—solid, dependable strength. Emmett Hughes, his speechwriter and biographer, has said that this

> physical fact symbolized a political fact. The man, throughout the campaign of 1952, seemed in firm and sure command of himself and all around him . . . even when his own instinct did bow to another's urging. This easy air of personal authority seemed, of all hopeful facts of 1952, the most promising for the future.

Yet he never behaved like a self-conscious hero. He was simple and friendly and, to an electorate ever distrustful of a military man in the presidency, it was evident that this trim, erect, confident officer was no proconsul. He had an essentially warm personality and, to young and old, General Eisenhower was kindly Ike, the liberator, not the conqueror.

His boyish grin added to this impression. John Mason Brown has variously described his smile in such superlatives as "all conquering," "a radiation of light," and possessing a "spread and radiance . . . beyond the invention of commercial artists."

Eisenhower's reputation for not being an intellectual was doubtless more of an asset than a liability. John Mason Brown has also pointed out that he "said these simple things to a people whose basic hopes are simple. Among the imponderables of the election was the appeal of Ike's earthbound oratory, with the occasional elegance of its plain phrases and the incontestable honesty and fervor of his beliefs."

The term "father figure" has been used, time after time, to describe Eisenhower's appeal in a troubled era, when people were longing for reassurance and for someone onto whose shoulders they could safely shift the country's problems. It has been suggested that many felt that tried and true Ike could somehow resolve the difficult issues that Adlai Stevenson was so clearly identifying and raising. It may be that the comforting prospect of a great war hero piloting the ship of state through dangerous international shoals, while, as a kindly, dependable

family man he restored sound principles and honorable practices to the business of government at home, was the key to
Eisenhower's overwhelming popularity. Whatever the combination of reasons, Eisenhower's name was magic, and few
doubted that he could win.

The Citizens for Eisenhower, having from the outset declared their intention of disbanding—win or lose—after the
convention, proceeded to do so. But there was an immediate
outcry from Citizens groups around the country who wanted to
reorganize for the presidential race. Very shortly they were
back in business.

Walter Williams felt that they should take a new name. He
reasoned that, to Taft and his people, the Citizens for Eisenhower represented the foe. It would be difficult for Taft followers, Williams believed, to join the enemy army that had licked
them. Williams proposed the name "Americans for Eisenhower-Nixon." But the old name was finally retained, adding only
that of the vice presidential candidate. The Citizens for Eisenhower had an important identity nationally and it was felt that
confusion would inevitably result from trying to reactivate the
same groups under a different name.

William E. Robinson, chairman of the board of the *New York
Herald Tribune* and a close friend of Eisenhower, in a letter to
Williams on July 23, advanced another reason. He said, "I think
there's a worry about the term 'Americans.' The foreign-born
and the first-generation elements, together with certain race-
conscious groups, might take some offense at an unintended
implication." Robinson also envisaged the organization of sepa-
rate bodies called "Democrats for Eisenhower" and an "Independents—or People's Crusade for Eisenhower." Apparently, he did not visualize the Citizens encompassing them all.

The immediate task facing the Citizens was once again to
change the thrust of the organization's activities. Their original
purpose had been to show Ike that he had such widespread
citizen support that he would agree to become a candidate for

the nomination. Once that had been achieved, they had focused their activities on the selection and persuasion of convention delegates. Now they must, for the most part, leave strictly Republican activities to the party organization and concentrate their efforts on wooing Independents, Democrats, and Republicans-in-name-only, who were ordinarily indifferent to politics and often stayed at home on election day. Walter Williams and Mary Lord saw the possibility of the reorganized Citizens attracting all of these groups, and they determined to plan such an operation.

Ralph Cake describes the purposes and the value of these amateurs from the standpoint of a professional politician who, unlike so many members of the regular organization, recognized their usefulness. "They were called upon to do the job that a Republican couldn't do, because we had to go out to the Independents and the Democrats."

The Republicans, Cake commented, were

> a minority party, and the Democrat who might vote for you would never come into the Republican headquarters to do it. He wouldn't want to speak to a Republican as such. But he would talk to a person who wasn't directly connected with the party organization. And you could get people to work for you. You first get them to give you a dollar, and then they'll start working.

General Lucius Clay, who described his politics as having "never been a Republican, never been anything" (adding that any background or affiliation he had had always been Democratic, "except I was for Eisenhower"), devoted his time, after the campaign got under way, to raising money for the Citizens for Eisenhower. He said he felt that he could make a better contribution to the campaign by "trying to get Independents to join in supporting Eisenhower than as a Republican."

Stressing later that the Citizens "was a very successful organization," Clay observed that there were more registered Democrats than Republicans in the country and "we had to get votes away from the Democrats or get voters out who had never voted for either party." He also pointed out that the Republican party couldn't get Democrats, "but an Oveta Culp Hobby (former director of the Women's Army Corps) in Texas or James Byrnes (secretary of state under Truman and governor of South Carolina) in South Carolina would be a Citizen for Eisenhower but not a Republican for Eisenhower." He saw the Citizens as "a vehicle by which men and women of great stature" could— and did—join "and were for Ike and still not be run out of their own party. They never became Republicans."

Describing how the Citizens planned to operate, Stanley Rumbough, who remained as vice chairman of the reorganized body said:

What we tried to do was supplement the Republican national campaign . . . volunteer precinct workers to cover the areas where the Republicans had no organization whatsoever, to do everything that a political organization in an election campaign should do, and to do it with volunteers and Independents rather than with regular political workers.

The reactivated Citizens were almost immediately embroiled in a major row. Before the convention, the Republican National Committee had ignored them until they showed clear signs of success, at which point the Committee had become antagonistic. Now they demanded that the Citizens be put under their jurisdiction. They wanted to absorb them. A meeting between the two groups was arranged for August 1 at Eisenhower's personal campaign headquarters, now established at the Brown Palace Hotel in Denver, Colorado. Among those present at the conference, which was called for the general purpose of deciding on overall strategy for the presidential campaign, were Eisenhower, Richard Nixon, Arthur Summerfield, chairman of the Republican National Committee, and a number of other party officials, together with Walter Williams, Mary Lord, Rumbough, and Willis.

Summerfield argued against an independent Citizens' operation, claiming that the disastrous friction between its counterpart, the Willkie Clubs, and the regular organization in 1940, had been a major factor in Willkie's defeat. He also brought up the danger of arousing the latent bitterness of the Taft people if the Citizens groups were to continue. Williams and Mrs. Lord knew that no Democrat and few Independents would work under the auspices of the Republican National Committee, so they argued forcefully for autonomy. They agreed to clear their money sources with the Republican National Committee, but otherwise they stood firm for political independence.

Mrs. Lord later described the negotiations as a "very emotional and rather difficult time." Rumbough reports that, when the National Committee could not be convinced by logical arguments, the Citizens said:

> "We'll go our way and not bother to coordinate with you"—at which point they readily saw that one area they could not control is the free movement of Citizens. Because this happens to be the United States you can't control something of this nature, and if we wanted to work on our own, they had to coordinate with us or let us go our own way.

Eisenhower, backed by Sherman Adams, decided in favor of autonomy for the Citizens, with one member of the National Committee to be appointed as liaison with them, and all fund-raising to be cleared in advance.

This was the culmination of the Republican National Committee's attempt to subordinate the Citizens' movement to their own committee. But until the end of the campaign, and throughout the entire Republican organization, there continued to be considerable hostility, more on the part of the regular organization than the Citizens. The local politicians naturally tended to feel, "Who are these newcomers and what right do they have to operate in my territory?" As has so often been demonstrated, organizations that are ineffectual feel threatened by newcomers, while strong and effective organizations usually welcome help. So there were differences in various parts of the country, depending upon the leadership of the Republicans locally.

Immediately following the conference, Arthur Summerfield, the chairman of the Republican National Committee, issued a statement in which he said:

> A discussion took place this afternoon on the question of continuing the work of the Citizens for Eisenhower Committee. . . . It was unanimous that a citizens organization working with the regular Republican organization would make a vital contribution to this campaign. . . . We are interested only in one goal—the election of Dwight D. Eisenhower and Senator Nixon and a Republican Congress this November.

On August 3, in a supplementary and much clearer statement, Eisenhower and Summerfield announced

> that the Citizens for Eisenhower-Nixon organization will be continued and expanded, and that they have asked Mr. Walter Williams to act as director, and Mrs. Oswald Lord as co-director.
> This organization will operate with its own personnel as a separate and special agency of the National Eisenhower-Nixon campaign.

"From then on," Mr. Rumbough reports, "the Citizens ran with a fairly free hand during the election period, putting their main emphasis on supplementing the Republican national campaign by trying to cover precincts where the Republicans had no organization."

It was at this meeting in Denver that General Eisenhower suffered a shocking personal disillusionment—one which reinforced his attachment to his idealistic amateurs and made him even more cynical about the party professionals whose tactics at the time of the "Texas Steal" had almost shattered whatever illusions he had. He told Sherman Adams that he had assumed that his selection as nominee had been based on his broad grasp of international affairs gained from his leadership in World War II and at NATO. He believed that the party saw him as the man best equipped to bring peace to the world. But at the end of the conference he muttered to Adams, "All they [the professionals] talked about was how they could win on my popularity. Nobody said I had a brain in my head." Eisenhower did not talk much about this disillusionment, but many times after that he would comment, almost emotionally, that he always felt invigorated by the Citizens' meetings, "because I feel their enthusiasm for me is genuine."

The representatives of the Citizens went back to New York, free to develop and implement their own program, subject only to the agreed-upon financial clearance with the National Committee. It was apparent that their activities should now be divided into two distinct but mutually reinforcing categories: serious political work and "hoopla," the latter having proved such an effective and attention-getting part of the Citizens' operations during the convention.

In the political area, they organized along the lines of their preconvention operation, now considerably broadened and focused on their new constituencies. They established a women's division under Mary Lord and, as she described it, in a telephone interview, "We worked with women and the men with men, but we coordinated our work." They commenced by making a precinct-by-precinct study of the country's voting patterns, concentrating mainly on those big cities where the Democrats had customarily won by small margins. They did not concern themselves with normally Republican precincts, leaving them to the regular party organization.

They then developed a handbook which described this strategy and emphasized the crucial importance of concentrating their efforts where they would do the most good—specifically in these marginal precincts. The brochure, of course, included the usual suggestions and directions for calling on people, for house-to-house and apartment-to-apartment canvassing, and for the best utilization of all of the standard campaign and get-out-the-vote techniques. The handbook put strong emphasis on working harmoniously with other established groups, with particular stress on the regular Republican organization. It was also clearly stated that the Citizens would disband immediately after the election and that they had no interest in job patronage.

It was essential to keep hammering at the latter points. Over-eager amateurs all too often ruffle partisan feathers. Whereas in some areas, notably those where the regular organization had favored Eisenhower before the convention, the professionals welcomed or at least cooperated with the Citizens, in other places, especially in preconvention Taft strongholds, they never ceased regarding them as the enemy.

Dr. Charles Masterson, an early Willis-Rumbough recruit, recounts what the Republican leader in his own area of Brooklyn asked him at the end of the campaign.

> "Well, if you were such a hot Republican, how come you were working for Citizens for Eisenhower?" He thought that was an alien force. The fact that most people credited Citizens for Eisenhower as a very important factor in the election of the President seemed to him almost a cause for chagrin.

The Citizens, of course, developed a great many special-interest groups. Rumbough reports that

> under Citizens for Eisenhower were many divisions, Jews for Eisenhower, German-Americans for Eisenhower, all ethnic groups you can think of. Doctors for Eisenhower, Lawyers for Eisenhower, bankers, every type and area we could think of where you could stimulate interest. And then, of course, those subdivisions became

national in scope. Each city had a Youth for Eisenhower, which was one of our most potent groups—kids in their twenties.

And, of course, there was one enormous body that needed no developing. Eisenhower had been a popular commander in World War II and the three million Americans that had served under him in Europe could still be counted as his loyal troops. They and their families were a vast pool of potential workers and voters. Also, as they had before the convention, the Citizens worked through already established organizations. They reactivated their contacts with such bodies as the National Council of Negro Women and with ethnic, business, labor, and farm groups, both at the national and local levels. Mrs. Lord recollects that they worked with about twenty-five different national groups. With their far-flung preconvention network of Citizens eager for action, and new clubs and new recruits rapidly swelling the numbers, they were able to put together a fairly effective precinct organization by the time the campaign opened officially in September.

One ingenious device thought up by the women and used most successfully by them was called the Shoebox Operation. A woman was assigned a two-block area for which she was responsible. Then she was given three shoeboxes—one marked "Sure Republican," one marked "Still on Fence," and one "Democrats, No Hope at All"—in which were filed the names of all the women in her area. By election time, these leaders should have arranged for coffee parties and small block parties, and talked to every woman in their areas. As conversions took place, the name of the convert would be moved into the appropriate box. On election day, the block leaders were responsible for seeing that baby sitters and transportation to the polls were arranged for all who needed them, provided their names appeared in the proper boxes.

Meanwhile under Langhorne Washburn's auspices, the spectacular Eisenhower Bandwagon was touring across the country.

The Bandwagon—a combination of the convention hoopla and the primary campaign sideshows put on wheels—rolled into the towns on Eisenhower's speaking schedule a day ahead of their hero to drum up excitement about his visit.

The success of the Bandwagon during the preconvention and convention periods resulted in its being sent, almost immediately after the convention, to Philadelphia where Eisenhower was to make one of his first campaign speeches. There was great concern that he would not be able to fill the hall. So the Citizens, calling on their successful primary and convention techniques, went into action. The repetition of these successes at Philadelphia made it evident that the Bandwagon should become part of the national campaign.

The Bandwagon was a rented, twenty-five-ton, Eisenhower-Nixon tractor-trailer. It carried a jeep, two huge "We Like Ike" barrage balloons, helium to inflate them, and specially designed "Ike" dresses in all sizes. These were designed by a Citizen, the wife of Arthur Gray, Jr. Half of the dresses were cleaned every day while the other half were being worn. "We Like Ike" parasols and thousands of buttons and pamphlets were also on board. Marty Snyder, Eisenhower's mess sergeant, came along too. Both the cab of the truck and the jeep were equipped with public address systems. There were additional sound trucks, too, and trucks for anchoring blimps and trucks loaded with confetti for throwing out of windows, bags of which were distributed to offices along the parade route the day before Ike's arrival.

An advance man had preceded the Bandwagon by several days, so all was in readiness, including an editorial in the local paper and saturation television and radio spots for Eisenhower, which lauded the General and announced his imminent arrival. Willis reports that the editorials were gotten "on the basis that this wasn't political, this was a great military leader that had never been in the city, and it was time to honor him properly, and all that sort of thing."

Girls and local bands were recruited for the parade. As

soon as the Bandwagon appeared, the balloons were hoisted. Citizens unloaded the jeep and drove it from one end of town to the other, blaring out Ike campaign songs—"I Love the Sunshine of Your Smile" was a favorite. At the same time, the sound truck announced the forthcoming rally and parade. Snyder was usually with the jeep and now got off at street corners to give personal reminiscences of Eisenhower as he handed out mimeographed copies of the General's favorite recipes.

The candidate's arrival was the signal for the parade to start. First came the jeep, then the Bandwagon—both playing catchy campaign songs. The Bandwagon was loaded with pretty girls (volunteers from the local Junior League, the high schools, and other groups) in their colorful costumes, giving out "I Like Ike" buttons and pamphlets. Then came the General's car, with the candidate, arms upstretched, enveloping the crowds with his captivating grin.

Behind him came the bands. One union band was always hired and paid. After it marched any number of grade- and high-school bands who volunteered "just for the fun of playing," and where there were special marching bands such as Papa Celestine's in New Orleans, or the mummers' bands in Philadelphia, they were recruited too and added to the din and enthusiasm.

As the triumphal procession rolled along, confetti and ticker tape rained from office windows. Eisenhower soon became adept at dodging large, unopened parcels of both. He also quickly learned that it was less painful and more courteous to catch the bouquets of roses that women tossed into his car then to try to knock them off their course. The bystanders, now whipped to a frenzy of excitement, fell in behind the bands and marched with the General to the rally.

Often there was also a torchlight parade at night, with searchlights playing on the barrage balloons. The effect was so dramatic that the Citizens called these evening events "ethereal nocturnal splendor."

Despite these extraordinary efforts "to create the right atmosphere," Arthur Gray remembers riding out of town in a cab after one of their most successful days and discovering, to his utter dismay, that the cab driver was quite unaware that Eisenhower had been in town. And this was not an uncommon occurrence, said Gray:

> With the parade, with the radio, with the editorial, with sometimes a torchlight parade at night—we'd get these flares, railroad flares, and distribute them up and down the streets, in front of Eisenhower —with all that going, there'd still be people who didn't know he'd been there. So every technique we could dream up and think of . . . we used.

The Bandwagon carried a team of four volunteer drivers, and the minute their job was finished and they had hauled down and stowed the balloons, they set off, driving in relays all night, to the next day's stop.

The Eisenhower Bandwagon "became a trademark of the whole campaign—the jeep, the truck, the candidate," said Willis. And Gray reported that "Ike said the first thing that he would do was to look up and see if the barrage balloons were there, and then he knew everything was under control when he hit a town."

In 1952 the Bandwagon covered twenty-six states and thirty-five thousand miles. When, in the 1956 campaign, plans were being made to revive it, a report on its history and purpose stated:

> It has become the symbol of President Eisenhower, and it represents the spirit of Citizens for Eisenhower. . . . [It] provides a focal point for local and national publicity—an emotional rallying point for millions of Americans. As an instrument of distribution for campaign materials, it is unsurpassed. It sparks parades and spontaneous demonstrations. . . . The now-famous Eisenhower barrage balloons are valuable for front page picture coverage and for their great crowd-drawing appeal. . . . The Eisenhower Bandwagon leaves a city

or town with an atmosphere of confidence, enthusiasm, and Eisenhower.

Solid evidence that the 1956 campaign managers believed in the Bandwagon was their decision to have six thirty-ton trucks that year with all of the usual equipment supplemented by a reverse projection screen on the back of the bandwagon which, after dark, would give repeated showings of an Eisenhower film.

The 1952 campaign rolled on toward election day. With his Bandwagon twenty-four hours ahead of him, Eisenhower covered much of the country by train rather than plane. Life on a campaign train is the distilled essence of the campaign itself. With everyone working at incredibly close and inconvenient quarters, passing acquaintances become passionate friends, incompatible co-workers become deadly enemies, ordinary problems loom as major crises, hard work is accelerated to frenzied activity, and both seriousness and humor are raised to the nth power.

Into this supercharged atmosphere exploded the bombshell of the Nixon Fund. Eisenhower was campaigning through Iowa in September when he first learned that the vice presidential candidate had, in 1950, accepted contributions from California backers to help defray his personal political expenses. The details of this controversial fund and its subsequent handling by the Republican National Committee, by Nixon himself in his nationally televised "Checkers speech" arranged by the committee, and finally by Eisenhower have no place in an account of the activities of the Citizens except insofar as their group entered into the imbroglio that resulted.

When the *New York Post* disclosed the story of the fund, a great many Republican papers, including Nixon's strong supporter, the *New York Herald Tribune,* either asked that he be dropped from the ticket, or, as in the case of the *Herald Tribune,* advised him, editorially, to withdraw. The ensuing arguments rocked the train, with the National Committee and the pros, as usual, on one side and Eisenhower's personal entourage and the Citizens on the other. Sherman Adams reports, "Many of his [Eisenhower's] close personal friends and supporters, especially from the political Independents and the Citizens-for-Eisenhower groups, lost no time in opposing Nixon."

In a revealing comment on the general attitude of Independents, Emmett Hughes observed that these people "felt vastly more concerned with the political fate of Eisenhower than with the political embarrassment of the party." When Eisenhower finally decided to retain Nixon as his running mate, the brouhaha subsided.

With tensions running high on an overcrowded, overworked campaign train, even trivial occurrences are magnified out of all proportion. Mildly funny incidents become hilarious and one particular bizarre accident delighted all on board. In the middle of the night, a very proper middle-aged lady wearing only her nightgown came screaming out of her stateroom, her nightgown covered from top to toe with Ike pins. A box of a thousand pins, stored above her berth, had tipped into it, and she had rolled onto them. Not knowing what had stung her, she shot into the crowded aisle—a human pincushion for Ike.

Adlai Stevenson made one twelve-day whistle-stop trip by train through the eastern states, but Eisenhower's campaign train covered 20,871 miles around the country, and was, as Willis put it, "probably one of the last big train operations."

Willis and Rumbough took turns riding on the train. At every stop, local political leaders are brought aboard a campaign train in order to meet the candidate and discuss how the best possible job can be done in their areas. At the following stop, these leaders disembark and a new group is brought aboard.

Rumbough and Willis were on the train to see that representatives of the local Citizens were also brought on and given an opportunity to participate in these discussions with the party leaders and the candidate. It also enabled the two vice chairmen to contact their local organizations and help coordinate the work of these grass-roots groups with the Republican regulars. The fact that many of the Citizens were not Republicans made this a particularly ticklish job. The candidate's visits provided excellent opportunities to demonstrate the value of cooperation between rival groups. Joint operations could put on far more impressive welcomes, parades and rallies, and create a more genuine atmosphere of mass support than could groups in competition.

Of course, in places where the Republican party was weak, or—as in most of the South—almost nonexistent, the Citizens were often the whole show. They provided a basic organizational stronghold in these areas. Without them it would have been impossible to hold any big rallies for a Republican candidate in many of the southern states. In places which had been strongly pro-Taft, the Citizens frequently met with antagonism. Far worse, from the standpoint of electing their candidate, Gray reports that they "went into a lot of areas where we were surprised to find that the Republican organization would rather lose than have Eisenhower win. . . ." Gray attributed this, in part, to their fear that, in the event of an Eisenhower victory, they would not be in a position to deliver what they had been promising for the past twenty years.

Politically, the Citizens continued to operate as amateurs and functioned as independently as they had before the convention. But many of the highly skilled professionals from the public relations and advertising fields who had volunteered their services to the campaign were assigned to the Citizens. One of them, Frederick A. Zaghi, business manager of the television/-radio department of the advertising firm of Young and Rubicam, reports that the agency's head, Sigurd Larmon, "held many meetings with key members of the Citizens for Eisenhower groups—planning strategy and making recommendations."

Zaghi himself started with the Citizens at the time of the New

Hampshire primary, where he was responsible for preparing a brochure "to be distributed to all the people in the state of New Hampshire to try to woo the delegates over to Eisenhower rather than Taft." Zaghi stayed with the Citizens until after the election and was "involved in brochures, commercials, and buying time on television and radio." He was also sent around to give help to the head of the Citizens in each state.

Zaghi reports that it was the Citizens for Eisenhower that provided the television coverage for Lodge's dramatic fight in the Texas delegate struggle at the convention, which was, many believed, "the turning point" for Eisenhower's nomination. Zaghi's list of the people who were part of the operating group of the Citizens, after the convention, reads like a section of *Who's Who,* and he adds that there was "also a large staff of writers, directors, producers, advertisements, radio commercials, television commercials from Young and Rubicam." Most of the material was cleared by Herbert Brownell.

During 1952, Young and Rubicam worked with the Citizens the entire time. Zaghi reports, "We supplied them with what they needed—sometimes even financed their operation on radio and television." This help may account for the conflicting recollections of Gray and Willis. The former says that "we didn't use television. That was out of our economic wherewithall," while Willis reports that they "had a large television and radio budget and top television people." Stanley Rumbough agrees with Willis, and cites a book, *Spots for Eisenhower,* prepared at the end of the campaign by the well-known advertising expert Rosser Reeves. Reeves not only points out the use of television by Citizens, but gives specific figures and the names of people involved. With lively cartoons and impressive figures, it documents the contention that this was a major project of the Citizens for Eisenhower.

The opposition questioned the propriety of such professional "selling" of a presidential candidate, particularly by the so-called amateur Citizens. But the Eisenhower people countered this criticism by saying that, as new techniques were developed —such as those in the related fields of public relations and advertising—and, as modern methods of mass communication, such as television, became available, it was not only proper but necessary to make use of them to get their message across to the greatest number of people. Certainly this has been the philosophy and the trend in every campaign since then.

Nonetheless, there remain the two plaguing problems of the dangers of "image making," and of the increasingly astronomical costs and therefore politically corrupting influence involved in the extensive use of the mass communications media in political campaigns. In any case, the pioneering methods of the Eisenhower Citizens and campaign officials proved extremely effective.

Before the campaign was over, there were about eight hundred people working at the Hotel Marguery headquarters. Zaghi says that "everyone had something to do—there was no stepping on toes." The vast majority simply arrived at the Citizens headquarters and offered to do anything. Arthur Gray says that

> all the people who came in to help didn't want anything out of it. That . . . refers . . . to, who wanted to go to Washington? But people would come in and say, "Give me anything, let me lick stamps. I want to help. I just believe in this man and everything that he stands for, and I want to do a job. What can I do?"

Often the stamp lickers proved to have invaluable talents. Gabriel Hauge is cited as "a classic example" by Arthur Gray.

> [Hauge] came into the Citizens office and just wanted something to do. This was in the early days, March, April. He was put to work trying to develop a little brochure to express the Eisenhower philosophy. All over people were saying, "Well, now what does Eisenhower stand for, on civil rights, economics"—this that and the other thing? Gabe came in and, from speeches [Eisenhower] had made at

Columbia and speeches he'd made at SHAEF, put together an Eisenhower philosophy that was our research material. Gabe Hauge went on to become a speechwriter for Eisenhower.

Until the campaign was over, he served in the dual capacity of research director both for the candidate's personal campaign and for the Citizens. After the election, Eisenhower asked Hauge to go with him to Washington as his assistant for economic affairs.

He is now president [later Chairman of the Board] of the Manufacturers Hanover Trust Company, and a very fine fellow. But . . . you know, he just came in and said, "What can I do?" He was obviously far more capable than the job he started with, and grew and grew, doing more important things.

Another volunteer was Alfred Hollander, executive vice president of Gray Advertising Agency and president of Gray International, as well as a successful theatrical producer. Arthur Gray says:

He just came in to help, and he helped prepare Ike for his television appearances. Never wanted to go to Washington, never wanted to do anything else, just, "What can I do to help?" And so he ended up by coaching and teaching [Eisenhower], preparing him for the camera and all that sort of thing—then walked away from it, back to his business. There were many people that just didn't want anything out of it, they just wanted to help.

In reviewing the history of the Citizens, Charles Willis remembers:

The exciting part to me is that part before all the big shots got into it, and when we were starting the spark and suddenly found ourselves almost covered with enthusiastic volunteers, whom we were hard put to keep busy with our limited staff. . . . But it was something, I don't know how often it could be done, because the ingredients were just perfect. The country seemed to want a change, and had a great leader. It was spontaneous. . . . I think all we were was the spark that came along at the right time.

When I think back on the magnitude of what we undertook, we had no idea what we were doing.

When Willis was asked if he had at any time regretted having cofounded Citizens for Eisenhower, he replied, "No, it was just one great twenty-four-hour day, until the thing was over."

For an amateur ad hoc body, the Citizens became remarkably well organized, efficient, and effective. The press and public who read the October 16, 1952 edition of the *Eisenhower-Nixon Club News* would have found the following item: "After three days on the Campaign Train out west, Walter Williams, National Chairman of Citizens for E-N reports: 'General Eisenhower is "humbly grateful" that close to a million citizens are working for his Crusade.' " Another article in the same issue, less than three weeks before the election reads: "There are 5,104 Clubs across the nation and more popping up daily—and in excess of a million workers are beating the bushes for Ike. Let's go for two million!"

But a million or more enthusiastic and well-organized volunteers is a powerful and impressive task force, as indeed the Citizens for Eisenhower proved itself to be.

On Monday, November 3, around midnight, the strenuous campaign of Eisenhower, his professionals, and his amateurs came to an end. The country would go to the polls the following day. But that Monday morning the *New York Times'* front page carried a disturbing headline. By now Eisenhower's army of workers had become virtually certain of victory, but the banner headline, reflecting the unanimous findings of the country's public opinion polls, read: "ELECTION OUTCOME HIGHLY UNCERTAIN, SURVEY INDICATES." The result of the *Times'* own survey showed that "neither Gen. Dwight D. Eisenhower, Republican, nor Gov. Adlai E. Stevenson, Democrat, can be regarded as of now as certain of election." This survey and all the others took into account the unprecedented number of still undecided voters who held the balance of power. Theorizing that those Independent votes would divide roughly evenly between the two candidates, when each citizen faced his moment of truth in the voting booth, the pollsters predicted an unpredictably close election—a toss up, in fact.

As in the 1940 Roosevelt-Willkie contest, a campaign which had also inspired widespread citizen activity, a record number of voters turned out on November 4, 1952—nearly thirteen million more than had voted only four years earlier for Truman and Dewey. But the Independent voters confounded the pollsters and, instead of splitting evenly, they moved en masse. The results were a landslide for Eisenhower. He received not only fifty-five percent of the popular vote, but 442 of the 531 electoral votes cast.

The Eisenhower-Stevenson contest was unique in two respects—the unusually high caliber of both candidates and the extraordinary personal magnetism of each as evidenced by the active and dedicated volunteer organizations which each inspired. And, when it was all over, most Americans of both parties still "liked Ike," while over a hundred thousand concerned citizens who had voted for Eisenhower for various reasons took the trouble to write to Stevenson to express their admiration or affection for him personally, and their sorrow that, under all the circumstances, they had felt in conscience bound to vote for "a change."

Looking back from the vantage point of 1967, Arthur Gray, Jr., gives an interesting analysis of the necessity for a Citizens for Eisenhower organization:

There was a vacuum created by people who were internationally minded, but also conservative in their domestic policy. At that time, either you were an internationalist and a liberal on domestic affairs, or you were an isolationist and, let's say, stood for sound conservative business. There was no place in either party for one to be an internationalist and sound on business, and Eisenhower filled this great gap for . . . millions of guys who were overseas and could no longer be blind to what was going on in the world, and yet were not ready to go along with a New Deal type of business philosophy. They wanted individual initiative, but they also wanted the United States to be very much involved in what was going on in the world, because they recognized that it was essential. . . .

So that was the tremendous gap, I think, that he filled. It took people from both parties. But because of the bad name that the Republican party enjoyed (or did not enjoy) there were so many people that, number one, would not write out a check to the Republican party, number two, would not vote Republican in the beginning; that's why Citizens for Eisenhower was created. . . .

At that time, in 1952, there was a whole generation of people who grew up to believe that Republican represented Hoover, represented the depression, represented, you know, everything evil. That's why there was a need for Citizens. Now they have a Citizens for every candidate, and it's just a way of making out more checks. But I think there was a definite philosophical need for Citizens for Eisenhower, because the bridge between the Democrat and Republican labels was too great to go directly.

Stanley Rumbough, however, has said recently:

I have to disagree with some of Arthur Gray, Jr.'s conclusions. Citizens for Eisenhower was established very simply (months before the Republican convention) because we didn't feel that the Republican party was going to nominate a candidate who could defeat the Democrats. Charlie Willis and myself felt that the majority of the people of the United States, whether Democrat, Republican, or Independent, would find General Eisenhower desirable over the incumbent administration.

Reminiscing about some of the accomplishments of the Citizens, Rumbough said, "One other aspect that I feel is rather unique to Citizens for Eisenhower was that at the conclusion of the campaign there was excess money in the coffers." This fact alone should qualify it for the Guiness book of records! But, Rumbough added, "In the truly idealistic approach which symbolized Citizens, after all expenses had been paid and storage space arranged for the files, that money was returned on a prorated basis to all contributors."

Before ending the story of the 1952 Citizens for Eisenhower, a word must be said about its two successor organizations in 1954 and in 1956, because the phenomenon that was first observed in Andrew Jackson's campaigns was repeated—with a new variation in 1954. The Citizens had demonstrated their ability to recruit Independents and Democrats. They had shown they were able to rouse ordinarily apolitical Republicans. And they had operated most effectively. So now, just as the professional politicians in Jackson's campaigns of 1828 and 1832 appropriated the Hickory Clubs' name for their party organizations and adopted many of the amateurs' symbols and techniques, so did the regular Republican professionals organize Citizens for Eisenhower in 1954 and 1956. But in 1954 they went even farther than the Jacksonians had, as Eisenhower was not running that year.

Using the rationale that the President needed a Republican Congress to support his programs, they organized Citizens for Eisenhower-Doe, using the appropriate candidate's name in the various senatorial and congressional districts. Thus they added the luster of President Eisenhower's name to the attractions of the office seeker, whether he was a fine, upstanding bonafide Eisenhower man or a scraping from the bottom of the Republican barrel. This transparent ruse was quickly seen for what it was by former Citizens and the public at large. Stanley Rumbough notes that "In 1954, all top officers were receiving financial compensation. In my opinion it is impossible to have a truly volunteer organization if the leadership is being paid. A certain feeling of resentment and greed surfaces so that a volunteer sometimes feels as though he were being used." Very few people joined who would not have been equally willing to work under regular party leadership, and there is little evidence that the 1954 so-called Citizens was particularly effective.

In 1956, with the Citizens infiltrated, at all levels, with Republican professionals, it presented a tarnished image and, though there was an attempt to revive it in its original form, this proved impossible. The idealistic amateurs of 1952 did not flock into it and Theodore White's observation about revolutions and upheavals fossilizing into structures appears to be valid for amateur movements as well. But if it is true that imitation is the sincerest flattery, then the selfless Citizens for Eisenhower of 1952 have a right to hold their heads high.

Cornell Capa. Magnum Photos

Adlai Stevenson, the Governor of Illinois. His volunteer supporters made it impossible for him to refuse the nomination for Democratic candidate for President, which he did not want, in 1952.

VI

The Governor

Adlai Stevenson's nomination was another miracle that "couldn't happen," but did. As in the case of Wendell Willkie, it seems evident that, without the contribution of a group of determined amateurs, Stevenson's nomination would never have come about. But here the similarity ends. Willkie's eagerness for the nomination, his cooperation for months before the Republican convention with his amateur advisers, and his acquiescence in the organization of Oren Root's Willkie (for President) Clubs—all contrast sharply with the frustrating circumstances of Stevenson's supporters.

The Governor of Illinois did not want the nomination. He did not want to be president. In 1952, he wanted to run as he was committed to do for a second term as governor. When, between January and March of that year, pressures steadily mounted on him to declare himself a candidate for the nomination—or at least to indicate that he would not refuse if it were offered to him—Stevenson answered every newsman's questions with strong negatives. He consistently refused to allow his name to be entered in any primaries, and when, despite this, Oregon admirers entered it in theirs, and he could not legally withdraw it, he asked his fellow Democrats there to vote for the only other Democratic candidate on the ballot—Estes Kefauver.

He tried in every possible way to discourage and thwart the activities of a mushrooming nationwide Stevenson for President movement, headquartered in Chicago. When this group persisted in spite of him, he would have no truck with them and insisted that the leaders of his Stevenson for Governor Committee should continue to organize for his reelection in Illinois. He also instructed them not to take part in—or have any contact with—the Stevenson for President organization. By convention time, the Governor had been so successful in convincing both the delegates and his amateur supporters of his adamant position that much of the draft-Stevenson-in-spite-of-himself hope had faded and the majority of his followers had either given up in discouragement or decided to throw their support to a variety of second-bests.

Only the original nucleus of the now almost defunct National Committee Stevenson for President remained united in their belief that a draft was not yet impossible, and that Stevenson could not in good conscience refuse it if it came about. On July 16, 1952, just five days before the convention opened, they quietly set up diminutive headquarters in three bedrooms at the Conrad Hilton Hotel, with almost no money but a sizable staff, only one of whom received a slim salary. Their unheralded arrival was the antithesis of the chaotic hurly burly of marching bands, parades and frenetic activity that accompanied the establishment of the traditional huge eye- and ear-catching headquarters of the major candidates which were being established at the same time. Equally striking was the contrast to the ebullient descent of Willkie's amateur hordes on Philadelphia in 1940. Yet it was this tiny band of dedicated men and women who, under totally different circumstances and using very different means, performed the equivalent function in securing the nomination for their reluctant candidate that Willkie's amateurs did for their aspiring one.

Stevenson's reluctance was genuine and deeply felt. To try to understand both his peculiar fitness for the presidency and his unwillingness to assume the office it is necessary to look into his background. His ancestors came from North Carolina and reached Bloomington, Illinois, by way of Kentucky in 1852. Both on his father's and mother's side, Adlai's forebears contributed substantially to the intellectual, cultural, and political life of their times. His father's family were Democrats and Presbyterians, his mother's were Republicans and founders of the Bloomington Unitarian Church. When asked about his own affiliation, Stevenson remarked that he inherited his father's politics and his mother's religion. His Republican great-grandfather, Jesse Fell, was a close friend of Abraham Lincoln. His Democratic grandfather was vice president of the United States under Grover Cleveland, and his father was Illinois secretary of state. Adlai came naturally by his extraordinary attachment to his home state and his keen sense of duty to his party and his country.

Born in 1900, educated in the Bloomington public schools, at Choate preparatory school, Princeton University, and at Harvard and Northwestern Law Schools, Stevenson worked for a time on the family-owned newspaper, the *Bloomington Pantagraph*, before moving to Chicago to join one of the city's finest and most respected law firms.

Among the many organizations on whose boards he was to serve, the Chicago Council on Foreign Relations won his heart earliest and kept it always. First, he helped to build it. Later he developed his gift for public speaking from its platform. After he became its president in 1933, it became a standard joke that members came to meetings more to hear his felicitous and witty introductions of the council's illustrious visitors than the speeches that followed. But his maiden effort at political persuasion was deflating. A story that he told about himself was that, in 1936, as he left the auditorium following a speech at Carleton College, Minnesota, in support of Franklin Roosevelt, he heard a student comment, "It was a good speech, but who was he for?"

Meanwhile, Adlai had married an attractive, bright, spoiled, and self-centered Chicago girl. The wedding was a major social event in Chicago; though the groom had come from what the inner circle of Chicago society thought of vaguely as a small town "somewhere downstate," the bride, Ellen Borden, was one of their own. They had three sons, the eldest of whom, his namesake, is today carrying on the family tradition in Illinois politics. Adlai served a prolonged stint in Washington during the early days of the New Deal, receiving generous leaves of absence from his largely Republican law firm. In 1934, he was made a partner of his firm, Sidley, McPherson, Austin and Burgess, whose name, Stevenson irreverently commented to Edward McDougal, Jr., one of his new partners, "sounds like a trunk falling downstairs."

An interesting aspect of Stevenson's entire career is that, as well as can be ascertained, he never sought a job or an office until 1956, when he actively campaigned for the Democratic presidential nomination after his 1952 defeat. But jobs sought him. And in the spring of 1940, following the outbreak of the war in Europe the previous September, he was "drafted" to head the controversial William Allen White Committee to Defend America by Aiding the Allies, an unenviable task in isolationist Illinois.

For three years, his wartime service was as personal assistant to the secretary of the Navy, Frank Knox; toward the end of this period, the President "borrowed" him to head a mission to Italy to recommend measures for the relief and rehabilitation of that devastated, demoralized country. Stevenson's report not only became the basis for rehabilitation in Italy, but in other European countries as well. Toward the end of the war; he served as a member of the United States Strategic Bombing Survey on the northern front.

Stevenson's long association with the United Nations began in 1944, when he was appointed special assistant to Secretary of

State Edward R. Stettinius to work with Assistant Secretary Archibald MacLeish "in matters relating to postwar international organization." His first assignment with MacLeish was to "sell" to the American public the draft proposals for a constitution for a world organization, drawn up at Dumbarton Oaks, Washington, D.C., by representatives of the United States, the United Kingdom, and the Soviet Union. In 1945, he handled press relations for the United States at the United Nations Conference on International Organization, the preparatory conference for the United Nations held in San Francisco. That fall, while serving in London as deputy to Stettinius, chief delegate to the Executive Committee of the Preparatory Commission for the United Nations, Stettinius fell ill, and Stevenson proved an effective and respected replacement. In 1946 and 1947, he served as alternate U.S. Delegate to the first and second sessions of the United Nations.

In 1947, circumstances first cast Stevenson in the role of a reluctant candidate. The Illinois Democrats needed a "blue ribbon" slate to run against incumbent Senator "Curly" Brooks, a staunch isolationist, and incumbent Governor Dwight Green, whose original "reform" administration had—in eight years— degenerated into a morass of corruption and broken pledges.

When a committee, headed by his old friends, Hermon D. (Dutch) Smith, Louis A. Kohn, and Stephen Mitchell, broached to Adlai the possibility of running for the Senate against Brooks, he was naturally interested. But when Smith discussed the proposal with Colonel Jacob Arvey, powerful boss of Chicago's Democrats, he discovered that Arvey was staunchly committed to Paul Douglas, who was already campaigning for that office. Arvey, however, was greatly taken with Stevenson and subsequently urged him, instead, to run for governor. Stevenson was deeply dismayed. He felt confident that his interest and experience had prepared him for the Senate where his background in foreign affairs would be invaluable. He had had *no* background in state government. He demurred for some time, but finally his strong sense of obligation to his party and to public service prevailed. His candidacy was announced on December 30, 1947.

Characteristically, once he had made his decision he campaigned for the better part of a year with energy, conviction, and eloquence—as though this were the prize he had sought all his life. In November 1948, this Chicago lawyer, who the previous January had been well known in Washington, highly respected in Chicago, but virtually unheard of in the rest of Illinois, won the governorship with the largest majority of votes ever recorded in the state.

The crowd that jammed into the barracks-like Chicago headquarters of the Stevenson for Governor Committee on election night was a remarkable conglomeration. Hordes of volunteers, many of them Republicans, who had launched, raised a large part of the money for, and practically run Stevenson's campaign, were jostled and squeezed between Democratic ward committeemen, precinct captains, and party workers, and all the best and the worst of Chicago's Democratic machine. Downstaters had come, both Democrats and Republicans from almost every county, convinced that Stevenson was the man to restore honesty and efficiency to Illinois government if he could oust the Republican incumbent who had sullied it.

Diminutive Colonel Jacob Arvey, the powerful and respected Democratic boss, beaming broadly, was exchanging political views and gossip and his own estimate of Stevenson's chances with many of Illinois's more conservative business leaders. These chances had appeared to be nil until about three weeks before, when the bookies (but not the polls) began to give Stevenson a slight edge.

Illinois elects its governors in presidential years. But the crowd, the din, and the excitement at these headquarters, whose bare walls the volunteers had festively covered with flags, bunting, and posters showing Stevenson in every conceivable situation, from running a tractor on his farm to heading a

St. Patrick's Day parade, might have made one believe that he was the only candidate running that year. But regular Democratic headquarters at the Morrison Hotel must have had its share of party regulars, too. For incumbent President Truman was also at the finish line of a neck-and-neck race with Republican Thomas Dewey, with the national odds favoring Dewey.

As the radio began reporting early returns, mostly from Democratic Cook County, both Stevenson and Truman took sizable leads. Immediately, huge sheets of white paper and stubby little pencils appeared on the tables and so-called experts began frantically calculating their projections. But their normal human inaccuracies, plus the see-sawing presidential race, only added to the uncertainty of the outcome and increased the hubbub in the milling crowd.

Stevenson's lead was, surprisingly, larger than Truman's, which elicited wild cheers from one segment of the crowd. As the returns from normally Republican downstate came in, Truman's lead shrank while Stevenson's actually increased. Wilder cheers from the Republican volunteers!

Tension continued to mount until around midnight, when Stevenson had taken such a commanding lead that the crowd started focusing part of its attention on the presidential race. "Look what's happening to our *other* man," could now be heard all over, amidst the continuing uproar. For the race for the presidency was still undecided, with Dewey slightly ahead.

But long before the final presidential returns were reported, the official Illinois tally came over the radio. Stevenson had won. Pandemonium broke loose. Republicans kissed Democrats. Conservative suburban matrons and precinct workers from "the back of the yards" hugged each other ecstatically. It was an orgy of triumph and pride—pride in their candidate's great campaign against supposedly insuperable odds and in their own part, large or small, in his glorious victory.

When the final national returns were eventually reported, it became official that their neophyte candidate had carried Illinois by a record 527,067 votes, while the incumbent President had squeaked through by only 33,612. Some stand-pat, never-split-your-ticket Republicans later bitterly accused Stevenson's Republican workers of having carried Truman in "on Adlai's coattails."

There were two postscripts to that memorable evening—one tragic, the other amusing. The following morning, the Governor-elect arrived at his headquarters looking drawn, despondent, and utterly beaten. When two of his campaigners, who were also among his oldest and closest friends, expressed concern, he confided to them that his wife of twenty years, who had sat grim-faced during most of last night's celebration, had told him at the end that she was going to divorce him.

A day or two later, however, the members of the Stevenson for Governor Committee were delightedly circulating around headquarters copies of two telegrams. Just before the election, a Dewey man had wired a Stevenson worker, "Stevenson has no more chance of winning than I have of peeing up Niagara Falls." The day after the election, the Stevenson supporter had replied, "Please wire immediately date and time of great experiment." It is hoped that Stevenson got copies of these, too, and had a good laugh.

During the next four years, the Governor streamlined Illinois's financial system, reorganized state purchasing practices, doubled state aid to schools, put the formerly patronage-ridden state police on the merit system, reformed the welfare system with special emphasis on improving the deplorable conditions in Illinois's mental institutions, launched an overdue highway and road construction program, tightened up mine safety laws, fought for—and lost—a fair employment practices law, fought for—and lost—the calling of a constitutional convention, but won the first major constitutional revisions in eighty-two years, and attracted and appointed top experts into high-level posts regardless of political affiliation. When 1952 dawned, the character, wit, personal appeal, and outstanding administration of

Illinois's Governor had focused national attention on him in a crucial election year.

When, on January 24, 1952, it was learned that, at the invitation of President Truman, the Governor of Illinois had spent the previous evening in Washington with him, the curiosity of both press and public skyrocketed. Had the President, who had kept people guessing as to his own intentions about running again, asked Stevenson to run in his place? What had been Stevenson's answer? Coincidentally, *Time* magazine already had Stevenson's picture on the cover of its next issue due to come out two days later. They quickly updated their cover story to include the White House visit and commented, "Whatever the truth behind the rumors, this much was evident: in a cold season for the Democrats Adlai Stevenson is politically hot, and Harry Truman feels the need of a little warmth."

But it was not only people at the top who were showing interest in Governor Stevenson's candidacy. Many rank-and-file Democrats and Independents saw in him the qualities they wanted in their president. By February, the Governor was writing to friends, "The pressures are *appalling.*" A small group of admirers in Chicago decided to do something about it and, in February, without consulting the Governor, they organized the Illinois Committee Stevenson for President.

The chairman was Walter Johnson, head of the history department at the University of Chicago. He also taught courses in political science. By 1952, he had published three books whose titles—*The Battle Against Isolationism, William Allen White's America,* and *The United States: Experiment in Democracy*—very clearly reveal his interests. His cochairman was a Chicago lawyer, George Overton.

The other members of the hard-core leadership were a real estate agent, two businessmen, four lawyers, a local newspaper publisher, two advertising men, a public relations counselor, and a housewife.

Johnson had run once for alderman—and lost. Otherwise,

these people were all political amateurs in that none had ever held or run for public office; nor had any of them had experience in the presidential nominating procedure or taken part in a national convention or campaign. But most of them were men and women who had felt deeply enough about local issues or candidates to have worked for a number of them. They had all rung doorbells, made speeches, prepared campaign literature, and helped organize political headquarters. One or another had worked for candidates for Congress, the state legislature, or the city council. A number were members of the Independent Voters of Illinois, and others had been active in the affairs of the American Veterans Committee. This added up to a considerable amount of talent and sound political experience, but it in no way prepared them to find their way through the intricate maneuvers of a national convention, much less to put pressure on its delegates.

When the committee first organized, however, such an operation was farthest from their thoughts. The full measure of their ambition was to help make Adlai Stevenson and his Illinois record better known throughout the country, to encourage the formation of local Stevenson for President groups, and to provide a national focal point for them. In addition to a voluminous correspondence, their activities consisted largely in the distribution of as much literature and as many buttons as their meager finances would permit. Their buttons simply read, "Stevenson," so that they could be used in the Illinois gubernatorial campaign should the Governor's desires prevail.

On March 21, the *Chicago Sun-Times* printed a picture of a huge pile of lapel pins simply saying "Stevenson" which the reactivated Stevenson for Governor Committee was distributing. The caption included the following: "Committee members insist the buttons are for Governor Stevenson's campaign for re-election. However, it was noted that plain buttons could be used in a presidential campaign too." As the Stevenson for Governor Committee was even more amateur than the Stevenson for President Committee, and under firm orders from the Governor to work and think only in terms of his re-election in Illinois, this devious idea probably never occurred to them.

At the end of March, Stevenson took determined steps to take himself out of consideration for the Democratic presidential nomination. On the twenty-ninth, President Truman, in the course of a routine Jefferson-Jackson Day dinner speech at which Stevenson was present, casually announced that he would not run for re-election. When the speech ended, the entire press corps descended on the Illinois Governor, asking the invariable questions with renewed intensity, while Stevenson answered negatively or parried them with increased determination: "I am still a candidate for Governor of Illinois and nothing else," or "no," he would not "try to get the nomination." As to the hypothetical question of whether he would accept if nominated, he would cross that unlikely bridge if he came to it.

The following day, on a long-scheduled "Meet the Press" program, he was subjected to merciless questioning. He maintained his steadfast position throughout this ordeal, but his thoughtful answers to the issues that were raised only added to his growing reputation.

Press and public interest in him and speculation about him mounted, and the Illinois Committee Stevenson for President shortly changed its name to the National Committee Stevenson for President. They intensified their efforts to create a nationwide movement and provide it with effective leadership. The press now began to take occasional notice of them and would peg a story about Stevenson's escalating popularity on information supplied by the committee.

On April 8, in the Illinois primary, Stevenson was officially renominated as the Democratic candidate for governor. A week later, on April 16, determined to eliminate himself finally from consideration as a presidential candidate, he issued a detailed statement in which, following an explanation of his long-standing position on the presidential nomination, he said, "To this I must now add that in view of my prior commitment to run for governor and my desire and the desire of many who have given me their help and confidence in our unfinished work in Illinois, I could not accept the nomination for any other office this summer."

It appeared that the Governor had at last succeeded in taking himself out of the race. The *New York Times* summed up the almost unanimous verdict of the press in the statement, "Stevenson seems effectively to have closed the door to his nomination."

The following day, Stevenson flew to New York to be present at a dinner at the Waldorf Astoria hotel honoring Averell Harriman. His instinct was to cancel out, fearing that his presence might somehow rekindle the interest that his statement had apparently effectively extinguished. But it was pointed out that dropping out at the last moment would be most discourteous to Harriman, an old personal friend, as well as disloyal to his party, as his presence was always a major attraction at Democratic gatherings.

He opened his short speech by remarking:

I am told that I am here at the head table by misrepresentation and fraud, that you invited a candidate for President but got a candidate for Governor instead. I feel like the weary old Confederate soldier, unarmed, ragged and asleep, whom some zealous young Union soldiers captured. "Git up, Reb, we got you now," they shouted. "Yea," the old fellow said, "and it's a heck of a git you got."

The remarks that followed, which the Governor intentionally kept brief, were of such quality that the audience was enthralled. The moment the other speeches were over, Stevenson tried to slip quietly away. He was trapped by a throng of excited Democrats and members of the press while Harriman stood virtually alone on the platform.

Despite the *New York Post*'s comment the following day that "the dinner for Harriman may come to be remembered as the starting point for a real draft-Stevenson movement," the Governor's unequivocal statement of the week before had done its work. Party leaders, convinced that a draft was now impossible, joined the camps of the avowed candidates. Many threw their support to Harriman or Kefauver. Colonel Arvey, Illinois's most influential Democrat and a strong Stevenson backer, after one final attempt "to draw the Governor into the race," gave up, believing a draft was now in the miracle category. Only the National Committee Stevenson for President, disheartened though they were, refused to give up. As one of them said: "If we give up, who will be left? We're the last hope."

To buoy themselves up, they clutched at two straws. One was that Stevenson had used the term "could not" rather than "would not" in his April 16 statement explaining why he felt unable to accept the nomination for any office other than that of governor. The other was the character of Stevenson himself. Though most of the committee members had never met him, and those who had knew him only slightly, his high sense of duty, his dedication to public service and his devotion to the principles of his party had shone through all he had ever said or done. The committee reasoned that if he were genuinely drafted by his party to run as their candidate for the highest office in the land, he could not refuse. The experts' conviction that the draft of an uncooperative and unwilling candidate would take nothing less than a miracle was not enough to discourage them.

The story of the arms'-length battle that ensued between the Governor and this determined and resourceful band of amateurs is unique in our political history. From the time the latter organized in February, until the day Stevenson was nominated in July, there was never one word of direct communication between them, except for a single brief telephone call from Stevenson to Walter Johnson on April 16, when he asked Johnson's opinion on a totally unrelated matter. Johnson subsequently learned that, at that time, the Governor "knew little or nothing" about their operation. When he did learn of their activities, he threw every possible roadblock in their way.

As the faith of the professionals and the public in the possibility of drafting Stevenson ebbed, so did the committee's plans for forming a strong national organization. Meanwhile, in April and May, in the course of carrying out earlier commitments to speak in Texas, California, and Oregon, Stevenson continued to discourage any lingering hope for his cooperation. *Would* he accept a draft? *Wouldn't* he accept a draft? To trap him, the question was asked so many times in so many forms that once in California he wearily replied to a reporter, "Why don't you put that question in German? It has been put in every other language it seems." When asked if his reluctance to run was because he was afraid of Eisenhower, he replied, "I am not afraid to run against Ike," and then smiling, "and I don't think Ike is afraid of me."

On July 11, the Republican convention nominated General Eisenhower. Immediately upon its adjournment the next day, July 12, Stevenson's office issued the following statement, undoubtedly prepared by the Governor himself: "He is a candidate for re-election as Governor of Illinois, and as he has often said, wants no other office. He will ask the Illinois delegation to continue to respect his wishes and he hopes all of the delegates will do likewise." This statement, Marquis Childs concluded on July 17, "was the final damper."

Coincidentally, on the twelfth, the National Committee Stevenson for President had mailed letters to all convention delegates and alternates giving Adlai Stevenson's unique qualifications to win the election and lead the country. The committee urged the delegates to vote for his nomination and announced the forthcoming opening of their own convention headquarters. The reaction from Springfield was immediate. Walter

Johnson, the committee's cochairman, received a telegram reading:

> Have just seen circular letter to delegates and am very much disturbed in view of my unwillingness to be candidate. Have consistently avoided trying to influence your committee's activities feeling that my position was manifest and that I could not properly ask you to cooperate as a friend if your group had other views in conflict with my wishes. . . . I do not want to embarrass you and I am grateful for your good will and confidence but my attitude is utterly sincere and I desperately want and intend to stay on this job with your help, I hope. Regards, Adlai E. Stevenson.

Unmoved, the committee wired back, in effect, that the decision about the nomination was not the Governor's to make, that the convention had the right to nominate any qualified American, even against his wishes if it thought him the best man. A nominee had the right to refuse to serve, but he was powerless to prevent the nomination. They reasoned among themselves that speculation about Stevenson and questions to him had centered on the point "will he accept?" whereas the cogent question was "will he refuse?" The committee phrased their telegram with the latter question in mind and sent it off, satisfied that they had trapped him at last in that no reply, they believed, would be a clear indication that he would not refuse.

By this time almost all of the party leaders who had retained the slightest hope finally had been effectively discouraged. A draft without at least some covert cooperation from a potential candidate would require a miracle. With his active opposition, it was clearly impossible.

Immediately after the Republicans vacated Chicago's amphitheatre and its many hotels, the Democrats started to move in. By the fourteenth (a week before the convention was to open), the headquarters of most of the presidential aspirants had already been set up in the Conrad Hilton Hotel, and the undaunted Stevenson for President people decided to push their own schedule forward by two days and to move into their Draft Stevenson headquarters on the sixteenth. Meanwhile, the Governor remained at his desk in Springfield and continued to make consistently discouraging statements.

On the fifteenth, the day before the new headquarters were to open, Colonel Arvey, Illinois Democratic chief, made a nationwide television broadcast in which he said he felt the chances of a Stevenson draft were "very, very slim." He also criticized the Stevenson for President Committee for continuing in opposition to the Governor's wishes and announced that he (Arvey) had asked them to disband.

Because the independence of the National Committee Stevenson for President from the Governor was obvious, the opposition had begun floating stories that the committee was acting as a front for the Illinois delegation and was in league with Arvey, who was secretly conspiring to engineer a draft. Some members of the committee felt that Arvey's speech gave them a splendid opportunity to scotch this rumor. Others were firmly opposed to getting into an argument with such a powerful opponent. A strong statement declaring their independence was drafted, but those opposed to it prevailed and the statement was not issued. The charge was never publicly denied and was kept alive throughout the convention and even lingered on afterward.

The press apparently was not impressed by the conspiracy theory, for on July 17, the day after the Stevenson headquarters opened, Marquis Childs and the Alsops both mentioned Arvey in their columns reporting the demise of the Stevenson draft movement. Childs said, in part, "Governor Adlai Stevenson has at last succeeded in eliminating himself. . . . Because of this grim determination, his good friend and patron, Jacob Arvey, boss of the party in Illinois, has had his hands tied. . . ." And the Alsops reported:

The movement to draft Governor Adlai Stevenson of Illinois . . . is now dead—at least for the first few ballots of the oncoming Convention. As of today, in fact, Stevenson is being counted right out of the Democratic picture, even by National Committeeman Jacob Arvey of Illinois, who took the leading part until recently in the powerful draft-Stevenson drive.

The *Chicago Sun-Times,* the *Louisville Courier Journal,* and other respected papers all gave similar reports. One can scarcely conceive of more dispiriting circumstances than those under which the National Committee Stevenson for President opened its tiny Hilton headquarters just five days before the convening of the Democratic convention.

But a surprise awaited them, or maybe they were the only people not really surprised. The very fact of their existence— perhaps their temerity in existing at all—gave those who had virtually abandoned hope an excuse for hoping a little longer. More important, their headquarters provided a meeting place for the unexpected number of interested or undecided delegates who turned up in droves, and for the working press who were becoming increasingly intrigued by the reluctant Governor.

By Saturday, the nineteenth, three days after opening, these unorthodox headquarters had been visited by over three hundred delegates, and the inundation of press and television people had forced the rental of five additional rooms. This was a huge expense for a group which needed to use its meager resources for literature and buttons. Though their expanded headquarters necessitated adding a few people to the payroll, most of the work was done by hundreds of devoted, unpaid volunteers.

Paul Ringler described the operation in the *Milwaukee Journal* of July 21:

Committees with Presidential candidates and toney headquarters are no novelty at this Democratic National Convention. They clutter up the place.

We give you, therefor, a Committee that is different. Almost fantastically different. It has no candidate. It has little money. It has headquarters of Spartan simplicity.

It is the National Committee Stevenson for President. . . .

The man it backs, Governor Adlai Stevenson of Illinois, keeps on insisting, as he has for months, that he is not a candidate for the nomination and doesn't want to be a candidate.

Yet the Committee, unimpressed, uninfluenced and unawed, goes right on working just as if Stevenson were as much a candidate as Alben Barkley, Estes Kefauver, Richard Russell, Robert Kerr, etc.

It's not only confusing, it is amusing.

One of the many problems created by this ambiguous situation was that the delegates and press consulted the Stevenson headquarters, as they habitually consulted those of all candidates, about the Governor's views and wishes. They requested information on appointments to be made, invitations to be sent, and the welcoming address he was scheduled to deliver as governor of the host state.

One day a very prominent member of the Ohio delegation arrived, asking to see Stevenson's campaign manager.

"Stevenson is not a candidate," was the reply. "There isn't any campaign manager. We have cochairmen and volunteers to interview delegates."

"Well," said the surprised delegate, "let me talk to Stevenson."

"Don't you know that this is a headquarters without a candidate?" he was asked.

"Well, with whom do I deal?" was his next question.

"We can't deal except that maybe we can give you a seconding speech to make," was the unexpected answer from Hubert Will, the member of the executive committee to whom he had been talking.

The delegate departed saying, "Oh! Well, keep in touch with me on the floor of the convention."

The committee kept in constant low-key contact with him from then until the moment the balloting began. They watched closely as the Ohio delegation was polled on the first ballot and their delegate cast his vote for Senator Richard Russell, as they had expected. On the second ballot, however, their hopes changed to worry when he stuck by Russell. But, on the third crucial ballot, he swung over and gave his vote to Stevenson.

Another confusing problem was that the hotel persisted in sending Stevenson's personal mail and telegrams to the committee. And the hotel switchboard kept putting personal calls to Stevenson through to the committee, while screening out others that should have come to them. In spite of the committee's constant efforts to make it plain that they were not authorized to speak for the Governor, receive his mail, or take his calls —quite the contrary—the confusion continued to the end.

On the final day of the convention, chaos reigned at the now frantic headquarters. Thousands of gladioli in tin tubs, addressed to Governor Stevenson, were suddenly delivered to them. They poured into the office space and then overflowed into the corridor. And still they kept coming, causing a major work stoppage and traffic jam. The mystery, though not the inconvenience, was finally solved when a volunteer managed to squeeze through the crowd with a card which read, "Congratulations to Governor Stevenson from the Wholesale Gladioli Growers of America."

Quixotic and confusing as the Stevenson for President organization appeared to outsiders, this small band of determined amateurs was putting together a very efficient operation. The leaders were assigned specific responsibilities. Four were put in charge of delegate contacts, three were in charge of volunteer assignments, four took responsibility for public relations, and four for office management. Three had the thankless task of handling finances. And three others ran communications and organization.

A service was set up, under the supervision of a very capable woman, to monitor, around the clock, all radio and television broadcasts and to clip all news stories. This information was digested and fed immediately to the group's executive committee. On July 15, this service passed its first test with high marks when they monitored Arvey's telecast and had the full text in the hands of the committee within minutes.

Interesting as was the committee's battle with the Governor and their determination to keep his standard flying in spite of him, the most fascinating aspect of their work proved to be the political operation that they were shortly drawn into. They had not planned it that way. At the outset of their convention operation, they had envisaged themselves as an information center where delegates and newsmen interested in Governor Stevenson could learn more about the man and his record. But it soon became clear to them that Stevenson had an astonishing reservoir of delegate interest and strength unknown to the delegates themselves.

The incredible potential of this untapped resource began to dawn on them. There was no doubt that it was there, but who realized it but themselves? And who, then, was there to try to tap it but their committee? But they knew so little about the involved politics of a national convention!

They analyzed the situation carefully, and decided that there were three moves that were essential and should be made immediately. Their information had to be circulated in order to combat the prevalent hopelessness in regard to Stevenson's candidacy. Those delegates sympathetic to Stevenson had to be made known to each other and their strength consolidated. And a nationally respected delegate had to be found who would be willing to put Governor Stevenson's name in nomination against his wishes. These were formidable assignments for a small band of obscure amateurs to undertake.

The committee relied heavily on the press to help in the first two efforts. They issued few press releases. Their pool of volunteers talked personally to each of the increasing number of press people who visited their headquarters. They discussed Stevenson's unique qualifications, explained his reluctance to seek the nomination, but stressed why, in good conscience, he could not refuse if drafted. They pointed out that an open, leaderless, grass-roots convention—such as that of 1952—would be ideal for drafting the best man, regardless of his personal wishes.

Finding a prominent delegate who would take the risk of nominating this unwilling candidate was quite another matter. The committee's resourcefulness and luck, however, appeared limitless. On July 14, they had telegraphed the popular and respected Governor of Indiana, Henry F. Schricker, inviting him to join the committee. Schricker called them immediately, asking them who they were and how they were operating. Though he refused their invitation to join on the ground that his acceptance might be construed as committing the whole Indiana delegation, he electrified Walter Johnson, to whom he was talking, by casually observing, "There is a statement in the Indianapolis papers that I am going to nominate Stevenson. I would be honored to do so, but no one has asked me." Johnson —though quite unauthorized—did so. That abruptly ended the conversation. There was no response from Schricker.

The committee turned again to the press to help them accomplish their third objective—to have Stevenson's name placed in nomination. A reporter for the *Baltimore Sun,* having overheard Johnson's end of the Schricker-Johnson conversation, headlined his July 18 story, without using Schricker's name, "Stevenson To Be Placed in Nomination." On the basis of this story, Johnson again called Schricker urging him to act. Schricker only replied that he would get in touch with Johnson personally when he arrived in Chicago on Sunday, the day before the convention was to open.

Johnson promptly relayed the gist of this conversation to a number of influential reporters, including James Reston of the *New York Times,* and this produced a rash of articles about the Stevenson committee trying to get Schricker to organize a draft. The committee's hopes seesawed that day. First they were raised by a report that, when Schricker was told a committee was going to call on him to ask him to nominate Stevenson, he replied, "That may not be necessary," then dampened by the news that Schricker had told friends that he planned to talk with Governor Stevenson before making his decision.

This worrisome state of affairs finally forced the Draft Committee to conclude that the best chance for nominating Stevenson was to wait for a deadlocked convention and then put his name in nomination. There were so many eager candidates vying for the job that there was every likelihood that a deadlock would occur. In such an emergency the convention was almost bound to turn to Stevenson. At that point, there should be no problem in finding someone to nominate him, and these pressures, combined with the Governor's patriotism and sense of duty, would force him to accept.

Still, the question remained: How could they get a firm commitment from some delegate to agree to nominate him when the time came? Governor Shricker was now only a faint hope.

On Friday, July 18, the day before Stevenson arrived in Chicago, a major break occurred. Archibald Alexander, former under secretary of the Army, a long-time friend of the Illinois Governor and a delegate and senatorial candidate from New Jersey, came into the headquarters and volunteered to put Stevenson's name in nomination provided no better-known delegate could be found to do it.

In view of the unofficial nature of the Draft Stevenson group and Stevenson's determined opposition to its activities, it took courage and deep conviction on Alexander's part to take this step. In addition, Alexander was well aware of the attitude of so many powerful professionals who felt that, under the circumstances, Stevenson had almost no chance of being nominated. Most professional politicians do not want to work for a noncandidate or, as Alexander put it, are in "fear of backing a loser or, even more embarrassing, a candidate who wouldn't run."

The release of Alexander's announcement gave a tremendous boost to the Draft Stevenson effort. One of the two major uncertainties had now been clearly resolved. Alexander reported that, within hours after his statement was published, he heard from delegates of at least twenty states, and many delegates paid their first visit to the committee's headquarters immediately after its release.

The Draft Committee skillfully utilized their delegate contacts and the press to circulate points they wished to make. Alben Barkley was too old to be president. Russell and Kefauver were both from the South and their strongest support was regional rather than national, and Kerr had little name-recognition throughout the country. Averell Harriman, former governor of New York, with the huge New York delegation committed to him, was a real threat. Furthermore, he was eagerly seeking the nomination. But all these candidates had been around for a long time.

Stevenson was a new face. His ideas were fresh and forward looking. His eloquence was already known to many of the delegates, as over the past four years as governor he had been invited to speak in a great many of the states. Increasingly, national attention and interest was being focused on the "fugitive from the nomination," as Edward Folliard of the *Washington Post* called Stevenson.

On Friday, July 18, the *Chicago Sun-Times* said, "Despite Stevenson's refusal to seek the nomination, and Arvey's public gloom over the possibilities of drafting him, there was a resurgence of Stevenson talk during the day." The same day, the *Christian Science Monitor* reported, "Governor Adlai E. Stevenson didn't plan it that way—and leading announced Democratic presidential aspirants certainly don't relish it—but the hottest conversation topic on the eve of the Democratic National Convention concerns the possibility of the Illinois Governor's being drafted."

On the seventeenth, the committee had started to produce and distribute widely a daily mimeographed handbill called "Stevenson Headlines," in which they quoted from the increasingly optimistic press stories around the country. In addition to

these dispatches, stories included on July 18 bore such headlines
as: "Stevenson Draft Grows as Dem. Deadlock Looms," *New
York Daily News;* "Gov. Schricker Gives Boost to Adlai Back-
ers," *Chicago Sun-Times;* "Governors Urged to Aid Stevenson,"
New York Times; "Schricker Eyed as Nominator," *Baltimore
Sun.*

The committee also put out occasional unorthodox background pieces. The day after the first issue of "Stevenson Headlines" appeared, they distributed an ingenious piece called "It
Happened in Chicago in 1880," which was intended to prove
that the draft of an unwilling candidate was not an impossibility,
because it had happened seventy-two years before, in Chicago,
to James Garfield. Apparently Garfield fainted when he was
nominated. But he went on to win the presidency.

By now the committee was convinced that Stevenson was
unquestionably the first choice of the majority of the delegates.
It was essential to dispel their fatalistic conviction that a draft
was, under all the circumstances, impossible.

On the same day—Saturday, July 19—that the Garfield piece,
which drew wide and favorable attention, appeared, Stevenson
flew up from Springfield to Chicago. As governor of the state
that was host to the convention, protocol demanded that he
welcome the delegates at the opening session. He was also a
member of the Illinois delegation. Both of these circumstances
created a dilemma for the reluctant Stevenson, who had tried
to stay out of the limelight and, since the arrival of the first
delegates, to keep as low a profile as possible.

He must have been even more disconcerted by his wild airport reception. Every member of the Draft Stevenson Committee was there to greet him with hordes of their followers. But
they were a small band compared to the huge shrieking crowd
of ordinary Illinois citizens that turned out for his arrival. A
large contingent of local politicians headed the official greeters
and the entire United States and foreign press, newsreel, and
television corps appeared to be there. They photographed and

questioned him mercilessly until he finally was given a moment to make a statement. He said:

> I shall never be a candidate in the sense that I'll ask anybody to vote for me here. On the contrary, I'll do everything possible to discourage any delegate from putting me in nomination or nominating me.
>
> I cannot conceive that, with all the willing candidates available and with all the talent and ability at its disposal, the Democratic party would turn to an unwilling candidate who is running for another office.

He added that he would do everything he possibly could to discourage Schricker and Archibald Alexander, two delegates reportedly ready to put his name in nomination.

The next day, Reston reported in the *New York Times* that Stevenson had taken "one more long step toward eliminating himself from the Democratic presidential nomination." But the committee had already tried to counter Stevenson's statement by issuing one of its own, repeating their conviction that Stevenson was "the strongest and most popular candidate" and that he "must and will accept a draft." The Governor, however, was making it more and more difficult for the committee's statements to carry weight.

As far as courting delegates was concerned, the Draft Committee used very low-key techniques. They were aided by the unprecedented number of delegates who dropped into their headquarters spontaneously. Visitors were welcomed at the elevators by the least experienced volunteers—young friendly housewives and students. Delegates were ushered into headquarters and introduced to the older and more experienced workers, members of the executive committee, lawyers, businessmen, and teachers, who interviewed them.

Surprisingly, a considerable number of strong Harriman, Kefauver, and Russell supporters visited the Draft Stevenson headquarters. In an effort to avoid the friction and bitterness that so often develops between the more ardent followers of various candidates, the greeters in the foyer were told not to argue with these visitors. They were instructed simply to say, "I prefer Stevenson. You are entitled to your view; but if you would like more information about Stevenson, we will arrange an interview with our delegate-contact people." This noncontroversial approach undoubtedly made it easier for these delegates later to climb onto the Stevenson bandwagon when their heroes showed signs of faltering. Pro-Stevenson delegates weren't interested in discussing his record—they knew it and they liked it. He was their man and, they felt, their most formidable vote-getter. But, under the circumstances, many seriously questioned whether he would accept if he were nominated.

Alexander's announcement of the eighteenth, however, had emboldened the Draft Committee to come to a firm decision. They made up their minds to put Stevenson's name in nomination during the nominating roll call, and not wait for a deadlock, as some leaders advocated.

They had now reached one of their goals and were making progress toward reaching the other two: overcoming pessimism about the possibility of a draft by publicizing the great amount of latent Stevenson strength among the delegates, and bringing those delegates together. Pessimism about the possibility of nominating Stevenson, however, was still their most formidable obstacle, and the supporters of other candidates were encouraging and spreading this pessimistic propaganda.

On the nineteenth, representatives from the Draft Stevenson Committee were invited to a pro-Stevenson meeting called by the national committeeman from Kansas. Arguments were fierce. Everyone had a point of view, but no delegate could convince another that his own was right, and probably were not sure themselves. The Stevenson committee soon became convinced that no one had the answer—they were all at sea. The meeting broke up with nothing decided and nothing agreed upon. Here they were, two days before the convention was to open, with no professional organizing the delegates, no floor leader selected yet, and the question of whether Schricker, Alexander, or someone else should put Stevenson's name in nomination not yet decided. The committee agreed that they must plunge head on into convention politics working with and through the delegates to help organize the draft.

Fortunately, among the pro-Stevenson delegates on the powerful Pennsylvania delegation were two active and respected leaders. James Finnegan, the president of the Philadelphia city council, was a slightly built, charming Irishman with a puckish look. His blue eyes always seemed to be darting about, taking in everything that was going on around him, and to be slightly amused by what he saw. Lewis Stevens was an old Princeton friend of Stevenson and a member of the council. They had both made earlier visits to the Stevenson headquarters and gone through their delegate files. Within an hour after the abortive meeting at the Kansas headquarters, Walter Johnson received an urgent invitation from Stevens and Finnegan to join them as soon as possible for a conference at the Pennsylvania headquarters.

Finnegan, Stevens, and another delegate, William Teefy, opened the conference with a leading question: "Did the committee's estimate of Stevenson's growing strength contain any serious flaws?" Johnson and freelance Washington writer Stuart Haydon, who had accompanied him, embarked on a comprehensive answer. They replied that, if there were errors in their calculations, "they were on the conservative side." They admitted that their peculiar position in not being able to speak *for* Stevenson, only *about* him, in not being able to make promises or offer compromises, and in having "no political coercive power" were serious handicaps to delegates working for his nomination. The committee could supply "no political tools." They stressed that delegates working for Stevenson have "only one concrete reward; the personal satisfaction that a dignified, competent and honorable man has been offered as the Democratic party's choice for the highest post in the land." They pointed out, again, the unbossed, uncontrolled makeup of the 1952 convention and the opportunity it gave the delegates to nominate their own man.

Johnson and Haydon then offered to help organize the nominating machinery if the Pennsylvania delegation would take the lead, and provided that they wanted the committee's assistance.

Before replying, Finnegan asked the inevitable, crucial question. He started by assuming the truth of all the National Committee Stevenson for President had said, and that everything had been done to secure Stevenson's nomination. *"How do we know he will accept it?"* Many people have tried to get him to commit himself, even privately—and he has refused to do so. What can you say that indicates he will accept the nomination?"

Another detailed reply by Johnson stressed Stevenson's character and conviction, using (by now) time-honored phrases: "in good conscience," "he has no right to refuse," "we believe him to be a man of good conscience who therefore will not refuse." He argued that if the Governor were going to refuse, he would have said so long ago and then he pontificated a bit on the nature of Stevenson's integrity. (Johnson apparently ignored Stevenson's deeply held conviction that it would be "presumptuous" to state his position on a nomination which he had so clearly stated he did not seek or want when it had not been offered to him and the probability of this happening was so remote.)

Johnson then permitted himself a good deal of rather dogmatic speculation about what "we feel that Stevenson believes. . . ." His peroration was an emotional appeal to the "American ideal of the office seeking the man" and the survival of the democratic process, and he closed by pointing out with justifiable pride what his committee of self-confessed idealists had accomplished in the past week: "Without funds, without traditional political organization, without even being delegates—one group has helped bring it about that Adlai Stevenson is *the* most serious contender for the nomination."

Johnson's presentation was evidently most effective. Later the committee was told that his and Haydon's "frankness and bluntness" were a major factor in the Pennsylvania delegation's decision to work with them. In any case, at the end of Johnson's statement he was asked if he could supply Stevenson buttons for the entire Pennsylvania delegation at their caucus the following day. Seventy buttons was a large order for the impoverished committee to supply, but by rounding up all that they had—including removing some from the shirtfronts of many of their volunteers—they were able to fill this welcome request. As they left, they were handed a check to have an additional supply made.

Sunday, the twentieth, was the hottest day—as far as both physical and emotional climates were concerned—of the pre-convention struggle.

That afternoon Governor Stevenson met for the first time with the Illinois delegation. Even the barrage of questions that he had faced at the airport had not been as difficult as this confrontation would be. How could he persuade his state's delegation not to nominate or vote for their own governor—an honor that any delegate would find hard to resist and a request that would be difficult to understand?

The atmosphere was tense as Stevenson entered the caucus room; he plunged straight to the heart of the problem that so deeply troubled him. He started by formally requesting that the delegation not nominate him or, should others do so, not vote for him. He reiterated that he wanted only to run for the office to which the Illinois Democrats had already nominated him, that of governor. And then he added, with barely disguised emotion, "I do not deem myself fit for the job—temperamentally, mentally, or physically."

Unfortunately, enterprising reporters, lying on the floor outside, their ears to the crack under the door, were eavesdropping at this closed caucus. The Governor's dramatic plea was spread across all the front pages the next morning, and provided powerful ammunition for other aspirants at the convention, and for the opposition in the presidential campaign.

Arvey was impressed by the Governor's sincerity and agreed not to nominate him, but added the proviso that, if Stevenson should be nominated despite all efforts to the contrary, Arvey would consider himself "relieved from any promise" not to work for his candidacy.

The Draft Stevenson Committee immediately released their own strong rebuttal to the Governor's action, stating their belief that, in spite of what he had said to the Illinois delegation, he "would not reject a genuine desire on the part of the nation to ask him to continue such service at a higher level." The following day, Paul Ringler had this to say in the *Milwaukee Journal:*

> One of the paradoxical things in this picture is that the Committee's major job since it moved into the Hilton last week has been to contradict the man who is its candidate, but isn't.
>
> Governor Stevenson will say: "I want no part of this business" and the Committee will rush out a statement that says in effect: "Pay no attention to this man."

That committee called a meeting for 11:00 P.M., inviting leaders from the states most organized for Stevenson: Pennsylvania, New Jersey, Indiana, and Kansas. These men were considered best equipped to head the draft on the convention floor. The purpose of the meeting was to pick out a floor leader and to select the delegate who would put Stevenson's name in nomination.

As governor of the host state, Stevenson was due to deliver the speech of welcome to the convention the next day. The committee had already obtained a copy of it, courtesy of the pressroom, which had received advance releases. Francis J. Myers, a dark, serious, heavy-set man and former senator from

Pennsylvania, read it aloud, and it was enthusiastically received.

The committee and the representatives of the four delegations agreed almost exactly in their estimates of the number of votes each of their states would give to Stevenson on the first ballot. The total was 178.5 votes. Former Senator Myers of Pennsylvania, a man respected by Democratic leaders of both the North and the South, agreed to be floor leader. And Governor Schricker was asked to place Stevenson's name in nomination.

Schricker's view that Governor Stevenson should be first asked if he would accept the nomination was overridden. But Schricker said he must consult with his delegation and would let the group know the following day. The meeting adjourned, having decided to meet at four the next afternoon, and the Draft Committee was left with the responsibility of inviting leaders of other delegations to be present. On the eve of the opening of the convention, the sentiment for drafting Stevenson had gained so much impetus that Doris Fleeson reported the next day in her *Washington Star* column that, "It now looks as though Governor Adlai Stevenson will be dragged protesting to the presidential altar by the Democratic party."

On July 21, the convention opened. By this time the well-publicized tug of war between the reluctant Governor and the Draft Committee had intrigued the delegates. Everyone—whether for him or not—was eager to see and meet this extraordinary politician who did not want to be president of the United States. As the delegates chatted in the aisles and searched for their seats, there were the usual shouts of greeting among old friends, but the single topic of conversation was Stevenson.

The Governor's appearance on the rostrum ended the suspense. Unexpectedly, it touched off an enthusiastic six-minute ovation from the floor and galleries alike, as surprising to the delegates as it must have been to the Governor.

In the next fifteen minutes, he managed inadvertently to give away all of his hard-won gains (perhaps one should more properly say "hard-won losses"). His short welcoming address was sober, exhilarating, poetic, and funny. And it stirred the convention as no delegate could remember it ever having been stirred before.

> Here, on the prairies of Illinois and the Middle West, we can see a long way in all directions. We look to East, to West, to North, to South. Our commerce, our ideas, come and go in all directions. Here there are no barriers, no defenses, to ideas and aspirations. We want none, we want no shackles on the mind or the spirit, no rigid patterns of thought, no iron conformity. We want only the faith and conviction that triumph in free and fair contest.

Referring to the Republican National Convention which had held its sessions in the same stockyard amphitheatre two weeks earlier, the Governor said:

> For almost a week pompous phrases marched over this landscape in search of an idea, and the only idea they found was that the two great decades of progress in peace, victory in war, and bold leadership in this anxious hour were the misbegotten spawn of socialism, bungling, corruption, mismanagement, waste and worse. They captured, tied and dragged that ragged idea in here and furiously beat it to death. . . . But we Democrats were not the only victims here. First they slaughtered each other, and then they went after us. And the same vocabulary was good for both exercises, which was a great convenience. Perhaps the proximity of the Stockyards accounts for the carnage.

The delegates seemed to recognize at once that this was no ordinary politician—no ordinary man. He appealed to the best in everyone there.

> This is not the time for superficial solutions and endless elocution, for frantic boast and foolish word. For words are not deeds and there are no cheap and painless solutions to war, hunger, ignorance, fear and the new imperialism of Soviet Russia. Intemperate criticism is not a

policy for the nation; denunciation is not a program for our salvation. Words calculated to catch everyone may catch no one. And I hope we can profit from Republican mistakes not just for our partisan benefit, but for the benefit of all of us, Republicans and Democrats alike.

And when he ended with, "Thus can the people's party reassure the people and vindicate and strengthen the forces of democracy throughout the world," the delegates responded with another spontaneous demonstration and tumultuous applause which only ended when he finally left the rostrum. As Reston summed it up in the *New York Times*, "The 'reluctant candidate' who has been trying to talk himself out of the Democratic Presidential nomination for the last five months, talked himself right into the leading candidate's role this morning with a fifteen-minute address that impressed the Convention from left to right. . . ."

The ecstatic Draft Stevenson Committee, their candidate having unintentionally cooperated with their plans, and the mechanics of the draft safely in the hands of competent professionals, now prepared to retire from center stage into the wings. One of the virtues of amateurs is that, for the most part, they are not power hungry; they generally work to advance a cherished cause or candidate rather than themselves. This was particularly true of the Draft Stevenson Committee. Their headquarters were now more than ever a magnet for delegates (many of whom had never visited before) and the press. There was still much for the committee to do.

The 4:00 P.M. meeting was held in the office of Illinois Congressman Sidney Yates because of the bedlam at committee headquarters. When Johnson once again asked Schricker if he would nominate Stevenson, the Indiana Governor replied decisively, "Yes, I will."

Myers and Finnegan were insistent that all those groups present should in the future work from the Draft Stevenson Committee's Hilton headquarters, and that the Draft Committee should continue to interview delegates and carry on their vote projection project through the final ballot. Myers, as floor leader, would undertake contacts with party and delegation leaders. It was decided to continue the committee's established policy of not sponsoring the customary ear-splitting parades and demonstrations through the hotel corridors, and 1500 "America Needs Stevenson" placards were to be ordered. Dignity would continue to be the theme of their drive for their noncandidate. When the Draft Committee suggested that Myers should now chair the meetings of the group, he refused. The committee which, he said, had "done an amazing piece of work with the press and the delegates" was to remain "an important part" of the picture.

In a press release following this meeting, Myers announced that

> a group of delegates representing twenty-five states asked us [at the Pennsylvania delegation meeting the night before] to assist in the Draft Stevenson movement. This magnificent coordination is the result of the tireless and at one time lonesome persistence of the National Committee Stevenson for President. . . .

By Tuesday, the twenty-second, the Stevenson bandwagon's momentum already seemed all but unstoppable. Raymond P. Brandt reported in the *St. Louis Post-Dispatch*:

> By a miracle greater than that which enabled Wendell Willkie to snatch the 1940 Republican standard from Governor Thomas E. Dewey and Senator Robert A. Taft, the 52-year-old Governor has been the beneficiary of a situation in which the draft notice is catching up with him while he is running away from it. . . . Unsolicited, the nomination appears to be his for the taking. It will be another miracle if it is not formally presented to him by the Convention.

Headlines from coast to coast reflected the same view, and these news stories were immediately mimeographed by the committee and distributed to the delegates.

Abruptly the brilliant convention spotlight shifted onto the Draft Stevenson headquarters, quite unprepared for the crowds of delegates that began appearing and the multitudinous demands now being made upon them. That same day, they added six more rooms to their headquarters, already expanded from three to eight rooms only three days before, borrowed or rented furniture, installed additional telephones, and hired a contingent of uniformed Andy Frain ushers.

Thanks to the assistance of R. Sargent Shriver, Jr., the manager of Chicago's Merchandise Mart, who later married Eunice Kennedy, an around-the-clock squad of city detectives was stationed in the fifteenth-floor elevator lobby to help the ushers preserve order in the milling crowd. And, at long last, contributions started pouring in. From February until the end of the convention, the committee had spent less than twenty thousand dollars, an interesting figure to compare with the astronomical sums spent by the committees of other candidates then —and since.

The morning of the twenty-second, the Pennsylvania delegation's Stevenson leaders moved into the committee's headquarters from which they worked when they weren't operating at the convention. One of Myers's first acts was to send telegrams to all national committeemen and state chairman asking them to support the Stevenson draft. Among those who joined the committee was a young Massachusetts congressman then campaigning for the U. S. Senate, John F. Kennedy, whose assignment was to organize senatorial and congressional candidates on behalf of the Stevenson draft—a project in which Michael De Salle, campaigning against Senator Bricker of Ohio, joined. Both of these men had very tough contests and needed the strongest name at the head of the national ticket. Like so many others, they were convinced that that name was Stevenson.

Before the convention opened, the Draft Committee had foresightedly rented a room in the Stock Yards Inn, next to the amphitheatre where the convention was to be held, and had shrewdly installed a direct telephone line to the convention floor. Now volunteers were stationed in this room to man the telephones during the sessions and pass messages back and forth between the floor leaders and headquarters. When the volume of these messages became too great for the direct line to handle, the telephone company and other neighboring offices provided the use of their telephones. Volunteers were constantly stationed at both ends of these lines to relay messages to the floor.

The committee's operations on the convention floor were seriously handicapped at the start. Because of their unorthodox operation, the Democratic National Committee refused to recognize the Draft Stevenson Committee, so they were issued no floor badges or passes. But those were the days before electronic entrance gates and personal photographs on badges and passes. It was relatively easy to borrow credentials from friendly delegates. The Pennsylvania delegation solved the committee's problem by lending them the badges of one of their alternate delegates and a sergeant at arms. Sharing these among them allowed working members of the committee to get onto the floor with no trouble.

Well in advance of the opening of the convention, the committee had assigned an experienced volunteer to the delegation of every state and territory. The rapport that these committee representatives developed with the delegations was often very personal. Although the Mississippi delegation never cast a vote for Stevenson, the woman assigned to them was gallantly taken out to dinner, made an honorary member of the delegation, and was even invited to attend their caucuses.

The Draft Stevenson Committee's success in bringing together and operating with the professionals produced odd reactions. The original charge that the committee was "a bunch of amateurs" had given way to the accusation that they had become "professionals." Other rumors were that the committee had "bowed out," or that the real pros had "moved in."

After Stevenson had told the President in March that he was not and would not be a candidate for the Democratic presidential nomination, President Truman had thrown his support to the seventy-four-year-old vice president, Alben Barkley. On the evening of July 21, Barkley withdrew as a candidate following labor's announcement that they would not support him.

This precipitated a stampede to Stevenson's bandwagon. Governor Elbert Carvel of Delaware climbed aboard, bringing most of his delegation with him, and offered to make a seconding speech for Stevenson. James A. Farley came on saying, in essence, that Stevenson was evidently the delegates' choice. A California mayor dropped into the committee's headquarters to say that their whole delegation was bound to vote for Kefauver under the unit rule. But, as soon as they could be released, "we want to get on your bandwagon." Doris Fleeson, a sensitive prophet, said of Stevenson in her syndicated column on the twenty-third, "It appears that he will be the object of a genuine draft on a very early ballot. He has made no commitments to any person, state or voting bloc. . . . He is under no obligation to the incumbent President of his own party. . . ." That day, James Reston described the Governor as "just a leaf on a rising stream."

By this eventful Tuesday, the Illinois delegation was growing very unhappy in its posture of involuntary abstinence. Arvey was determined not to break his promise to the Governor, but pressures both from within and without Illinois's powerful delegation were putting him in an increasingly difficult position. Neither he nor the other Illinois delegates relished the idea of being "left at the post when the Governor Stevenson Presidential race gets off to a flying start," as the *Chicago Herald-American* commented. Members of the delegation complained to Arvey that they would "look silly" if they did not give Illinois's votes to their governor on the first ballot. Presumably, the fact that the draft had been spearheaded by a group of volunteer Illinoisians, who had frequently fought the Chicago politicians on local issues, was an added goal.

Arvey went so far as to telephone Stevenson on the twenty-third, telling him that his nomination now appeared almost inevitable. In answer to Arvey's urgent query if he would accept if nominated, the Governor adamantly stuck to his position that he was a candidate for governor of Illinois and for nothing else. Nonetheless, the next day, when the Illinois delegation caucused, forty-six votes were pledged for Stevenson, three for Kefauver, and eleven were uncommitted but were thought to be for Stevenson. The chairman of the delegation later remarked, "We are not going to nominate or second anybody. We're respecting Governor Stevenson's wishes in that regard."

That same day, it became known that the votes of Indiana, New Jersey, and Missouri would, in each case, be overwhelmingly for Stevenson. Now that President Truman's candidate, Barkley, had withdrawn, Missouri could act on its own. Reliable press reports indicated that Connecticut, which was committed to a favorite son on the first ballot, would shift to Stevenson on the second, and that Maryland and a number of Rocky Mountain states would swing over if a genuine bandwagon seemed to be in the making. The committee also had word that the Stevenson sentiment in the New York delegation was so strong that Harriman was having a hard time holding the delegation's allegiance.

Two press comments summed up the responsible view of what was taking place at the Democratic convention. On the twenty-second, Roscoe Drummond had reported in the *Christian Science Monitor:*

This Convention is jelling so speedily, the prospect is that President Truman will have no opportunity to determine the presidential nominee—even if he could. . . . They say that Mr. Truman, who can recognize a trend as well as the next politician, is ready to give his favor to Governor Stevenson. The view here is that if he does not do so shortly, he will be waving at a bandwagon which has passed by.

And on the twenty-third, the Associated Press's Louis Brom-field said, "If Governor Stevenson wins the nomination, which now seems likely and, indeed, inevitable, he will have won it on his own."

The work of Thursday, July 24, started for the Draft Steven-son chairman, Walter Johnson, and a number of others at about 1:00 A.M. Johnson was awakened with the disturbing news that a serious controversy had developed about who was to have the privilege of putting Stevenson's name in nomination that day. Although both the pros and the amateurs on the committee had agreed, together with Schricker, that the Indiana Governor would be the nominator, Governor Carvel of Delaware, al-legedly backed by Colonel Arvey, had decided that he wanted the role. Convinced that Schricker was the ideal man for the assignment, not only as governor of an adjacent state but be-cause of his standing with Republicans and Independents, as well as with his fellow Democrats, the committee decided this must not be allowed to happen. Negotiations, accompanied by pressures and counter-pressures, went on for hours. It was finally agreed that Delaware, whose name would be called be-fore Indiana, owing to the current system of alphabetical roll calls, would yield to Indiana and Schricker would make the nominating speech, with Carvel seconding. Equal time would be given to each speaker, which left no time for any other seconders. Finnegan's terse comment about the whole episode was, "It's obvious what has happened. Everybody is on the bandwagon."

The names placed in nomination before Stevenson's were those of Senator Richard B. Russell, Senator Estes Kefauver, Senator Robert S. Kerr, Senator J. W. Fulbright, and Averell Harriman.

During this lengthy process, the delegates started moving around, visiting other delegations, and conferring earnestly with individual delegates. As many of the Draft Stevenson Committee members as could get on the floor had been assigned individual delegations to watch or, as diplomatically as possible, to try to firm up a wavering or undecided vote. They were moving about, too, trying to overhear bits of conversation or note who was talking to whom, and attempting to piece together their information and assess what it augured for their man. By the time "Delaware" was finally called and Carvel yielded to Governor Schricker of Indiana, the tense expectancy on the convention hall had grown almost to the breaking point.

The Indiana Governor spoke for twelve and a half minutes. He ended by saying,

> In Governor Stevenson's own words, "the world looks to America for dignity, sanity, and confident leadership." His own humility, dignity, and capacity for confident leadership have, to a unique degree, excited the imagination, caught the fancy, and fired the hopes of the American people.
>
> Ninety-two years ago, the nation called from the prairies of Illinois the greatest of Illinois citizens, Abraham Lincoln. Lincoln too was reluctant. But there are times when a man is not permitted to say no.
>
> I place before you the man we cannot permit to say no, Adlai E. Stevenson of Illinois.

As Schricker finished, pandemonium broke out. The *New York Times* reported, "It was then that the Convention really went wild," and the *Baltimore Sun* described the massive demonstration as "easily the biggest, noisiest, longest and most spontaneous outburst of this long day of nominating speeches." Governor Carvel's seconding speech was drowned out in the ecstatic uproar.

Stevenson, who had not returned to the convention hall since he had made his welcoming address, responded by issuing the low-key statement, "I had hoped they would not nominate me, but I am deeply affected by this expression of confidence and goodwill." His eager supporters noted jubilantly that this was a far cry from General Sherman's immortal phrase, "If nominated I shall refuse to run."

It was only at this point that, following a caucus of the Missouri delegation, President Truman's alternate announced that he had just received the President's instructions to cast his vote for Stevenson. And William S. White, in the *New York Times*, commented that "As the Convention struggled noisily forward through the fatigue of many hours the drive to select Mr. Stevenson, notwithstanding his reluctance, had become the first genuine draft movement since the Republican party demanded James A. Garfield in 1880."

The speeding Stevenson bandwagon ran into two roadblocks on Thursday evening and Friday morning. The first was the bitter fight that developed over the seating of delegations which would not sign the so-called loyalty oath, a resolution aimed chiefly at the southern states which in 1948 had run their own "Dixiecrat" candidates under the Democratic banner. When Minnesota challenged the seating of Virginia, South Carolina, and Louisiana, all of which had refused to sign, the battle was on. As *Life* commented, "In no time at all the Democrats were fighting just like the 1952 Republicans as America sat in front of its T.V. sets." The final outcome, at 2:00 A.M. Friday morning, after nearly fourteen hours of wrangling, was the seating of all three contested delegations.

Meanwhile, attention had been completely diverted from the Stevenson draft—indeed from any consideration of candidates —and the Kefauver-Harriman forces took immediate advantage of this to call a stop-Stevenson meeting under the guise of a widely publicized "liberal-labor caucus."

Though attempts were made by conveners of the caucus to prevent members of the Draft Stevenson Committee from attending, the committee ignored these warnings and three of their representatives were present as observers. At the end, the caucus had not been able to agree on a stop-Stevenson candidate. As a result of the confusion engendered by this caucus, members of the old guard, headed by Senator Thomas C. Hennings of Missouri, tried to revive Barkley's candidacy with a view to gaining control of the party machinery via the National Committee. This, too, proved to be an abortive effort to derail the bandwagon.

After all of the ferment leading up to the actual voting, the balloting proceeded in a very orderly manner, thanks to the convention chairman, Sam Rayburn, who was evidently determined to conduct it with fairness and dignity.

An hour before the roll was called, the Draft Stevenson Committee which, on Saturday, had estimated that Stevenson would receive a minimum of seventy-five votes on the first ballot, and had revised it drastically on Sunday to 178.5, was now predicting that he would receive 272. When the first ballot tally was announced to the convention as 273 for Stevenson, Finnegan remarked to Hubert Will, a member of the committee, "That's the trouble with dealing with you amateurs—you're not accurate!"

Out of the 615.5 votes needed for the nomination, Kefauver led Stevenson on the first ballot with 340. Immediately behind Stevenson was Russell with 268. The others were far behind; Harriman had 123.5, Kerr had 65, Barkley had 48.5, Dever 37.5, Humphrey 26, and Fulbright 22. Incidentally, Stevenson's alternate on the Illinois delegation voted, as instructed by Stevenson, for Harriman.

On the second ballot, Stevenson, Kefauver, Russell, and Barkley all increased their votes, while the others slid. Kefauver was still in the lead with 362.5, while Stevenson remained in second place with 324.5.

The third roll call was the crucial one, as many delegations which had been committed to other candidates for the first two ballots were now free to vote their convictions. The great majority of these had indicated to the committee that their choice would be Stevenson. Following the second ballot, there was an agonizing dinner recess, during which time the New York delegation caucused.

But dinner was the last thing on anyone's mind. Representatives of every candidate started scurrying around, putting heavy last-minute pressure on the delegates. The Draft Stevenson people, whose watchful eyes seemed to be everywhere, moved in immediately, bolstering delegates they considered doubtful with their own now-powerful arguments: "No convention has ever been offered such an opportunity. Stevenson is clearly the people's choice. We know now that he is the choice of the majority of the delegates. He is the finest type of American, and the only candidate who can beat Eisenhower. Don't fail our country and our party at this critical time by offering them anything less than the best."

Immediately after the convention reconvened, New York's Democratic state chairman read a statement from Harriman, who was withdrawing in favor of Stevenson and urged his followers to throw their support to him. Governor Dever of Massachusetts followed suit, assuring the convention that Stevenson would accept. Then, state after state swung into the Stevenson column and, when Utah's switch of its twelve votes put him over the top and the motion to make the nomination unanimous was enthusiastically adopted, the reluctant Governor, the overwhelming choice of rank-and-file Democrats, became the official Democratic nominee for president. Clearly this was one of those rare instances in our history when a cherished American ideal had been realized. The office had sought—and *found* —the man.

Governor Stevenson, meanwhile, had spent the evening with his family and a few close friends at William McCormick Blair, Sr.'s house, alternately watching the proceedings on television and withdrawing to his own room, to be alone, meditate, and no doubt pray, to gain strength for the ordeal which, with every passing minute, he knew now, was inexorably approaching. As the balloting proceeded, and it became evident that there was no way that a Stevenson landslide could be stopped, friends urged him to start for the amphitheatre so that there would not be such a long wait between his nomination and his appearance to accept it. It was now past midnight and they were worried that many of the weary delegates and spectators might go home. But Stevenson was adamant. He would not set out for the convention until their decision became final.

He was watching television when it happened. His nomination was made unanimous. Immediately he was surrounded— everyone congratulating him, shaking his hand, hugging, and kissing him. Even members of the Stevenson for Governor Committee, who had stood by him in his long fight to avoid this moment, appeared jubilant. Only the Governor looked pale and shaken. But he was composed and had obviously gained some inner strength from those periods of meditation during the long evening.

Then, accompanied by a motorcade of his family, friends, co-workers, reporters, television and newsreel people, and a cordon of police and secret service men, the candidate set forth shortly after midnight for the ride to the amphitheatre.

The shortest route led through dimly-lighted residential streets, from the affluent near-north side to modest streets, lined on both sides with small houses set cheek by jowl. They were solidly packed with cheering families, many in pajamas or bathrobes, waving sheets and pillow cases for flags.

To the exhausted delegates and visitors it seemed far more than the hour that it took to get the Governor from Chicago's near-north side onto the floor of the convention. But no one regretted the seemingly interminable wait when, at the side of the President, who had flown to Chicago for the finale, Stevenson walked to the platform to deliver his historic acceptance speech:

> . . . I hope and pray that we Democrats, win or lose, can campaign not as a crusade to exterminate the opposing party. . . . Even more important than winning the election is governing the nation. . . . When the tumult and shouting die, when the bands are gone and the lights are dimmed, there is the stark reality of responsibility. . . . Let's

face it. Let's talk sense to the American people. Let's tell them the truth, that there are no gains without pains, that we are now on the eve of great decisions, not easy decisions, like resistance when you're attacked, but a long, patient, costly struggle which alone can assure triumph over the great enemies of men—war, poverty and tyranny —and the assaults upon human dignity which are the most grievous consequences of each.

As he closed, there was a moment of almost reverent silence, similar to the moving stillness that paid tribute to Abraham Lincoln's Gettysburg Address, and then the whole convention erupted—inside, the delegates, the galleries, the guards; outside, where the proceedings had been broadcast to waiting thousands, the people! With cheers and tears, spontaneous marches and riotous demonstrations, their pent-up tensions and emotions released at last, they joined ranks behind the man whose eloquent words made them proud that, win or lose, they knew they had chosen greatness.

The exhausted Governor, his motorcade followed by hundreds of horn-blowing adherents, drove back to the Blairs' house through street celebrations that seemed to be gathering momentum as their radios blared out the details of Stevenson's victory.

The next morning, following a brief sleep, Bill Blair delivered the following note to the Democratic nominee.

Adlai,

I am keen to have a chat with you before I leave town. I will be taking a brief rest and then want to go to work for you in any way I can be of help.

It was a great speech last night.

Averell

It is not the purpose of this book to try to analyze all of the facets of this campaign or others included here, but to tell the story of the amateurs who participated in them and to try to assess their special contributions.

The American Political Science Association's study in its report on the 1952 Democratic convention evaluates the work of the committee as follows:

> Perhaps it can be concluded from all this that the Stevenson nomination would have been arranged even if the Draft Stevenson Committee had not taken it upon itself to make the necessary arrangements. At the same time, however, the question remains as to whether a draft arranged by the convention management would not have taken on a coloration that might have prevented the reluctant candidate from accepting. . . . At any rate, it seems fair to conclude that the activities of the Draft Stevenson Committee did much to make the Stevenson nomination a genuine draft, however much stage management was also being undertaken by other kingmakers.

Without underestimating the fact that it is the delegates who ultimately cast the votes that choose the nominee, all the evidence makes it impossible to escape the conclusion that, if the National Committee Stevenson for President had not existed, Adlai Stevenson would not have been the nominee in 1952.

At a minimum, from February until the end of the convention, this small but dedicated group kept alive and fanned the spark of hope that Stevenson was draftable, in spite of his adamant position and the resulting pessimism of almost all of the professionals.

At the convention, they provided an information center and meeting place for those delegates and members of the press curious about the Illinois Governor and his record. They brought interested delegates together and they collected and reproduced news stories from around the country and circulated them to the delegates and national press. Perhaps their greatest contribution at the convention was uncovering the enormous amount of latent pro-Stevenson feeling that existed among the delegates, and helping to create channels through which it could express itself.

Finally, they were instrumental in bringing together the leaders of the Pennsylvania, New Jersey, Indiana, and Kansas delegations, which became the nucleus of professionals that headed up the convention draft, and they helped to organize the machinery through which the will of the convention could be realized. The important, probably the crucial, role that the National Committee Stevenson for President played in nominating Stevenson is not a matter of debate. It is a matter of record.

Cornell Capa. Magnum Photos

A typical whistle-stop of Adlai Stevenson's campaign train in 1952, aboard which the author made arrangements for local volunteers to meet the candidate.

VII

"Madly for Adlai"

Adlai Stevenson has been called "more than anyone . . . the patron saint of the amateur politicians." One biographer after another has given him credit for revitalizing the tired old Democratic party by infusing it with new ideas, new life and new people. These people were a fresh breed, too; enthusiastic, idealistic, many of them young veterans of World War II who had returned, determined to do what they could to preserve the ideals for which they had given so much. As president, they wanted a man who shared these ideals and, when Adlai Stevenson had finished his acceptance speech at the Democratic National Convention in 1952, hundreds of thousands of them knew instantly that they had found him.

In his eulogy to Eleanor Roosevelt many years later, Adlai Stevenson asked the rhetorical question, "Who can name what she was?" By what combination of qualities and behavior had a shy, awkward, insecure young girl matured into "the first lady of the world"?

Who can name what Adlai Stevenson was? What were the qualities inbred in this small-town American boy that so deeply moved the convention and the television public as they watched and listened to him accept his party's nomination? And why was it that, in twice losing the presidency, he became the beloved idol of countless millions both at home and throughout the world? It has been said that "Adlai Stevenson . . . brought more honor to the Presidency in seeking the office than any who have since held it."

Beloved is a word not often used to describe a public figure, but it has been applied time and again to Governor Stevenson. No doubt this was because of his extraordinary ability to communicate.

His genuine interest in people created instant bonds and lasting loyalties. It was the usual experience of anyone ending a one-to-one conversation with Stevenson to realize that he had been asked more questions than he had asked, that he had talked more about himself than Governor Stevenson had about himself, that he had expressed more dogmatic views than the Governor, and that, throughout, he had had the concentrated attention of a keen listener.

A group chatting around a fire or a spellbound political audience would break up feeling like better, prouder people because Adlai Stevenson had talked to them as equals. He had spoken to the best in each one—to their intelligence, their idealism, their decency, their integrity, their compassion, their vision of America. And he made them laugh again and again.

Barbara Ward has described the Governor as having a quality which the Africans call "nommo"—the Bantu word for the "gift of making life larger and more vivid for everyone else." Somehow he seemed to communicate to those around him his zest for life and his care for life in all of its grandest and humblest aspects.

Physically, Adlai Stevenson's medium height, his stocky—later somewhat rotund—figure, his crooked nose (broken, it was said, in a political fist fight as a small boy in Republican McLean County), his bald head—even his friendly blue eyes and his quick warm smile—did not add up to any standard of great good looks. Yet few Adonises have inspired the affectionate popularity that was his both at home and abroad. The answer to what Adlai Stevenson was lies in what he made of those whose lives he touched.

Governor Stevenson had been an amateur, himself, when he ran for governor of Illinois in 1948. This was the first public office he had ever run for and the only one he ever won. Because, at that time, very few politically-oriented citizens gave him even an outside chance of winning, his Stevenson for Governor Committee had been spearheaded almost entirely by his close friends and most starry-eyed admirers—all the rankest of amateurs.

In April 1952, when Stevenson was renominated in the Illinois primary to run for a second term, he asked the leaders of his 1948 Stevenson for Governor Committee to reactivate it and start immediately organizing for his reelection. But national speculation about him as a presidential candidate had turned any attempt to set up a gubernatorial committee into an exercise in futility. The reenlistment or recruitment of volunteers for this purpose proved to be virtually impossible that spring. In spite of his determined and well-publicized statement of April 16, "I could not accept the nomination for any other office [than that of governor] this summer," and the prevailing view in the press that he had finally succeeded in closing the door to his nomination, his eager volunteers of four years earlier were either adopting a let's-wait-and-see attitude or enthusiastically joining the presidential Draft Stevenson group.

The leaders of the Stevenson for Governor Committee (disrespectfully referred to by the Stevenson for President people as "The Wedding Party" because of their close personal ties to the Governor) were unwilling to disregard Stevenson's urgent request that they work only for his reelection as governor and shun all contact with "the Conrad Hilton group," as the Stevenson for Governor Committee, in turn, called the Draft Stevenson people because they had established their early headquarters at that hotel.

There was great dismay when an occasional member "defected" to the latter organization. Furthermore, the gubernatorial committee was split on the issue of the presidency versus the governorship. Aside from fruitless discussions about how to reactivate local groups and raise funds before the end of the Democratic convention, the meetings were usually taken up with spirited arguments between members who felt that Stevenson would bring such distinction and talents to the presidency that he owed it to his party and his country to make himself available and those who pointed to his personal desires, to his "unfinished work in Illinois" so brilliantly under way, to four more years of "seasoning" in government, and to the fact that, after twenty years of Democrats in office and the so-called "mess in Washington," this was not a propitious year for anyone who headed the Democratic ticket. Many members of the Stevenson for Governor Committee were then, and some still are, bitter because they were convinced that the Draft Stevenson people were, against the Governor's personal wishes and best judgment, "leading a man down a dead end."

Another running argument concerned the "moral right" of any committee or group of individuals to set themselves up as arbiters of a man's destiny in direct opposition to his wishes. Those who argued against this right reinforced their position by pointing out that it was an even more dubious question under existing circumstances. It was becoming increasingly evident that there was strong sentiment in the liberal wing of the Republican party to nominate a popular war hero, General Eisenhower. With such a leader riding the crest of the time-for-a-change sentiment that was already sweeping the country, what chance would *any* Democrat have? Illinois needed Stevenson. He would have a better opportunity in 1956—or, if he weren't nominated or failed then, there was still 1960. Why risk him in a year when a Democrat had such severe odds against him? The argument continues to this day among Stevensonians. Those who worked for Stevenson's presidential nomination in 1952 say to those who wanted him saved until 1956, "What makes you think he would have been nominated in 1956 if he had not run in 1952? The defeated nominee, as titular head of the party, is almost always given the nomination the next time around. The 1952 nominee would have had it sewed up in 1956." The Stevenson for '56 people did some research and discovered that in the course of one hundred years, from 1848 through 1948, only three defeated candidates had been renominated by their party: Grover Cleveland twice, in 1888 and 1892; William Jennings Bryan twice, in 1900 and 1908; and Thomas E. Dewey once, in 1948.

Each of these men had had unusual staying power. Cleveland's case was unique. He had first won in 1884. In 1888, he ran as the incumbent president, but lost. In 1892, the Democrats gave their popular former president another chance, and he won.

Dewey was a thoroughgoing party man who wanted the presidency badly, had worked long and skillfully to get the nomination, and had the support and confidence of the then-dominant elements in the Republican party. And Bryan was the outstanding orator of his era.

The argument that a party will not turn again to a man who has once shown reluctance to seek the presidency when certain party leaders wanted him was countered by citing Eisenhower's experience. In 1948, his supporters did not force him into the position of having to make General Sherman's irrevocable statement or having to accept a nomination he did not want when neither he nor the country was ready. In 1952, as became evident, the timing for Eisenhower could not have been better.

But without benefit of hindsight, the Stevenson for Governor people in 1952 were convinced that there was far less risk in waiting for the presidential nomination in 1956. Even assuming a defeat that year, they could count on Stevenson's unique gifts and qualifications to secure the nomination in 1960, when his opponent would be an ordinary mortal, not a living legend. Needless to say, the Republicans on Stevenson's nonpartisan gubernatorial committee were not thinking in those particular terms, but the division over whether or not his wishes should be respected in 1952 was, surprisingly enough, rarely along partisan lines. These meetings and the arguments came to an end on July 25, when the Democratic convention chose Illinois's Governor as their candidate for the presidency.

In 1952, both candidates would campaign in a very different world than the one in which Willkie had waged his fight against Roosevelt at the height of World War II. By the spring of 1950, all of mainland China had been taken over by the Chinese Communists. Mao Tse-tung's government was in control, and Chiang Kai-shek had fled to Taiwan, where he reestablished the old government, which the United States continued to recognize instead of Mao's.

Russia, no longer our wartime ally, had become our peacetime competitor. She had launched her fifth five-year plan in 1951, and economic planning had begun in her satellites.

President Roosevelt had died in April 1945, and his vice president, Harry Truman, had automatically succeeded him. In 1947, under Truman, the Marshall Plan, designed to help in the recovery of devastated Europe, was launched. By 1952, its objectives—to promote international trade, to shore up the various European currencies, and to help expand Europe's production—were all being realized at an amazing rate.

Economic planning by individual governments was now being undertaken almost routinely. The degree of government control and dictation varied—from the Soviet countries' government ownership of the means of production, to France's Monnet Plan, in which the government was authorized to plan but have no direct control over private firms. The United States, most of Western Europe and Japan—the market economies— used monetary and fiscal policies to promote economic development. But the United States was one of the few, along with France, that had not taken some steps—if only small ones—to nationalize some of their industries.

The less developed parts of the world were starting to be heard from. Their agricultural production, largely still on a subsistence level, was not keeping up with their population increases. Some were experimenting with industrial development, most were trying to export some of their raw materials or scarce agricultural products. They were no longer in a mood to tolerate famine and starvation, to which they had been so long resigned. And independence movements were spreading throughout Asia and Africa.

By 1952, the United States had become the acknowledged leader of the free world, and its own economy was in good shape and steadily on the up-turn. And the world was at peace.

One would have thought, perhaps, that at such a moment in their history, the American people might not have feared another Democratic administration, might even have preferred it to a return to the party of Hoover. And perhaps they would have if the Citizens for Eisenhower and the liberal Republicans at the convention had not prevailed over the Taft forces and nominated an admired and respected national hero, Dwight Eisenhower.

A day or two after the Democratic convention had closed, the chairman of the now disbanded Stevenson for Governor Committee, Hermon Dunlap ("Dutch") Smith and I, cochairman of its women's division, were invited by Governor Stevenson to come to the executive mansion in Springfield to discuss establishing national headquarters and national leadership for the presidential volunteer groups that were already springing up and organizing from coast to coast. We were both surprised when he asked us if we would assume the leadership. We had expected that this would be the role of those who had headed the preconvention Draft Stevenson Committee. As a result of this committee's contacts in the field and their work at the convention, they now had considerable national experience and connections, while the political experience of the Stevenson for Governor Committee had obviously been confined to Illinois.

As Stevenson was a man of strong loyalties, it is probable that he decided as he did because Dutch and I had been among those who early had encouraged him to run for governor, who had headed up the volunteer work in his successful gubernatorial campaign, when he was thought to have no chance and no experienced people were "available," and because we had scrupulously respected his wishes in recent months.

It must have been difficult for the Stevenson for President group to understand and accept this decision. But a measure of the decency and selflessness of these self-appointed crusaders was that, if they were disappointed, they kept it to themselves. As soon as the new national organization was established, they turned over all of their files to us and cooperated in every way to help elect their candidate president. Many members of the "Conrad Hilton group" were among the first to volunteer.

Before the Springfield meeting with the Governor and his staff broke up for the night, the question of a name for the new organization was tossed around. "Clubs" had been used by Willkie and "Citizens" by Eisenhower. Everyone wanted something new. It was decided that all would put their minds to the problem overnight and convene for breakfast with recommendations. The Governor was the first person to be asked for his suggestions the next morning, and he tentatively ventured, "What would you think of 'Volunteers for Stevenson'? It has a good ring and says what it is." Everyone agreed enthusiastically, not only because they genuinely liked the name, but because apparently no one else had had a single inspiration during the night.

It was gratifying to the amateurs and typical of Stevenson that he felt their participation in the campaign was important, and from the outset he took great personal interest in their organization. In any table of organization (something which never showed up in any Stevenson campaign), the Volunteers would have appeared in a prominent and relatively independent spot in the free and easy hierarchy.

Stevenson had already demonstrated his interest in talented amateurs by attracting many into state service. Most of his personal aides and appointees in Springfield, who were in good measure responsible for maintaining the quality of his administration, had been political neophytes recruited from law offices, law faculties, or the business community. Now he was showing the same tendency in recruiting the leadership of his campaign.

He chose, as his campaign manager, Wilson Wyatt, a man of quality and personality, a former mayor of Louisville, Kentucky, who had managed several Kentucky campaigns and had served as administrator of housing in Washington. But Wyatt's approach to politics was much closer to that of the Volunteers than that of the standard "pols."

Withstanding strong pressure from President Truman, Stevenson replaced Frank McKinney, Truman's appointee as chairman of the Democratic National Committee, with Stephen A. Mitchell, an able Chicago lawyer who had been chief of the French division of the Lend-Lease Administration and advisor to the State Department on French economic affairs and, as a concerned Illinois citizen, had been one of those in the earlier Draft Stevenson effort to make him governor of Illinois. This was an unlikely background for the tough job of chairman of the Democratic National Committee.

The Governor persuaded his invaluable personal aide and appointment secretary in Springfield, William McC. Blair, Jr., to continue in his role. He also appointed Carl McGowan as his chief consultant and planner. Though fresh from the Northwestern University law faculty four years before, McGowan was now a seasoned veteran of state government. But he had had no experience in national campaigns. It was he who recruited the fabulous group of political neophytes to work on the candidate's speeches.

Headed by Arthur M. Schlesinger, Jr., the young Harvard historian who had already made a name for himself with his Pulitzer Prize-winning book, *The Age of Jackson*, the other amateur members of the "Elks Club" were Willard Wirtz, law professor and an old friend of Carl McGowan's, and later secretary of labor in the Kennedy administration; John Bartlow Martin, an author; and William Reddy, a Kansas City editor. They worked together with three veterans of the White House and State Department: David Bell, Robert Tufts, and Sidney Hyman. Others who had had no previous experience in a political campaign were a young Harvard economist named John Kenneth Galbraith; Jack Fisher of *Harper's* magazine; Eric Hodgins, connected with the Luce publications and author of the best seller, *Mr. Blanding Builds His Dream House;* Bernard DeVoto, an authority on conservation and a historian of the American West; and Herbert Agar, author, journalist, and personal friend of Stevenson. These five turned up on occasion for specific assignments, together with David Cohn, the only pro in that category, who was lent by Senator Fulbright of Arkansas.

These men were literary craftsmen of the highest order, but largely political amateurs. The measure of their dedication was that they continued to devote their time and talents to doing research and composing speech drafts for the Governor, who regularly discarded them, rewrote them, or revised them so thoroughly as to make them his own. At the outset, most of these competent writers were upset by such cavalier treatment of their best efforts, but, as Kenneth Davis notes:

> All of them became convinced . . . that Stevenson was a far better writer of Stevenson speeches than any of them could ever be . . . [and] whatever resentment they may occasionally have felt was submerged in the pride they took in a political candidate who was so fine a master of their own profession.

In 1952, Stephen Mitchell and Wilson Wyatt were not professional politicians, but they were men of the Stevenson stripe, with a broad grasp of politics and human nature. They were quick to size up situations and to act decisively, and they worked at winning over the professionals. Also, because of their own backgrounds, they understood and encouraged the Volunteers for Stevenson. Their total accessibility to its leadership provided a useful bridge between that organization and the regular Democratic party.

In addition to Hermon Smith and me, as national chairman and vice chairman of the Volunteers, George Ball became our executive director, and proved a potent fundraiser, as well as a prime catalyst between the professionals and the Volunteers. He seemed to know everyone. Because of his contacts, he was away from headquarters a good deal, and Richard Babcock, a young Chicago attorney, was appointed deputy executive director and proved most faithful and able.

Roger Stevens, a great and loyal friend of Adlai's, volunteered directly to the Governor to raise money for his campaign, and probably raised more than anyone else. He was always extremely helpful to the Volunteers, especially when we needed money in a hurry. National television broadcasts demanded cash-on-the-barrel-head before a candidate went on the air.

Porter McKeever, executive director of the Chicago Council on Foreign Relations, resigned immediately after Stevenson's nomination and came to work for the Volunteers as national publicity director. Later Porter became president of the United Nations Association of the United States, and subsequently senior assistant to John D. Rockefeller III in his many philanthropies.

Porter's first imaginative and miraculous coup was to get together, in less than two weeks, a collection of Stevenson's speeches, with a foreword by John Steinbeck, printed by a major commercial publisher and available to the public at one dollar a copy. He had the idea one morning. Debs Myers pulled together copies of the speeches (twenty-one of them) that after-noon; they telephoned Steinbeck in New York, who immediately agreed to write the foreword, and did so overnight, and Debs Myers and Ralph Martin wrote a brief biography. The handsome eight-by-eleven, slick-covered paperback, with an excellent color photograph of Stevenson on the front, was being typeset within forty-eight to seventy-two hours from the day the idea first occurred to Porter. Fourteen days later it was in the bookstores.

Everything in Stevenson's campaign had to be thought of in terms of an extremely short time frame. The Eisenhower people had already bought up a tremendous amount of prime television time. But Lou Cowan (Louis D. Cowan, who later became president of CBS) was then producing the popular "Whiz Kid" program and "packaged" many more. He volunteered to schedule the Governor's television and radio time and, under the circumstances, did a magnificent job. Much as he admired him, Stevenson was the despair of Lou, and others, because he was simply oblivious to the strict limitations of television and radio time and often delivered his peroration after he had been cut off the air.

We had a number of field organizers, all of them volunteers. One was Stanley Karson, a young aide to Senator Lehman. Lehman had been national chairman of the Harriman committee, but Stan had been so taken by Stevenson that, when he was nominated, Stan had asked the Senator for a leave of absence to work for the Volunteers. He was originally sent out, as he describes it, "to rescue the North Ohio Stevenson Volunteers from the hostility and apathy of the regular Democratic organization under Ray Miller, the Democratic boss of Cleveland," but he also worked closely with the student groups nationally.

Unlike Rumbough and Willis of the Eisenhower Citizens who had "divided" the country more or less in half between them, the Volunteers divided it into a number of sections and assigned specific field organizers to each one. Among them were Hubert

Will, who had been very active with the preconvention Draft Stevenson Committee and is now senior district judge of the district court of northern Illinois, Ben Heineman, Donald Petrie, and a number of others, who not only were in charge of organizing their "territories," but were always at the ready to catch a plane if we suddenly got an SOS call from any of them.

An invaluable member of our office staff, Florence Medow, had been one of the first to volunteer from the Draft Committee. Her complete familiarity with their (now our) files, her contacts, her devotion to the Stevenson cause, her hard work, long hours, and unruffled good humor made everyone's job easier. And she never asked for anything for herself. To me, Florence represents the ideal of a volunteer.

An incident connected with the launching of the Volunteers for Stevenson was somewhat frustrating to its new leadership. Governor Stevenson was to open his official campaign at a large nationally televised dinner rally in Denver, Colorado, on September 5. Because the Volunteers were sponsoring the television program, it was decided that Dutch Smith and I should accompany the candidate. In order to give us maximum publicity, we were to fly out on the Governor's plane. When we landed in Denver, Stevenson, his son Borden, and Dutch and I were to wait until all the other members of the campaign party had gotten off. Then the new Volunteer leaders were to walk down the ramp with the Governor and his son. The press was briefed in advance on the identity of the newcomers and, as the four descended from the plane, flash bulbs popped, newsreel and television cameras rolled, everyone was interviewed, and the occasion was counted a great success—until the next morning. On the front page of almost every paper in the country appeared the carefully arranged picture with the caption: "Governor Stevenson launches his campaign in Denver accompanied by his handsome son, his sister, Mrs. Ives, and an unidentified man."

There were a number of overriding compensations that evening, however. A Denver Volunteers' headquarters had been opened in August and, as they prepared for what proved to be a highly successful affair, twelve hundred new members were enrolled in the Volunteers in the course of purchasing their dinner tickets. In his opening remarks, the Governor said, "There is deep personal satisfaction for me in the fact that this, my first talk on my first extended campaign trip, is sponsored by the independents who are organizing around the country on my behalf." Later he identified "the distinguishing characteristic of the true independent" as the fact "that he finds deeds more meaningful than words" and, in using the term independent, Stevenson said he included "all those who wear a party label over their hearts but not over their eyes. . . ." At frequent intervals during his nationally broadcast television special, superimposed on the Governor's image was the message, "This broadcast is sponsored and paid for by the National Volunteers for Stevenson." As helping to pay for radio and television time proved to be one of the Volunteers' toughest assignments throughout the campaign, this, at least, was a satisfaction.

Governor Stevenson's Volunteers had a most important asset from the start. They did not have to fight for recognition as General Eisenhower's Citizens originally did. The Volunteers were welcomed by the candidate, his campaign manager, and the chairman of the Democratic National Committee—a far cry from the position of the postconvention Citizens organization. But, once the Citizens had won the backing of their chief, they had a more than compensating advantage. They were already a national organization with branches, chapters, and local groups in every state prepared and eager for the long-sought big push—the campaign for the presidency. The Volunteers were starting from scratch.

The first problem confronting the National Volunteers, once we had established headquarters in Chicago, was how to catch up with, bring under one umbrella, and give leadership and general guidance to Stevenson groups now forming spontaneously almost everywhere. Another was how to mobilize latent Stevenson interest in areas where there was no Volunteer organization, and how to find the best possible leadership in each individual area.

A related problem developed as soon as national headquarters were established. Enthusiastic unknown voices from all over the country began to swamp the switchboard with offers to help, to organize, or to head up Volunteer chapters or branches in their states or localities. Not only was the volume of calls overwhelming, but it was obviously impossible to know whether the man or woman at the other end of the line was an eccentric or a potential leader, a skid-row resident, with nothing better to do, or one of the area's most influential citizens. And, because so many spontaneous local groups had sprung up and organized themselves almost from the moment Stevenson had finished his acceptance speech, we had no way of knowing how many or where they all were or how to contact them. With less than three months in which to operate, it became imperative to find good state leaders as quickly as possible and work with and through them. A centralized operation was patently impossible and impractical, so a loose federation had to be the modus operandi from the outset.

The Volunteer headquarters staff, now augmented by a majority of the members of the old Stevenson for Governor Committee and many of those from the National Committee Stevenson for President, had enough political acumen and experience to recognize the importance of harmonious relationships with the professionals. We also knew that friendly, trustworthy pros could be most helpful in giving advice on the standing and backgrounds of people in their communities. Files from the Draft Stevenson organization—especially those compiled during the convention—turned up a number of such professionals, many of whom indeed proved cooperative in evaluating or recommending good independent leadership. Other sources were friends of the Governor. This was a vast reservoir of information, both Democratic and Republican in many parts of the country.

It was these operations that were assigned to the field organizers and to which they devoted most of their time—often at great personal, business, and professional sacrifice—for the duration of the campaign.

Dick Babcock, the deputy executive director, on whose desk usually landed the urgent telephone calls for help, in a later discussion with me about his role in the campaign, had this to say:

> It was going really from one crisis to another. There was always somebody in Oregon or Minneapolis who was annoying the professionals, or we were told we got the wrong guy, or the guy we thought was right wasn't doing anything, and I can remember having phone calls stacked up an inch deep.

These problems could sometimes be solved over the telephone, but usually they required a visit from one of the troubleshooters in the field.

Babcock also commented that the screening of state and local leaders

> was not always done on the basis of the way you'd do it a second time. I remember Paul Douglas [incumbent Senator from Illinois], when he asked me to handle his volunteer group in 1954, saying to me only half jocularly "It isn't that we want you to tell us what we should do. But, based on your experience in 1952, we want you to tell us the things we *shouldn't* do." In 1952, of course, our big problem was that we really had to improvise.

One other major problem in 1952 was, as it is in all campaigns, money. For the Volunteers this was particularly acute. The ordinary expenses of presidential campaigns had been greatly increased by the advent of television. The Democratic National Committee, recognizing its importance as a campaign technique and aware of the extensive use the other side was making of it, overcommitted themselves for television time and called on the Volunteers for help.

Dutch Smith and I were appalled when Steve Mitchell called us frantically from Washington on September 25 and asked us to take over thirty-eight contracts which they had signed. We were operating on a day to day basis, ourselves, never being sure when or where our next money was coming from. George Ball and Roger Stevens, who were in charge of fundraising, were being beset with requests for money from all sides. The cost of even one national television hook-up, whether it was for a single minute spot (which we didn't use very often) or a half-hour speech by the candidate, was astronomical. "We simply can't do it, Steve. We haven't the money. And we have our own commitments. It's impossible," Smith said firmly.

Mitchell was not satisfied, so Dutch immediately called a meeting attended by himself, me, our deputy executive director, our lawyer, the chairman of the Illinois Volunteers, and one or two others. Dick Babcock, the deputy executive director, jotted the following informal "minutes" in his notebook:

> Brown [the lawyer] reminded that National Committee expects and wants National Volunteers to take over all television-radio commitments previously entered into by the Democratic Committee. Wants us to sign thirty-eight contracts. National Committee said it was up to its limit on three-million-dollar limit and must get rid of some of these contracts. Smith had told Mitchell we had to take care of our primary obligations—our clubs, literature, payrolls, etc.
>
> Tenney [a lawyer and chairman of Illinois Volunteers for Stevenson]: "If we sign these contracts we can't rely upon any guarantee?" All agreed we would not sign contracts regardless of any guarantees or otherwise.

Later in the campaign, Dutch and I did sign a number of contracts at the eleventh hour, whether we had enough money or not, rather than forfeit an opportunity for our eloquent candidate to speak. We counted on getting the money by the time the program went on the air, and somehow we always did. But whenever our lawyer heard that we had signed, he would storm into Dutch's office or mine, or that of whichever officer had put his or her signature on the contract, crying, "Remember *I'm* not responsible. *I* can't keep you out of jail," etc., etc., until he ran out of steam or felt he had adequately chastised the official. A methodical, devoted, and upright friend of Governor Stevenson, he would solemnly walk into my office every evening and cross another day off the calendar, in evident anticipation of the time that his ordeal would be over. John Paulding Brown, who lived in Washington, had appeared on the doorstep of the National Volunteers' headquarters the day they opened and announced, "I'm here to work for Adlai's election. I've moved to Chicago until November 4. Tell me what to do." Being a competent lawyer, he was immediately employed, at no salary, for the duration.

Regardless of their financial worries in connection with their candidate's broadcasts, the Volunteers were always rewarded when he came on the air or when they heard one of his campaign speeches:

> When an American says he loves his country, he means not only that he loves the New England hills, the prairies glistening in the sun or the wide rising plains, the mountains, and the seas. He means that he loves an inner air, an inner light in which freedom lives and in which a man can draw the breath of self-respect.

Or:

> We have learned from the past, and more recently in the bitter experience of the two world wars, that today human freedom is indivisible. We have come to know that the basic human rights we cherish are linked with the fate of even the most humble and remote peasant. Whenever fundamental rights are denied, freedom is

everywhere threatened, whether it be in far-off Korea or in Cicero, Illinois.

And his followers all loved it when he made his point by dealing humorously with foolish speculation or accusations: "I have been much interested in the continued debate raging in the newspapers as to whether I am headed left, center or right. I think it would be more relevant to ask: Is the man moving forward or backward, or is he grounded?"

Once the spontaneous state and local amateur groups had been corralled and more or less integrated into the National Volunteers for Stevenson, their relationship to the national headquarters and their activities in the field were very similar to those of the postconvention Willkie Clubs and the Citizens for Eisenhower. Headquarters supplied them with lists of names in their areas, encouragement, advice, "how-to" pamphlets, campaign literature, buttons, bumper stickers, and anything that they requested which headquarters had available. The local groups were all asked to pay the costs and shipping charges of campaign material so that the national organization could afford immediate replacements. Most of them did. Some did not. Some probably could not. But they were never refused stock if it was available. They were also, of course, encouraged to undertake the usual variety of political activities.

For the same reason that the Citizens for Eisenhower had felt it necessary to organize throughout the South—the solid strength of the Democratic party and the weakness of the Republican—the Volunteers made no attempt to organize in several of the southern states, nor in a few in the North. They, too, concentrated their major efforts in the areas where the regular Democratic organizations were weak or ineffective.

The quality of performance obviously varied greatly between the thirty-four states that organized Volunteers for Stevenson statewide in 1952, and between local chapters within the states. In those days, the amateurs were not as knowledgeable or as well organized as they are today to do precinct work. Furthermore, the time factor worked against the Stevenson Volunteers trying to develop an efficient countrywide precinct operation in 1952, as they had to build their entire organization starting from scratch in mid-August. Most of the local groups lined up precinct workers and canvassed their areas, but, on the whole, there was greater use of speakers, sound trucks, radio and television programs, newspaper ads, rallies, coffee-meetings, literature distribution, election-day telephone campaigns, and getting voters to the polls. And, of course, there was the unending problem of fundraising.

State and local Volunteers organized special interests and minority groups into divisions such as farm, labor, veterans, women, young people, Puerto Ricans, Mexicans, and Negroes.

Young people were greatly attracted by Stevenson. They lionized him, as they saw in him an embodiment of the ideals in which they believed, and they admired his candor and intellectual honesty. He, in turn, had always enjoyed the young—talking to them and exchanging ideas with them. In March, at the time of the Jefferson-Jackson Day dinner, at which Truman had bowed out, many reporters were searching all over town for the Governor prior to the dinner. He was spending those two hours at a young people's cocktail party, given for him by Stanley Karson, then the twenty-six-year-old aide of Senator Lehman. The moment the National Volunteers organized Stan came to Chicago and joined our staff. In addition to his job as a field organizer, he was put in charge of supervising the rapidly self-organizing student groups throughout the country.

The Students for Stevenson were coordinated rather than organized by the National Volunteers. There was little time to organize them because of the lateness of the convention and the fact that the students would not be back on their campuses until mid or late September. However, great numbers of student groups sprang up on their own, often with the assistance of young faculty members who were taken by Stevenson's personal qualities. Some of these student organizations became focal points for community Stevenson Volunteers.

They were serviced from national headquarters, but were put in touch with the Volunteer leadership in each state where it existed. Each state chairman appointed a director of Students for Stevenson and, through him, the students worked under the Volunteers or in affiliation with them. Their activities included registering and handling absentee voting of pro-Stevenson voting-age students, circulating petitions, organizing or helping with meetings and rallies, fundraising to defray their own expenses, arranging for national speakers to come to their campuses, and recruiting as much student manpower as possible for their tasks. They also rang doorbells, but this was not as systematically organized as in the later campaigns of Eugene McCarthy (1968) and George McGovern (1972). Their enthusiasm and their contribution to the campaign were of a high order.

In October, a mid-campaign meeting of the National Volunteers for Stevenson was held at the executive mansion in Springfield, Illinois, and the Governor entertained everyone at dinner. Reports of progress, exchange of ideas, and inspiration were the purposes of this gathering. The numbers of student representatives and universities around the country amazed everyone.

This meeting, of course, was not just for students but for Volunteers from all over. John Hersey and Chester Kerr, co-chairmen of the Connecticut Volunteers, were there; Bill Mauldin, the well-known cartoonist; Alan Cranston, then a Volunteer, later Democratic whip of the Senate; and many others provided an exhilarating mixture. I believe that the Governor got as much inspiration as he gave.

Because of the shortness of time, the spontaneity and rapid proliferation of Volunteers for Stevenson at the grass roots, and the decentralization of authority, it was difficult for national headquarters to do more than be a coordinator, adviser, and supplier. But when members of the National Volunteers had an opportunity to visit some of these branches and chapters and see at first hand what they were actually accomplishing, it was an almost constant source of amazement and pride.

I was fortunate in being asked to represent the National Volunteers on Governor Stevenson's twelve-day whistle-stop train trip across the eastern states just before the end of the campaign. We left Chicago on October 22. As was usual aboard a campaign train, the candidate occupied the last car containing a small sitting room at the rear, five compartments (and a shower!), a dining room seating twelve at a tight squeeze, and a tiny kitchen and pantry. His eldest son, Adlai, Jr., was in the Marines, so was not able to be with us, but the two younger ones, Borden and John Fell, traveled with their father when they could get a day or two off from college or school. His immediate aides and his bodyguard took up the rest of the car.

Wilson Wyatt, the campaign chairman, and George Ball, our executive director and fundraising genius, would suddenly arrive at many of our overnight stops. Three telephones would always appear as if by magic at those stops and be immediately hooked up in the dining room. The telephone company had issued us numbers in advance and, when these two dynamic gentlemen were on board, high-level conferences flew over the wires for most of the night, incoming and outgoing calls vying for priority.

I lived in the car adjoining the Governor's with his sister and brother-in-law, Buffie and Ernest Ives; India Edwards, the vice chairman of the Democratic National Committee; and occasionally Letitia Stevenson, the Governor's aunt, who had last campaigned in 1885 (for Grover Cleveland), but was as game as any Volunteer a quarter of her age. Also in this car were the Governor's two invaluable secretaries, Carol Evans and Margaret Munn, and other members of his official family and staff. Among the Volunteers on board were Porter McKeever and Bob Tufts, and others who came and went.

Ernest Ives was no politician. He was every inch a Virginia gentleman—very sweet tempered and excellent company. He enjoyed talking to the reporters and I believe it was mutual. Counting all the newsreel and cameramen, and regular newspaper, wire service, and magazine reporters, we had between eighty-five and one hundred press people traveling with us at all times. One day, they sent Ernest the following poem:

> With apologies to you and Mrs. Ives,
> I'm the husband of the sister of the candidate,
> I'm a most unnecessary chap.
> Just the husband of the sister of the candidate,
> Who neither gets the praise nor takes the rap.
> Every fellow on the train has a duty clear and plain,
> At each whistle-stop he'll hop for fear he's late.
> It makes no difference what I do,
> For the reason, sad but true,
> I'm just the husband of the sister of the candidate.

My duties were much the same as those that Willis and Rumbough were performing on Eisenhower's train. I made arrangements for Volunteer leaders to come on board at each stop and ride to the next one, in order to meet, have a word, and shake hands with the candidate. This was one of my hardest jobs, as the Governor spent a great deal of time between stops mulling over his speech for the next one. He refused to have a set talk and always surprised those who traveled with him, especially reporters, by the new ideas and fresh quality of his whistle-stop speeches. But his inaccessibility frequently irritated the pros, especially those aboard only between stops, and they resented any time taken up by "those volunteers." After these missions were accomplished, I spent most of every day talking with those men and women, finding out what each group had accomplished, and what they proposed to do.

I passed on the techniques that other groups were using in

the all-too-few remaining days, made suggestions for election day activities, and gave encouragement and praise to these eager campaigners.

I recorded speeches which the Volunteers took back to the local radio stations, hopefully to be broadcast throughout the areas through which the train passed. And I was interviewed by countless reporters from the news and women's pages of the local papers, all eager for scoops on life on a campaign train, the work of the Volunteers, or personal anecdotes about the Governor. The days grew so crowded that I never even had time to read the morning paper, and I began to feel like the Governor, who, when asked one day his opinion of some news article, answered, "It's hard enough to try to make news without being expected to keep up with it."

At every whistle stop, Governor Stevenson introduced the three women who were part of his official party—his sister, Mrs. Ernest Ives; the vice chairman of the Democratic National Committee, Mrs. India Edwards; and the vice chairman of the Volunteers for Stevenson, myself. When he came to me, in a light allusion to the opposition's charges that he was a "captive" of Truman, he would sometimes add "and she isn't a captive, either, even if she is a Republican." Or he would comment that "a convert is a Republican who becomes a Democrat. A traitor is a Democrat who becomes a Republican." Two years later, I changed my inherited Republican registration to Democratic. The whistle stops were all different, and, much to the joy of the reporters, so were the Governor's speeches. They all scrambled off the train at each stop to hear what he had to say.

As we approached one stop in Ohio—that near Oberlin College—we were all nonplussed as we saw a sea of waving placards which appeared to read "Welcome, Bob Taft." Some people felt we should bypass the stop, but obviously we didn't. When we drew up to the platform and the signs became clearer, they said "Welcome, Bob Tufts," to our traveling Volunteer Oberlin professor.

The most glamorous couple that traveled with us for several days were Lauren Bacall and "Bogie." As Eisenhower, or perhaps his troops, the Citizens for Eisenhower, seemed to have captured Hollywood's most prominent stars right after his nomination, we were both delighted and proud to have two of the best and nicest on our team. Lauren (or "Betty," as we all soon called her) was the first Stevenson convert in the Bogart family. Bogie had earlier declared himself for Eisenhower. But after he had met and talked to Stevenson and had heard him speak, he switched and became as strong a Stevenson supporter as his wife.

Betty and Bogie had offered to do anything they could for Stevenson—not just as entertainers, but as workers. It was decided that one of their most useful contributions would be to ride on the campaign train. The advance publicity that they were aboard was practically guaranteed to attract large crowds to our whistle stops. They willingly agreed, and their regular appearances on the observation platform functioned just as they were supposed to.

On Sunday, October 26, after we had spent one of our overnight stops at the Statler Hotel in Boston, I met Bill Blair at breakfast, looking quite disconsolate. I asked him what was wrong and he said, "I've had the most miserable night. At about 2:30 A.M., my telephone rang. It was Betty. She said, 'Bill, were you the person who sent word that Bogie and I would have to leave the train?' I had to confess that I was."

"My God, why did you do that, Bill?" I asked. "They've done a terrific job."

"That's just the trouble. They've been too successful. You've noticed that when we get to each whistle stop the crowd starts shouting, 'We want Bogie, we want Lauren,' instead of 'We want Adlai.' In trying to help, they're taking the stage away from him. Besides, because of these fans at every stop, it's impossible to keep on schedule. You've seen that, ever since the Bogarts got on board, we've been running later and later. The train can't start while people are standing on the tracks and practically climbing onto the observation platform. You remember that we were so late yesterday the Governor almost missed his first speech last night."

"What did you say to Betty?" I asked Bill.

"I told her the situation and said I was going to tell the Governor that they had had to leave unexpectedly to help warm up Madison Square Garden."

As this rally was still three days off, it seemed a rather lame excuse, but he knew that the Governor would be furious at such treatment of these good friends and illustrious Volunteers, and Bill had to handle it the best way he could.

The Bogarts, of course, understood at once, and quietly disappeared. They remained loyal and valuable campaigners to the end, and Betty and the Blairs are still fast friends today.

Governor Stevenson's train traveled through twelve states in twelve days and made eighty-four stops. There were big crowds of enthusiastic Volunteers at every one of them. Overnight stops were made in the larger cities such as Buffalo, Cleveland, Albany, Boston, New York, Philadelphia, and Chicago. Enormous parades, with the Governor riding at the head, escorted us to rallies at vast auditoriums packed with Democratic party workers, Volunteers, and the usual cheering Stevenson enthusiasts carrying posters and waving "Madly for Adlai" signs. At Madison Square Garden it was estimated that seventeen thousand people who could not get in stood outside throughout the evening. The crowds had grown larger and more ardent at every stop and euphoria increasingly possessed the train.

In the smaller towns, the candidate popped out and spoke from the lectern built on the observation platform of the rear car, or was paraded to the main squares of the towns, where temporary platforms were usually provided. All of the local leaders—both professional and volunteer—always tried to clamber onto these shaky structures with the Governor. Once they all narrowly escaped injury when one of the platforms collapsed. Stevenson calmed the ensuing pandemonium by taking over the microphone and saying that it was most gratifying to find so many people trying to get aboard the Democratic platform.

At the overnight stops and at many of the smaller ones, I had opportunities to visit the bustling local Volunteers headquarters —usually rented or donated storefronts. And, in connection with the large rallies at which the Governor spoke, there was almost always a Volunteers dinner or reception at which I was expected to speak, as well as one or more run by the regular organization. Stevenson would always appear at all of them.

At headquarters, we had been seriously concerned that we had not been able to organize door-to-door campaigning as systematically and efficiently as we knew it should be done. Both conventions had opened later than usual that year—the Republicans on July 7, and the Democrats on July 21. But the Citizens for Eisenhower had been active for months prior to their convention, and had national files and personnel ready and available to go into action the day their candidate was nominated. The Volunteers had not even had a name until the first of August, much less national files and known volunteers to call upon. With three months and four days to go, we had had to rely on our decentralized method of operation—and doorbell ringing was our biggest worry. We sent out instructions on the best way to operate, and the best approach once the doorbell had been rung, and stressed the importance of this method. We kept in close touch by telephone, and then we hoped.

But we need not have worried. Our Volunteers were wiser and more resourceful than we knew. One of my greatest and happiest surprises was to discover how thoroughly most of their canvassing operations were organized. By the end of October, I was able to report to our Chicago headquarters that the re-markable achievements of the local Volunteers, which had sprung up and developed such active and efficient organizations in so short a time, were far beyond anything that I and my colleagues could possibly have anticipated only ten weeks earlier.

My recollections of the whistle-stop trip are a blur of exciting and happy memories of the Governor talking sense earnestly or humorously from the observation platform, from the railroad embankment, from town squares, auditoriums, and field houses. On one occasion, speaking from the top of the embankment to a crowd gathered below, the Governor remarked, "The opposition is always accusing me of talking over the heads of the people. I'm grateful to you for giving me that opportunity today."

I remember Buffie Ives's tact and graciousness in always being available to people or for the myriad chores she was called upon to do, but never attempting to take over. I especially remember the kindness and helpfulness of a real pro, India Edwards, in treating this Volunteer as a friend and equal on all occasions—setting a new standard for this sort of relationship. I can see the golden autumn landscape of the eastern states rolling by our windows, and I can hear the shrill toot of the cocky little steam whistle that was attached to the railing of the observation platform to signal our departure from each stop, and the strains of the loudspeakers striking up the Democratic campaign song, "The farmer's farming every day—don't let them take it away," as we rolled out of town.

But most of all, I remember the bustling activity of the Volunteer headquarters in every big city, little town, and village; the hard work, devotion, and enthusiasm of every individual Volunteer; and their absolute dedication to their candidate and the ideals for which he stood and with which he had imbued them. I heard from many of them for years after the campaign was over, and my profoundest satisfaction has been to realize that the inspiration of Adlai's campaign—win or lose—had made a lasting impression on all those who participated in it.

One woman with whom I talked by telephone and corresponded during the entire campaign and afterwards, but whom

I had never met, had organized an extremely active Volunteers for Stevenson in Eau Claire, Wisconsin. A year or two later, I was invited by the *Chicago Sun-Times* to a reception in honor of their new columnist, Ann Landers. When I was introduced to the guest of honor, a petite, vivacious brunette, this eminent stranger practically threw her arms around me. "At last!" she said. "I'm Eppie Lederer. I'm the gal who organized the Eau Claire Volunteers for Stevenson." She has become a valued friend, and Eppie—or Ann—is today as loyal a Stevensonian as ever.

Governor Stevenson was given a great deal of advice during the campaign, some of it useful, some of it funny, all of it well-meaning. The most touching advice he received was given during our whistle-stop trip. It was not given to him by me, but I was often the bearer of it. It was heartening to discover that, while the vast majority of newspapers in the country—around ninety percent, I believe—were editorially supporting Eisenhower, the great majority of the working press was for Stevenson. Whenever I went through the press car, I almost always was given a message to take back to the Governor. "Tell him to say this at Erie." Or, "He ought to make such and such a statement tomorrow." Or, "He really shouldn't let so-and-so ride in the car with him; he's not the Governor's kind of guy." Once, when he disappointed them by repeating too often a funny story about a baby named "little Jimmie," they sent him a petition saying, "We have just cut little Jimmie's throat. Please bury him." That is the last we ever heard of Jimmie.

His aides felt he should wave more. It happened that one of them mentioned it to him right after he had ridden through Baltimore with the candidates for mayor and governor—both sizable politicians. "Damn it," he said. "How could I wave, pinned between d'Alessandro and Mahoney?"

With advice heaped upon him, pressures mounting daily, and almost no sleep, it seemed amazing that he kept his good temper and his humor throughout the campaign. Near the end, in

Pontiac, Michigan, he spoke at a rally packed with Eisenhower supporters. There were a lot of cries of "I like Ike." "So do I," was Adlai's surprising reply, "but please give me a chance to make my speech." The crowd stopped shouting and listened.

In some states, Stevenson himself, and the Volunteers for Stevenson, were powerful agents for political reform. New York and California were outstanding examples of this. During my lengthy and informative interview with Theodore White in June 1972, he described the history of reform in New York and the role played in it by Stevenson and his amateur workers as follows:

> Adlai Stevenson is the pivot figure of modern American politics. . . . The new world begins somewhere with Adlai. You have to see the Democratic party as it really was—a fine party, founded two months after the Constitution was passed, by a bunch of amateurs, actually. A paper hanger, an upholsterer here in New York—Moody was his name—founded something called the Society of St. Tammany, which was the beginning of the Democratic party in the United States, or, as you remember, Tammany Hall. Those amateurs became the most corrupt professionals over the years.
>
> But about 1948, when Truman was reelected, the Democratic party had a very nice structure. Everything had its place. There were the southerners, there were the union people, the big-city machine bosses, a handful of professors gravitated to the thing, and the general idea was that the bosses would deliver their troops at the polls, the troops would vote the way they were supposed to, and the President would share out the graft with the bosses. The President was supposed to run war and peace and make sure the people had jobs. The President ran the country well. The bosses could offer no criticism. It worked rather well too. . . .
>
> Now, with Adlai, there is a new rhetoric and that new rhetoric begins to echo across the country and begins to call in different kinds of people. Mind you, Adlai's period was in that time of a tremendous burst of education in the United States. The country was changing. We were going from a million college students to eight million. The country was full of educated people, people whose ears would be attuned to a new rhetoric, a new type of discourse, and you had the beginning of citizen influence in politics. Willkie was a very elite

white-glove-ladies and Ivy-League gentleman. It think it was with Adlai when citizen participation really began. He blew the trumpet and people flocked to his rhetoric, but there was nowhere—no units, no regiments, no companies—that they could join, because all the units and regiments were commanded by bosses whom they loathed. So they had to form their own organizations. There were two states that were particularly important—California and New York—and where the citizens movements really were launched.

White was outspoken in his contempt for the bosses:

At the same time, the reform movement in New York City began with a lot of young people wanting to help Adlai Stevenson and not being able to do so, and knowing that the bosses here in New York, the old-fashioned bosses, didn't care a hoot whether Adlai was elected or not. They probably preferred Eisenhower. The young kids in those days were fighting for control of clubs, so this was very rough stuff. It all began here in this neighborhood with a bunch of young lawyers and their friends who were appalled at the corruption of the courts of New York and were called into politics by Adlai Stevenson's rhetoric. One by one, these reformers in New York have picked off club after club in Manhattan—I don't think there are more than four or five old-fashioned Tammany Clubs left. There are quite a few left in Brooklyn. In the Bronx, the organization is declining. In Queens, the leader now has decided to join the amateurs.

Lloyd K. Garrison and John J. B. Shea, who were among the leaders of the reform movement, agree with White, but point out that attempts at reform in New York County were not new in 1952. Earlier efforts had put together and supported multiparty or fusion tickets. Occasionally, one of these endeavors to sweep the Tammany rascals out was successful—but only for a single term. With the brilliant exception of Fiorello La Guardia, who was a master politician before he became New York's three-term fusion mayor, the reform administrations were inept at discovering and using the levers of power, or actually disdained them. They were themselves regularly swept out for lack of accomplishment, and the voters returned Tammany to power.

The post-World War II reformers, many of them young veterans of that holocaust, concluded that the way to lasting reform was to work actively *within* the Democratic party, to infiltrate the local Democratic clubs with "good guys," and to insist on the membership having a voice in policy making and candidate selection. When, because of the closed Tammany hierarchy, this plan proved to be unworkable in many areas, they formed insurgent Democratic clubs in the same districts, and put up their own candidates in the primaries against Tammany's "bad guys." For example, they backed Lloyd Garrison and Dorothy Schiff, publisher of the *New York Post*, in a successful primary contest against the Tammany district leader and coleader.

In 1952, and again in 1956, Lloyd Garrison headed up the New York Volunteers for Stevenson, which he had taken a leading part in organizing. It was in the 1952 campaign that the Volunteers played the most significant role, because Adlai Stevenson at that time was scarcely known in New York. Garrison was a distinguished New York lawyer who had served in a number of public capacities: first as an assistant to Attorney General Mitchell in the Hoover regime in charge of a nationwide bankruptcy investigation; then as dean of the University of Wisconsin Law School, during which time he got to know Stevenson in Chicago; then as chairman of the first National Labor Relations Board; and, during World War II, as counsel and later chairman of the National War Labor Board.

In the early winter of 1951, Lloyd had arranged for the governor of Illinois, Adlai Stevenson, to come to New York and address the National Urban League, of which Lloyd was then president. The morning preceding the dinner, he took Adlai up to Harlem, where they spent several hours with the Urban League people, so that Adlai could have a first-hand acquaintance with some of the problems and difficulties confronting

Negroes. Then he gave a luncheon for him at the Harvard Club, with about forty leading citizens, including Paul Fitzpatrick, the state Democratic chairman, attending.

Garrison knew some of the ins and outs of local politics; the year before, he and Dorothy Schiff had run in a primary election in their district for the Democratic State Committee against the Tammany Hall district leader and coleader, man and woman against man and woman. They both ran as the candidates of the Lexington Democratic Club, the first reform club in the city, which had been organized by a group of able young men and women, among them Jack Shea, already a prominent lawyer who devoted a lifetime of service to good government. During the contest which the Lexington Club had persuaded Lloyd and Dorothy to engage in, members of the club went out every evening ringing doorbells and speaking on street corners, and so did Lloyd and Dorothy. To their astonishment, they were elected by a wide margin. The Tammany Hall leader and coleader then resigned and gave up their posts to the reformers. That was the start of the whole Democratic reform movement in the city, which brought into public life many young men and women who went on to serve the city and the state with great distinction. Thomas K. Finletter, who had been secretary of the Air Force, Senator Lehman, and Mrs. Roosevelt gave the reform movement great help, and later took leading parts in Stevenson's campaign.

After Adlai was nominated, Lloyd and Tom Finletter, representing the Volunteers, met every week for luncheon in a private room in the Century Club with Carmine DeSapio, the sinister-looking boss of Tammany. The black patch he wore over one eye made him appear more sinister than he actually was, and he bore them no ill will, in spite of their reform activities. Through these unpublicized luncheons, they were able in a quiet, off-the-record way to coordinate the campaign activities of the regular organization and the Volunteers.

"The major cause of this new good-government movement

was Adlai E. Stevenson, the Democratic candidate for President in 1952 and 1956," says Edward Costikyan, a leader of the young New York reformers of that time.

> Stevenson was essentially a good-government man. An intellectual, a gentleman, an idealist, he set out to prove, and he did prove, that an honest man could remain honest within the context of the obligations created by whole-hearted devotion to a political party. . . .His amateur followers decided to follow his example: to plunge into the political maelstrom, to replace the hacks that had failed, to school themselves and their followers in the techniques of political action. As he was loyal to the institution of the Democratic party, so were they. As he had demonstrated the possibility of the good-government tradition functioning in the context of an organized political party, so would they. As he had engaged in the drudgery of campaigning in primaries and general elections, so would they. As he had engaged in political maneuvering without destroying his integrity, so, by God, would they.

Great numbers of these men and women, captivated by Adlai Stevenson, had first found in the Volunteers for Stevenson the ideal channel through which to work for his election. Reformers took the lead in organizing Volunteers branches throughout the metropolitan area. And dedicated citizens from all over poured into them, offering "to do anything" from stuffing envelopes and ringing doorbells to organizing other Volunteers headquarters.

Costikyan points out that, after each of Stevenson's defeats, a very large number of these Volunteers, called into politics by Stevenson, stayed active. They organized local Democratic clubs throughout what Costikyan calls "the heartland of Stevenson supporters," midtown, as well as the East and West Sides of Manhattan, or joined existing clubs and provided most of the troops and many of the leaders for New York's great reform army of the 1950s.

Following Stevenson's 1952 defeat, the New York reform movement was given added impetus and a new source of power when Eleanor Roosevelt, Senator Herbert Lehman, and Thomas K. Finletter, all strong Stevenson supporters, joined it in a public statement denouncing the bosses for the arrogant way in which they dictated the nomination of candidates for high office. Soon afterward, Senator Lehman declared war on Carmine de Sapio, and a few years later, in a primary contest, the reform movement succeeded in ousting de Sapio from his district leadership. This led to de Sapio's resignation as party boss and shattered the county organization.

Other prominent citizens who helped create and actively assisted the reform movement were Francis W. H. Adams, a lawyer who had served as police commissioner under Mayor La Guardia; Irving Engels, another prominent lawyer and chairman of the American Jewish Committee; and James Lanigan, one of Stevenson's most active supporters in 1952. Probably the most important contribution of the reform movement has been its election to public office of countless first-rate young men and women who, as congressmen, state senators, assemblymen, city councilmen, and judges, are helping to infuse new vigor and integrity into the political life of New York.

In California, the reform tradition is a legacy of the Republicans and, in particular, of Hiram Johnson. When Johnson was elected governor in 1910, he and his followers in the progressive wing of the Republican party determined to break the hold that the Southern Pacific Railroad had at that time over the state government. To do this, they believed that the power of political parties had to be curbed, and they embodied this view in a series of successful legislative acts. The direct primary had already supplanted the party convention in selecting party candidates. To this the reformers added a presidential primary, the direct election of United States senators, the elimination of the party circle from the ballot, nonpartisan election to city and county offices, and crossfiling to permit running as a candidate in both parties without disclosing his own party affiliation. (Much of this legislation has since been repealed or superseded.)

In trying to eliminate a corrupt regime, they all but destroyed the party system in California. The legal organization of parties was "fragmented and reduced to impotence." These "reforms" of forty years earlier had, by 1952, created a political vacuum which opened unusual opportunities to organized amateurs in the absence of entrenched political machines to thwart them.

Any group coming in from outside of California to spearhead the organization of an independent political operation for a presidential candidate, as the Volunteers for Stevenson did in 1952, was confronted with a bewildering set of circumstances, because so many competing bodies had meanwhile moved in to fill the vacuum.

For a variety of reasons, the Republicans had had the advantage under the Johnson laws and, in 1952, the Republicans held all of the statewide offices, both United States Senate seats, nineteen of the thirty congressional seats, and eighty-three of the 120 state legislature seats. The professionals seemed helpless and the nonprofessional Democrats, for a number of reasons, had made no serious attempts to change the situation.

Since about 1940, there had been a few insignificant and scattered Democratic clubs organized on occasion to support individual candidates or liberal causes, but it was not until 1952, when Stevenson's nomination spurred countless thousands of Californians to action on his behalf, that the amateurs finally became a significant cohesive force in the Democratic party. Volunteers for Stevenson mushroomed seemingly overnight. And many of the existing clubs were brought together under the banner of the Volunteers which found fertile ground in California. Other men and women joined already extant independent Democratic clubs, or formed new ones, often calling themselves "Adlai Stevenson Clubs," that never disbanded.

The alchemy of a campaign is mysterious, but potent. In 1952, by election day, it had worked its spell on Stevenson's amateur supporters across the country. Even many of those who had been the greatest skeptics at the outset now believed that their candidate would win. Eisenhower's October 24 pledge to go to Korea if elected had given the coup de grace to Stevenson's chances in the eyes of many of the pros. But the Volunteers, being less accustomed to reading political signs and portents than the professionals, with no political future as a bulwark in case of defeat, and possessed of a passionate devotion to this man who had opened new horizons to them, had become increasingly confident of victory. The electorate, now that they had been exposed to the warmth, wisdom, tolerance, and sparkling humor of Adlai Stevenson could choose no other candidate.

Although there were undoubtedly election night parties at most Volunteers headquarters throughout the country, a great many workers simply descended on Springfield, Illinois, to be with their beloved hero when he won or—inconceivably—lost.

The executive mansion was a milling throng of ardent emotional well-wishers—family and friends of the governor, staff members, politicians, volunteers, press, radio and television people, and the Secret Service. Anyone who passed by a microphone was likely to be grabbed by a newsman and asked to make a prediction or give his or her impressions. As the bad news started arriving and began to mount, Dutch Smith and I, under the firm instructions of the campaign chairman, Wilson Wyatt, were continuing to make confident predictions of ultimate victory.

The scene in the Leland Hotel Ballroom a few blocks away, where a huge crowd was awaiting the Governor's appearance, was no different—just a bit more crowded, if possible. And there was a constant stream of people traveling between the two.

Late in the evening, when there was no further doubt as to the outcome, the Governor left for the Leland Hotel followed by his enormous entourage. Here in the ballroom he made his concession speech to General Eisenhower, including these words:

We vote as many, but we pray as one. With a united people, with faith in democracy, with common concern for others less fortunate around the globe, we shall move forward with God's guidance toward the time when His children shall grow in freedom and dignity in a world at peace.

Then, human as he was, he looked out at his tearful colleagues and campaign workers and characteristically added a touching personal footnote.

Someone asked me, as I came down the street, how I felt, and I was reminded of a story that a fellow townsman of ours—Abraham Lincoln—used to tell. They asked him how he felt once after an unsuccessful election. He said he felt like a little boy who had stubbed his toe in the dark. He said he was too old to cry, but it hurt too much to laugh.

By this time men and women, old and young, pros, volunteers, reporters, and cameramen alike were sobbing unashamedly.

By a popular vote of 33,936,252 to 27,314,992, and an even more decisive electoral vote of 442 to 89, Governor Stevenson lost the election in a defeat very nearly as crushing as Wendell Willkie's.

With the Stevenson campaign having been headed almost entirely by amateurs, the professionals may have had more than the usual provocation to grumble, which, of course, they did. And when the election was lost, many of them, looking for the inevitable scapegoats, blamed the defeat on the amateur nature of the campaign.

But even working, as they did, in coordination with the party, the devoted and hard-working amateurs, from coast to coast, could not turn the tide of opinion that was running against the Democratic party after twenty years in office. And even so gifted a campaigner and so splendidly qualified a presidential candidate could not beat an authentic American hero. Many close to Stevenson felt that he knew this from the start. But he campaigned with all of the vigor and conviction of a potential winner.

This gave heart to his volunteers throughout the campaign. And they gave heart to him. Their enthusiasm, as they preached his gospel, came in droves to meet him at airports, rallys, and whistle stops, and brought others to listen to what he was saying, was an enormous encouragement—to the point that, at the end of the campaign, even he began to believe in the possibility of winning.

But the greatest tribute his volunteers paid him, and one of the most enduring legacies of his campaign to his party and his country, was that, when Stevenson lost, they did not desert him or his principles. From all over the country, he was besieged with pleas to "let us keep the Volunteers going for 1956." When he called a meeting of the leaders of the National Volunteers and instructed us to disband at once, as he was determined "not to maintain a personal political organization," the New York reform movement took on new strength and vigor from the infusion of fresh blood from the disbanded Volunteers. In California, as James Q. Wilson says: "The enthusiasm for Stevenson transcended his defeat. Having discovered politics and an intellectually gratifying leader, the new club members were anxious to continue after 1952 in hopes of electing him in 1956." It was these enthusiastic Stevenson amateurs who were responsible for the organization of the California Democratic Council (CDC) in 1953.

In November of that year, a convention attended by over 500 delegates was held in Fresno. A constitution was approved for a California Democratic Council composed of the local clubs with statewide officers elected at conventions. It provided that the council could endorse certain candidates and perform some of the ordinary party functions prohibited to the state, central, and county committees under the Johnson legislation. Alan Cranston, later elected United States senator from California, became its first president. The following February, the council's first state convention was held at which Democratic candidates for the United States Senate and other offices were endorsed. These endorsements were of great symbolic, as well as actual, significance.

As in New York, so it was in California. It was the amateurs —"educated people, people whose ears would be attuned to a new rhetoric, a new type of discourse," as Theodore White put it, who had answered when Stevenson first "blew the trumpet" —who now flooded into the CDC, determined to work again for Stevenson's election in 1956, and meanwhile to direct their energies to improving the quality of politics in California. By 1956, when Stevenson suffered his second defeat, the lively CDC was doing just that. In an interview, former Governor Edmund G. Brown, Sr., of California, had this to say:

> Adlai Stevenson was the catalyst who sparked the founding of the California Democratic Council. Even though we lost, we wanted to do something that would carry on the greatness and spirit of Adlai Stevenson's appeal to the people. The CDC was primarily responsible for my election six years later in 1958. [The opponent he beat was Richard Nixon.]

And Edward Costikyan points out: "By the time of Governor Stevenson's death, many of his followers had installed themselves in significant party offices throughout the country. New York's reform movement was staffed, almost to a man, with Stevenson supporters. And the people of the country at large had come to an increasing awareness of the compatibility of political activity with integrity."

And in 1956, with the Democratic National Committee headed by an old pro, Paul Butler of Indiana, and Stevenson's campaign run by that master politician and admirable man, James Finnegan of Philadelphia, Stevenson lost more decisively than in 1952. It was then that even the most avid scapegoat hunters were forced to admit the potency of some of the real factors that led to Stevenson's two defeats: the widespread feeling that the Democrats had been in power too long, the feeling that the country was in a mood to relax rather than to innovate, and the safe feeling of having the country run by a war hero and "father image." In 1952, in a rare moment of exasperation, Stevenson had exclaimed, "I'm running against George Washington!"

Nonetheless, his party chose him to lead it for a second time in 1956. His misfortune was that his opponent, again, was Eisenhower, then the incumbent president, and Stevenson was again defeated.

He lived nine more years, until 1965, during which time he continued to serve his party and his country well and with distinction, both in private life and as America's ambassador to the United Nations. His views, as expressed in his writings and speeches, continued to make headlines throughout the world. And he lived to see countless thousands of his volunteers plunge into local, state, or national politics, determined to talk responsible sense and try to make the people's business as decent a profession as Adlai Stevenson showed them it could be.

Cornell Capa. Magnum Photos

The author *(standing right)*, vice chairman of the Volunteers for Stevenson, whom she represented on his campaign train, together with *(left to right)* his sister, Mrs. Ernest Ives, and Mrs. India Edwards, is introduced by the candidate to the crowd at a whistle-stop.

VIII

The Role of
Volunteers in
Campaigns Since 1952

Since the Eisenhower-Stevenson campaign of 1952, there has
been no campaign that has spontaneously inspired such a tremendous outpouring of private citizens eager to join in political
action. Nevertheless, volunteers have played a useful, if not an
indispensable, part in every subsequent presidential election
except Nixon's. So much has been revealed about the methods
of Richard Nixon, from his first campaign for Congress through
all the subsequent disclosures about CREEP (the Committee to
Reelect the President in 1972), that it is clear why no vestige
of a true volunteer movement ever developed on his behalf.
Indeed, it was the amateur Citizens for Eisenhower who, during the 1952 campaign, were in the forefront of those who
urged Eisenhower to drop his running mate, Nixon, from the
ticket at the time of the scandal over the Nixon Fund. What a
different political history we might have had if Eisenhower had
taken the advice of his devoted amateurs!

In stressing the vital role of volunteers in presidential contests, I must draw a distinction between campaigns where the
candidate is seeking the presidency for the first time and those
in which he has already been elected and is running for another

term. The campaign for a first term is normally accompanied by more excitement, more difficulties, more unknowns, and more need of all the help it can get than the campaign for a second term. An incumbent president has much more ready and seasoned assistance to call upon than one running for the first time. He is supported by a well-established machine, by members of his administration who have become known to the public, and by an array of governors and senators who were elected with him and may be indebted to him in various ways, to say nothing of the special interests whom he has rewarded. The first-time runner lacks all these advantages and can therefore make more of an appeal for volunteer help.

For example, when President Eisenhower ran for a second term in 1956, it was almost a repetition of Andrew Jackson's second campaign. The professionals took over all of the lists, trappings, slogans, gimmicks, and even the name, Citizens for Eisenhower, and ran it as a subsidiary arm of the party.

It is true that the reactivated Volunteers for Stevenson (now Volunteers for Stevenson-Kefauver) worked as hard as ever in 1956, knowing that the "father figure," now that he was president of the United States, was an even more formidable opponent than their hero had faced four years earlier. But Jim Finnegan, Stevenson's campaign manager, sized up a different problem for the Stevensonians in a rerun. He told Walter Johnson during the 1956 Democratic convention, "The trouble is, this time all of the professionals think they're eggheads, and all of the eggheads think they're pros." It is never the same the second time around.

In the 1960 presidential election, Senator John F. Kennedy brought the young, "the best and the brightest" into the campaign, but he had not been induced to make the run by volunteer action as Stevenson and Eisenhower had been. There was no spontaneous coast-to-coast mushrooming of Kennedy clubs, Citizens for Kennedy, or Volunteers for Kennedy before the nomination. Instead, from Kennedy's base in the Senate, the amateurs were recruited in a very orderly way before the convention, and particularly afterward. They were assigned to work under three able and politically-experienced intimates of Kennedy's: Theodore C. Sorensen, Kenneth O'Donnell, and Lawrence F. O'Brien. Sorensen and O'Donnell had been senatorial assistants to Kennedy and, after the latter's election to the presidency, Sorensen became counsel to the President and served through 1964. O'Brien had been organizational director of Kennedy's two senatorial campaigns and his campaigns for the nomination and the presidency. Afterward, he served Kennedy and Lyndon Johnson as assistant for congressional relations and personnel and became, successively, postmaster general and chairman of the Democratic National Committee.

These three men were real pros, unlike the zealous but inexperienced amateurs who tried to guide the volunteers in the first Stevenson and Eisenhower campaigns. After Kennedy's nomination, these pros pursued disappointed Stevensonians. Many eventually joined up and worked dutifully, if not jubilantly, while others simply sat the campaign out.

David Broder, in his book, *The Party's Over,* recognized the very important role which volunteers play in a presidential election, with particular reference to the Kennedy campaign:

> The organizational secret of Kennedy politics was so simple it was often overlooked: it was a politics of personal involvement on a massive scale. It was laid out publicly, at the time of John Kennedy's presidential campaign, by Lawrence F. O'Brien in the manual for Democratic Precinct Workers:
>
> "Volunteers are essential to the success of any political campaign. . . . There is no such thing as having a surplus of volunteers. There are any number of ways of recruiting volunteer workers, including asking persons who have offered their services to the candidate. Asking persons who have returned worker cards . . . indicating they will perform some specific volunteer function in the campaign. Asking college and high school students. Asking members of political civic, church and social clubs. Asking persons who express a desire for political participation and experience. Asking persons who have

worked in previous political campaigns. Asking elderly persons who may be willing to perform light political chores, such as addressing envelopes. Asking members of Democratic state, city, county and town committees. Asking members of labor unions. . . . Asking the wives, husbands, sons, daughters, sisters, brothers, fathers, mothers, aunts, uncles, cousins, and friends of everyone in the preceding categories. . . .

"It is the responsibility of campaign headquarters to make certain . . . that everyone who volunteers to work is given an assignment. It is terribly discouraging to a person who has volunteered to work in a campaign not to be given something to do. More than that, it is a sure sign of an inefficient campaign organization."

In 1964, the Republican candidate, Barry Goldwater, attracted more genuine volunteers than the incumbent President Lyndon Johnson, running on his own for the first time after finishing out John F. Kennedy's brief term. But Goldwater's volunteers, though devoted to their conservative candidate, represented ideologically and geographically but a small segment of the voters. There was no amateur movement on a national scale for Goldwater.

By contrast, when Senator Eugene McCarthy ran for the Democratic presidential nomination in 1968, his campaign was spearheaded and largely manned by a multitude of enthusiastic and idealistic amateurs who managed to coalesce into a nationwide organization. They were mostly students who were activated by his courageous stand against our involvement in Vietnam at a time when no other prominent figure would speak out against it. Unfortunately, they often attributed to him qualities and positions which he did not have. They created their own McCarthy image, and dropped out of schools and colleges to work to get him the nomination. When he disagreed with positions that they themselves had ascribed to him, they felt he had let them down. But they still plugged on because he had been the original lone voice to speak up on the only issue that mattered to them—

the senseless immorality of the Vietnam War.

McCarthy's volunteers, on the average, were so young that his campaign became known as the "Children's Crusade." Despite their inexperience, they helped McCarthy to garner forty-two percent of the votes in the New Hampshire Democratic primary held on March 12, 1968. This rousing result stunned President Johnson and led to extraordinary consequences. On March 16, Senator Robert Kennedy, who had been a critic of the administration but had only lately spoken out against Vietnam, entered the primary campaign. On March 31, the discouraged President withdrew from the race. On April 27, Vice President Hubert Humphrey, who had supported the war, announced his own candidacy for the nomination.

The anti-Vietnam forces were now divided between Senator McCarthy and the doomed Senator Kennedy. Before his assassination in June, Kennedy had modeled his primary campaign organization on that of his brother, the late President. His staff and closest advisers were old Kennedy pros and the dynamic Kennedy family. He had some difficulty in attracting volunteers for, though many of his volunteers were strongly anti-Vietnam, McCarthy's early and courageous stand had already attracted the great majority of those most concerned—aggressive activists with lots of initiative. However, added to the magic of his name, Bobby Kennedy had extraordinary personal charisma and sex appeal. Probably a great many of his volunteers joined up for the thrill of working with Bobby and his clan rather than for any specific issue or policy which he stood for. Because of the professional character of his readymade staff, his volunteers were usually not given as much significant work as the McCarthy amateurs, who were continuously asked questions such as, "Do you know anything about North Dakota?" "Will you do an analysis of their delegation for me? I need help." But Kennedy kept their allegiance and they helped him win the crucial California primary. Then disaster struck. As Kennedy, accompanied by well wishers, was leaving the Ambassador

Hotel in Los Angeles, where his great victory was being celebrated, a demented Jordanian immigrant named Sirhan shot and fatally wounded him.

As the whole country mourned, shock, grief, and bitterness abruptly drained the McCarthy campaign of the exhilaration and sense of mission that motivate volunteers. Divisiveness plagued the McCarthy efforts from then on.

At the strife-torn National Convention in Chicago, not only did the establishment dominate the Democratic National Committee and the convention machinery, but President Lyndon Johnson and Vice President Hubert Humphrey controlled the federal government as well. It must be remembered that it is always more difficult (though not always impossible) for insurgents to prevail when the leader of their party is the incumbent president than it is when their party is out of power, as in the cases of Willkie and Eisenhower.

The McCarthy volunteers' quest for delegates had met with little success. The convention nominated Humphrey on the first ballot. Out of a total of 2622 votes, the roll call gave the Vice President an overwhelming 1760.25, McCarthy 601, and McGovern 146.5, with a scattering of also-rans. Senator Edmund Muskie of Maine was nominated as his running mate. Then the convention endorsed President Johnson's Vietnam policy while frustrated and embittered antiwar demonstrators were clashing angrily with the police outside the amphitheatre and throughout Chicago's streets and parks. After losing the nomination, McCarthy abdicated his antiwar leadership and his young followers, disillusioned, resentful, and disoriented, simply fell apart. McCarthy, as a political force, ceased to exist. The Republican nominees, Nixon and Agnew, won the election by a large margin.

After the election, as a result of the bitterness caused by the Democratic convention, the party rules were changed so as to give effective control to the majority of elected delegates. Senator George McGovern, a strong liberal, was chairman of the committee that drew up the changes. They obviously enhanced the potential role which volunteers could play in future conventions.

In the 1972 campaign, he sought the Democratic nomination. So did Humphrey, with Muskie's backing. They were powerful and moderate men, and so well known to the voters that McGovern faced a formidable task. His preconvention strategy was to campaign hard to win the support of the so-called "new politics" constituency represented by the political activists, both professionals and amateurs, who had worked in the 1968 McCarthy and Kennedy campaigns. Many of these volunteers had subsequently gone to work in state and local elections across the country. McGovern expected that the political networks they had established could be easily revived; indeed, in some cases, these had remained more or less intact. He seemed to have an ideal grass-roots base on which to build.

McGovern knew, from watching the progress of the previous McCarthy campaign, that McCarthy volunteers were self-starters. Once they were involved in the campaign, they would need minimal supervision and very little morale boosting or prodding from the national organization.

But McGovern's efforts to garner the backing of the new politics constituency were never completely successful, despite his charismatic personality. Hubert Humphrey had regained more of his old appeal and prestige than people realized. Many former volunteers decided for various reasons that state or local elections were more crucial than the national election. In spite of these defections, McGovern managed to win the nomination. The Republicans renominated the incumbents Nixon and Agnew.

McGovern made many inept moves during the presidential campaign which lessened the support for his candidacy. Many volunteers would work only for candidates that they "believed in"—they did not work for a candidate merely because he was a Democrat or a liberal, or because he was running for president.

There were, however, other volunteers who worked for McGovern with enthusiasm and ability. Marjorie Benton is an excellent example. Her first political work was in 1949 as a volunteer for her father-in-law, William Benton, in his successful campaign for United States senator from Connecticut. She volunteered in the Stevenson presidential campaigns of 1952 and 1956, did "a little" work for John F. Kennedy in 1960, and was thoroughly involved in McCarthy's campaign eight years later. But she says that her major effort, both pre- and postconvention, was in 1972 for McGovern. Marjorie Benton is still technically an amateur, as she has never run for public office or held a party post. But there are few practicing politicians today who know more about American politics than she does.

Another enthusiastic McGovernite who got his start volunteering for McCarthy in the summer between his graduation from college and entering law school was Gene Pokorny. He was one of the top leaders in McGovern's citizens' organization and, as state coordinator for Wisconsin, is given full credit for McGovern's win in their primary—his first big victory, and a major factor in his nomination. "Boy, he pulled it out of the hat in Wisconsin in terms of the campaign," one fellow volunteer remarked of Pokorny.

In 1976, the campaign of the incumbent President, Gerald Ford, was waged to the daily accompaniment of fresh Watergate disclosures. Though obviously a decent man, Ford's unpopular pardon of Nixon, his low-key campaign and lackluster personality did nothing to stem the severe erosion of public confidence in government in general, and in his administration in particular.

Under the circumstances it seems surprising that the Democratic nominee, Jimmy Carter, a new face, a former governor, unsullied by affiliations with the discredited government, did not become a rallying point for Independents and disillusioned members of both major parties.

There were many reasons for this. One was the unusual number of aspirants for the Democratic nomination in 1976. At one point, eleven serious contenders were formally entered in primaries or seeking the endorsement of state caucuses or conventions, in addition to the usual favorite sons or stalking horses. Each had his followers, and by convention time Democratic loyalties were either hopelessly divided—or confused. Indeed, when Jimmy Carter finally emerged as the nominee, no one had a clear impression of the man or what he stood for.

This lack of clarity was due largely to his astute perception of the possibilities of the primaries. He reasoned that the notoriously small turnout in primary elections gave relatively few people great influence on the outcome. He saw a state-by-state grass-roots campaign in each primary state as the best possibility for an unknown candidate. If this candidate familiarized himself with the geography, the ethnic makeup and the urban, suburban, small town, and rural mix; if he understood the issues and prejudices, the simplest hopes and most exalted aspirations of the people of each individual state; if he met not only with the leaders, but with the people, individually or in small groups rather than rallies; if he shook enough of their hands, and slept under enough of their roofs—if he did all this, he could win.

Jimmy Carter decided he was the man to prove his theory. He knew that he was at his best in small gatherings. People who have been privileged to participate in some of these sessions attest to the fact that he is very, very good. His intelligent grasp of facts and issues and his ability to energize people under intimate conditions are exceptional.

Jimmy started his campaign long before most of the other aspirants had surfaced, and he briefed himself thoroughly on all aspects of the state he was about to tackle. His folksy talks at factory gates or senior citizens' picnics were a great success, and he relished hobnobbing with the neighbors on the front porches of his overnight hosts. Everywhere he went he made friends.

Furthermore, in Indiana he could say what the Hoosiers wanted to hear, and in Indiana he could, and no doubt did, genuinely believe that what was best for them was best for the country. In New England, however, or in the western states, he could enunciate—and believe in—different priorities. Carter's campaign for the nomination was not a national campaign, but a series of individual statewide campaigns. For Carter it was an intelligent and clever strategy, and it worked.

But when he emerged as the Democratic nominee for president, of all the people, the question began to be asked nationwide: "What does Candidate Carter stand for?" A good man, yes. A religious man, yes. One who wants the best for the country, yes. But we don't know what he thinks is best, or how he plans to achieve it.

Volunteer groups, of course, got together for Carter in many states but, to the end, his most cohesive supporters were his closely-knit band of Georgia colleagues, many of them pros from his gubernatorial days, who had helped him devise and carry out his unique and successful primary strategy.

IX

The Making of Volunteers

What special attributes must a candidate have to activate hundreds of thousands of dedicated followers throughout the country to work with passion and selflessness for his or her nomination or election? What constitutes the mystical pull between a great political leader and the people? The most frequent replies to these questions are: "He must be a man who cares" and "one must feel that he is 'untainted' by politics." Amateurs are strongly attracted by individuals they feel are independent and willing to speak out forthrightly, regardless of consequences.

But it is that indefinable force called magnetism, casting its aura around a man and his views, that makes a leader charismatic. Wendell Willkie's biographers variously refer to his "personal" magnetism, his "political" magnetism, his "animal" magnetism, and his charm for women. And men and women who profoundly disagreed with Adlai Stevenson's political views were strongly attracted to him as a human being. Magnetism is an indispensable ingredient.

Volunteers also need to feel *needed*. They are powerfully motivated if they sense that the establishment is not going to take their man or take their side of an issue unless they bring it about. Volunteers have shown in numerous campaigns that they will give tremendous loyalty to a leader who inspires trust, lifts their hearts, and makes them feel he needs their help.

Of course, in politics, as in anything else, it is not always selfless idealism or even a charismatic leader that stimulates an individual to join up with the amateurs. A variety of more practical or mundane reasons may prompt him, and some of them may give the professionals genuine cause for worry.

Personal Ambitions

There are men and women with political ambitions who feel that, by backing a winner at an early stage, they can achieve their goals for personal advancement faster—almost overnight, in fact, if their man is elected. The citizens' groups offer a quick and convenient way to bypass the closed-party hierarchy for, if one should decide to volunteer at regular party headquarters during a presidential campaign, how little would one be given to do? Obviously, here the only jobs fit for a novice are such routine ones as licking envelopes. This menial task must, of course, be performed at every campaign headquarters, but, as one envelope licker at a volunteer office remarked, "The glue may taste the same but it goes down better here." And even as the volunteer is engaged in this boring occupation, the candidate himself may be seriously considering the use of a speech draft or position paper that the worker has submitted—unthinkable at party headquarters.

Reformers' Aims

Reformers and reform groups, which have struggled, usually with limited recognition or success, against entrenched party organizations, often find these volunteer campaign groups ideal channels through which to mobilize and consolidate their forces, make themselves heard, and frequently achieve some of their long-sought reform aims. In 1952 and 1956, most members of the anti-Tammany clubs in New York City joined the Volunteers for Stevenson. When the campaign ended, many formerly apolitical volunteers went on into the clubs, and the momentum generated by these campaigns subsequently gave a tremendous boost to the clubs' membership rolls and effectiveness. Occasionally, in the case of two warring political factions, the outs, or the minority of the party professionals, may see a presidential volunteer organization as a medium through which to work for a candidate to whom the regular organization is not giving adequate support. This happened in New York City in Stevenson's 1956 campaign.

Psychological Needs

Some individuals join volunteer campaign organizations to satisfy a variety of their personal needs for status, power, identity, companionship, adventure—or to escape from loneliness or unhappiness or sheer boredom. The average citizen is frightened at the idea of trying to get into regular "party politics." To many it is a time-consuming, unsavory business in which novices are not welcome. Whereas working with their peers for a candidate they admire holds no terrors, and frequently it leads men and women with genuine interest and ability into party work—a plus both for the party and the individual. There is also a vast pool of mobile Americans to whom volunteer groups are a boon. It is estimated that forty million Americans move every year. Before they have had time to join local clubs or political groups in their new communities, campaign organizations often offer them unique opportunities for recognition and instant friendships.

The McCarthy people flew or bused members of their Children's Crusade from New Hampshire to California, stopping along the way to campaign in the primary states of Wisconsin,

Indiana, Nebraska, and Oregon. Hordes of other volunteers simply followed along. For many of these young people, their serious determination to help stop the war and end the draft was enhanced by the romantic appeal of travel, adventure, excitement, being away from home on their own, leaving school, meeting new friends, taking on adult responsibilities, and being treated as equals.

One enthusiastic teen volunteer felt that half the teenagers sign on for such nonpolitical reasons as an opportunity to meet the "bright young lawyers" who write position papers and speeches and supervise the young volunteers; as "a favor to a friend"; as a "requirement for a civics course"; or because he or she "is on a diet and needs something else to think about."

However, those who join a citizens' campaign organization for an ulterior motive are the exceptions. The overwhelming majority, young and old, are in it because they want to do all in their capacity to help the candidate of their choice become president of the United States. Sometimes, when power appears within their grasp, ambitions may soar, but there is ample testimony that most volunteers want nothing for themselves. They do not expect any reward at the end. The most persistent request of volunteers is simply for the opportunity, at long last, to meet or shake hands with the man whom they may never even have seen in person but to whom they have given so much of their time, faith, and devotion.

The most telling testimonial to this selflessness of the true amateur came from Dwight Eisenhower after he became president. "There were Republicans," he said, "who resented the Citizens (for Eisenhower)" and wished "to get rid of these volunteer politicians." At one point a woman party leader said to the President, "All they want is to get their fingers in the patronage pie; it is time we let them know that the Republican party is in charge." Eisenhower reports that his temper began to boil and he said to her:

It's true that I have been besieged by people seeking appointments for themselves or others and asking for every kind of favor a President could possibly grant. But I must tell you, to their everlasting credit, that not a single member of the Citizens' groups who gained entry to my office, has asked me for any kind of official or unofficial favor. Moreover, I have not been approached even indirectly by anyone suggesting that the Citizens and volunteers should receive political rewards of any kind for their help in the campaign. . . .

Women are frequently the mainstays of citizens' campaign organizations. Most women do not feel locked into the establishment as so many men do, and they are apt to respond more intensely than the average man to the emotional appeal of the issues; and, when they enlist as volunteers, they work with extraordinary devotion.

Women with school-age children can be particularly helpful. Many have time available during the school year and often put their children to work during the holidays. Even quite young children make splendid volunteers. One eleven-year-old Stevenson volunteer is reported to have licked envelopes all day every day until school opened. He kept his morale high by chanting softly to himself, between licks, "I'm sealing up another vote for Stevenson. I'm sealing up another vote for Stevenson."

Working in a citizens' group during a campaign is a great opportunity for young people. They have the essential qualifications for success—energy, initiative, self-confidence (sometimes a certain amount of brashness helps), willingness to put up with long hours and physical discomfort, and a penchant for the new rather than attachment to the old. In campaigns, there are never enough people to do all the jobs that need doing, so an intelligent, willing, and resourceful volunteer who joins up early often quickly rises to the top simply by filling the constantly appearing vacuums. Age is no deterrent to advancement, but the qualities of youth are a considerable asset.

Before closing this chapter, I must take note of a theme which keeps recurring when former volunteers discuss campaigns in which their candidates had enlisted their loyalties and their zeal. They nearly always express the conviction that "our campaign was unique"; that the experience of working for their particular candidate was special and never to be forgotten. For example, the 1952 chairman of the Illinois Citizens for Eisenhower, George A. Poole, told me in an interview on June 12, 1972 that: "The Eisenhower campaign, the Citizens for Eisenhower campaign prior to the convention, was and always will be unique. As we say about Bobby Jones winning the 'grand slam,' there will never be one again. His Citizens' campaign was unique and will always remain unique." And that same year, on November 13, 1952, following Stevenson's defeat, a Volunteer for Stevenson wrote to me that: "Having worked in a campaign such as ours must be something like having lived in Paris when you were twenty, or discovered the 'Ode to a Grecian Urn' in the midst of your first true love affair."

Ralph Martin in his biography, *Cissy, The Extraordinary Life of Eleanor Medill Patterson,* has most accurately and vividly described the peculiar exhilaration of a campaign to its volunteer participants—young and old:

> She learned that political volunteers are tied together by a most powerful bond—a dedication so deep that they forget family, friends, love, sleep, time, memory. The political campaign, short and intense, becomes their whole world, a world open only to those whose blood is true, whose eyes are wide, and whose hearts are full. In this world there is more heart than head, more hope than knowledge, more fervor, more faith, more love than anybody deserves.

X

Volunteers in a Changing Political World

What are the legacies that the early volunteers left to their successors?

The most important is the knowledge that citizen participation *can* count. If people care enough, if they work hard enough, if they concert their efforts, they can achieve their objectives even when opposing the professionals. Sometimes they fail. But sometimes they work miracles.

The pioneer amateurs left their successors with the conviction that politics is neither a dirty word nor a dirty vocation, that indeed it is the only instrument by which a free people can exercise their collective will in a democratic society. If one wants to be a doer—an accomplisher rather than a critic—one must regard politics with respect and gratitude. And one must participate. To do that effectively, one needs to study political methods, use them as best one can, and develop new and imaginative techniques, especially when the volunteer effort goes counter to the plans of politicians.

The volunteers learned that they had to work together and, if possible, in harmony with the professionals. Often, through these contacts, the amateurs acquired a new respect for politicians and politics and a greater awareness of the importance of the party system to our form of government.

As a result, following their campaigns, many men and women amateurs went into party politics in their home towns, worked for party candidates, and themselves ran for local or state office or for their state legislatures or Congress. But their interest in national campaigns never flagged, and many Willkie workers, for example, turned up twelve years later as leaders in Eisenhower's campaign.

And the same is true of the Stevensonians. Frustrated by the defeat of their candidate, deeply concerned about the issues he had raised, and animated by his respect for the political profession and his appeals to his followers to become active participants, great numbers of his volunteers moved into the mainstream of the Democratic party, both in 1952 and in 1956. The Republicans, with their man safely in office, were not so strongly motivated. Nevertheless, in smaller numbers, many of them followed the same route.

Referring back to the interview with Theodore White mentioned earlier, he summed up the legacy of Stevenson and the 1952 volunteer movement he inspired when he said, "Adlai Stevenson is the pivotal figure of modern American politics." There have been, as we have seen, and as White puts it, "amateur inrushes into politics from time to time and for a variety of purposes throughout our history." But White believes that "the new world begins somewhere with Adlai"—when he "blew the trumpet."

In 1952, politicians still regarded amateurs as a bore and a nuisance. If they could get some "white-gloved ladies," they might raise some money. Amateurs were thought of as a source of campaign funds. They were mainly middle-class elite. They were not supposed to work the precincts, man the polls, talk about judgeships, or have anything to do with the jobs reserved for the politicians. They were good for public relations—if they remained on the outside.

On the other hand, the Democratic party—especially in the big cities which were largely run by bosses and their hand-picked "machines"—was notoriously corrupt and patronage oriented. It was unthinkable that the amateurs would work with these machines, even if they had been welcome. As White pointed out, if they were to do any significant work, which they were so eager to do, they would have to develop their own organizations. And that was precisely what they set about doing, from the moment Stevenson accepted his party's nomination. The Citizens for Eisenhower, already operational for several months, also provided a home for Republicans, Independents and disaffected Democrats who would not or could not work within the party. It was these organizations that proved to be both the school in which its members learned their lessons in rudimentary politics and the bridge which enabled them subsequently to cross over into the professional sector.

It would be gratifying if this transfusion of new, innovative, and idealistic blood into the parties' mainstreams had transformed the parties. For a time, it appeared that it had, especially in the Democratic party, where names of people who had been neophytes in 1952 and 1956 reappeared, in subsequent campaigns, on the rosters of governors, senators, congressmen, and in many less conspicuous offices. One young woman, Joanne Alter, a hard-working Volunteer for Stevenson in 1952 and 1956, ran, a few years ago, for the unglamorous job of member of the Chicago Sanitary District Board. She won, and did an outstanding job—making the public interested in and aware of the ecological importance of proper sanitation in a large city. Subsequently, she had strong support as a candidate for nomination for lieutenant governor. Unfortunately, she lost that race, but is continuing, by her own stellar performance, to upgrade the Sanitary District Board.

Two generations of the children of those who worked in the Willkie, Stevenson, and Eisenhower campaigns have now grown up—or are growing up—in politically oriented households. They hear politics discussed at home and on television and radio. They take political science courses at school and college and many continue to involve themselves in local, state, or national campaigns. And eighteen-year-olds now have the vote, thus swelling the ranks of potential activists. Large numbers of young people have been in the forefront of those demonstrating against nuclear power and in favor of environmental protection and the reduction of armaments. In the new generation, with its new outlook, issues such as these may become the stuff of presidential campaigns, aided and fired by masses of eager volunteers.

It may even be that issues like these will, in the future, attract volunteers more powerfully than the personalties of candidates. There are signs that our modern-day political processes are not producing the quality of candidates who are likely to attract many dedicated followers. The presidential primary system, as it has evolved, has become so drawn out, expensive, and exhausting that few people of top stature care to subject themselves to the ordeal. This very fact, however, may challenge volunteers to work in primary contests in more organized and effective ways than in the past on behalf of men and women they believe in who might not otherwise be willing to take the plunge, and in support of causes that might not prevail without their devoted efforts.

At the local level, the primaries have largely eroded the base of the old city "machines" on which the state parties have been elected. As a result, party discipline and direction have been weakened, and the doors of opportunity have been opened more widely to organized volunteer efforts.

Whatever the future holds, several things are clear: Our democracy needs both the professionals and the amateurs. It is a sign of political health when both care enough about a candidate or the cause he is fighting for to join in the battle—either together or in opposition to one another. After a campaign, the parties are strengthened when knowledgeable volunteers join the established ranks and turn pro themselves. Even the amateurs who return to private life become better-informed citizens, with keener political interest and understanding and a greater readiness to return to public life when the need arises.

In spite of its inadequacies and contradictions, and the difficulties it faces in functioning, the strength of our form of democracy lies primarily in our strong two-party system. But a balancing strength is a national tendency, which de Tocqueville noted nearly 150 years ago, for independent citizens to "constantly form associations." The amateurs' readiness to join together to fight the parties' establishments when they disapprove of their positions, methods, or candidates; to work with the parties for candidates of whom they approve; and to support political and social reforms by applying mass pressure on both parties—this is America's unique contribution to the art of politics. It has served the country well, and is needed more than ever in these days of worldwide changes which concern us all.

Chapter Notes

I. YESTERDAY

3   "Americans of all ages, . . .": Alexis de Tocqueville, *Democracy in America*, trans. Henry Reeve; ed. Henry Steele Commager (London: Oxford University Press, 1946), p. 376.

4   "the popularity of Jackson rests . . .": Stefan Lorant, *The Glorious Burden: The American Presidency* (New York: Harper & Row, 1968), pp. 116–17.

7   "was not to be equaled until . . .": Irving Stone, *They Also Ran: The Story of the Men Who Were Defeated for the Presidency* (New York: Doubleday, Doran & Company, 1943), p. 141.

8   Political clubs for parade . . .: John G. Nicolay and John Hay, *Abraham Lincoln: A History*, 10 vols. (New York: Century Company, 1886), 2:284–86.

II. THE TYCOON

11   "I knew, of course, . . .": Marcia Davenport, *Too Strong for Fantasy* (New York: Charles Scribner's Sons, 1967), p. 259.

12   "not thinking like a typical American millionaire.": Donald Bruce Johnson, *The Republican Party and Wendell Willkie* (Urbana, Ill.: University of Illinois Press, 1960), pp. 50–51.

12   "criticized the Indiana law school . . .": Ibid.

12   "an outspoken condemnation . . .": Ibid.

14   "fair compensation . . .": "78.6 million dollars. Willkie's original asking price had been 94 million, the Government's original offer had been 57 million." Ellsworth Barnard, *Wendell Willkie, Fighter for Freedom* (Marquette, Mich: Northern Michigan University Press).

14 "built upon a tripod . . .": November 1, 1939.

15 "an intellectual and temperamental affinity . . .": Davenport, p. 269.

15 "ought to be the next president . . .": Ibid., p. 259.

16 an editorial about Willkie, . . .: Editorial, *Fortune* 21, No. 4 (April 1940):24.

16 "We the People,": "We the People," *Fortune* 21, No. 4 (April 1940):64–65.

17 "Mr. Willkie's Petition,": "Mr. Willkie's Petition," *Fortune* 21, No. 4 (April 1949):65.

19 "If the government keeps on . . .": Stone, p. 350.

24 He likes to earn the stuff . . .: Wendell Willkie, *This Is Wendell Willkie: A Collection of Speeches and Writings on Present-Day Issues*, intro. by Stanley Walker (New York: Dodd, Mead & Company, 1940), p. 23.

25 "both his strength and his weakness . . .": Herbert S. Parmet and Marie B. Hecht, *Never Again: A President Runs for a Third Term* (New York: Macmillan Company, 1968), p. 67.

25 "Miracles don't happen anymore": Johnson, p. 40.

26 "businessmen drunk with power, . . .": Parmet and Hecht, p. 82.

26 "sound in principle . . .": Ibid.

28 thoughtful, responsible American people . . .: Davenport, pp. 260–61.

33 the Gallup poll of May 8, . . .: George H. Gallup, *The Gallup Poll: Public Opinion 1935–1971*, 3 vols. (New York: Random House, 1972), vol. 1: *Republican Presidential Candidates: May 8, 1940*, p. 222.

33 Nine days later, May 17, . . .: Ibid., p. 224.

33 A month later, . . .: Ibid., p. 228.

33 "one of the most remarkable phenomena . . .": Parmet and Hecht, p. 112.

33 "had conducted an amazingly . . .": Ibid., p. 117.

34 I have no campaign manager, . . .: Ibid., p. 122.

34 "I'm not running for anything, . . .": Stone, p. 342, or *Saturday Evening Post,* June 22, 1940.

37 the committee's final report.: U.S. Senate, *Special Committee to Investigate Presidential, Vice Presidential, and Senatorial Campaign Expenditures*, 1940, 77th Cong., 1st Sess., Feb. 15, 1941, Rept. 47, p. 31.

41 "Guests, hell! . . .": Stone, p. 354.

41 "Are we to understand . . .": Parmet and Hecht, p. 144.

43 "a hell of sealed-in heat" . . .: Davenport, p. 270.

48 "I was at the nerve-center . . .": Davenport, p. 263.

49 The party of Harding, . . .: Johnson, p. 108.

III. WIN WITH WILLKIE

51 "cooperate with the Republican . . .": Johnson, p. 114.

53 "completely out of touch . . .": Parmet and Hecht, p. 211.

57 "opponents of force . . .": Willkie, p. 266.

57 "force of free enterprise . . .": Ibid.

57 "He agreed with Mr. Roosevelt's . . .": Johnson, p. 124.

57 Willkie would receive fifty-three percent . . .: Gallup, 1:238.

65 the question of a third term.: James A. Farley, telephone interview, New York City.

65 "only the strong can be free . . .": Barnard, p. 207.

65 Gallup gave Willkie . . .: Gallup, 1:243.

66 were forming in virtually every county.: *Report of Associated Willkie Clubs of Illinois,* October 21–24, 1940, Willkie Manuscripts Department, Lilly Library, University of Indiana, Bloomington, Indiana.

66 "more than half of that number . . .": *Report of Willkie Clubs of Illinois,* November 1940, ibid.

67 "hundreds of Peorians—eager to join . . .": *Willkie Club News: Peoria, Illinois,* October 22, 1940, ibid.

67 listed "suggested salient points," . . .: *Idaho Willkie Club News,* late September 1940, vol. 1, No. 2, ibid.

68 "almost broke the Democratic . . .": "The Willkie Campaign," *Journal of Politics* (May 1952), p. 256.

69 and had now reached 117.: Barnard, p. 557.

69 The electoral vote disparity . . .: Edward Franklin Cox, *State and National Voting: In Federal Elections 1910–1970* (Hamden, Conn.: Archon Books, 1972), p. 254.

69 "one of the most exciting . . .": Henry O. Evjen, "The Willkie Campaign: An Unfortunate Chapter in Republican Leadership," *Journal of Politics* 14 (May 1952):241.

IV. THE GENERAL

73 "a citizens movement which would ask . . .": The Reminiscences of Charles F. Willis, Jr. (1968), 50 pp., in the Oral History Collection of Columbia University, hereafter Willis, OHC (Eisenhower Administration Project).

73 "We thought either he or General MacArthur . . .": Ibid.

73 "Yes, and their integrity . . .": Ibid.

73 "he was already established . . .": Ibid.

73 "the concern about the Korean War . . .": Ibid.

74 "let's stop talking . . .": The Reminiscences of Stanley M. Rumbough, Jr. (1977), 43 pp., in the Oral History Collection of Columbia University, hereafter Rumbough, OHC (Eisenhower Administration Project).

74 "that New York was a dirty word, . . .": Ibid.

74 "Virgil, you have been standing . . .": Dwight D. Eisenhower, *Mandate for Change: 1953–56* (New York: Doubleday & Company, 1963), p. 5.

74 "General, there is nothing . . .": Ibid.

75 my decision to remove . . . : Ibid., p. 7.

75 "the necessary and wise subordination . . .": Ibid.

76 "conveniently overlooked.": Ibid.

77 "Since I was still an officer . . .": Ibid., p. 12.

78 "with politics almost the single subject . . .": Ibid., p. 16.

78 "I'm not interested . . .": Ibid.

78   "We decided," said Willis, . . . : Willis, OHC.

78   "was simply . . . to organize . . .": Rumbough, OHC.

79   "gave us encouragement, . . .": Willis, OHC.

79   "about how to set up stores . . .": Ibid.

79   "We didn't just pick . . .": Ibid.

80   "It was a pretty difficult thing . . .": Rumbough, OHC.

81   "for almost six months . . .": Willis, OHC.

82   And while he did not say . . .: The Reminiscences of Lucius D. Clay, Sr., 1977, 113 pp., in the Oral History Collection of Columbia University, hereafter Clay, OHC (Eisenhower Administration Project).

83   Mr. Eisenhower has never voted . . .: Sherman Adams, *Firsthand Report: The Story of the Eisenhower Administration* (New York: Harper & Brothers, 1961), p. 13.

83   he called a press conference, . . .: *New York Times,* January 7, 1952.

83   "gives an accurate account . . .": Kenneth I. Davis, *The Politics of Honor: A Biography of Adlai E. Stevenson* (New York: G. P. Putnam's Sons, 1967), pp. 257-58.

83   Under no circumstances will I ask . . .: Ibid., p. 258.

84   "our problem was solved, . . .": Adams, p. 13.

85   "I'll get the people, . . .": The Reminiscences of Jacqueline Cochran (1975), 105 pp., in the Oral History Collection of Columbia University, hereafter Cochran, OHC (Aviation Project).

85   "tied right in with . . .": Rumbough, OHC.

86   "We couldn't get rid of the people . . .": Cochran, OHC.

86   "was such an incredibly difficult task . . .": The Reminiscences of Arthur Gray, Jr. (1977), 32 pp., in the Oral History Collection of Columbia University, hereafter Gray, OHC (Eisenhower Administration Project).

87   On February 10 . . .: Eisenhower, p. 20

88   "Tears were just running . . .": Cochran, OHC.

88   I want you to go and see . . .: Ibid.

88   that the time had come . . .: Clay, OHC.

89   At this meeting . . .: Eisenhower, p. 21.

90   Although all involved seemed confident . . .: This memo is among the papers at the Dwight D. Eisenhower Library, Abilene, Kansas.

91   "Look, this is too big . . .": Rumbough, OHC.

91   It was either get us to come . . .: Willis, OHC.

95   "So what we did, . . .": Gray, OHC.

95   "Our candidate was not there. . . .": Ibid.

95   "Yes, it was natural . . .": Gray, OHC.

96   "received fifty percent of the total . . .": Herbert S. Parmet, *Eisenhower and the American Crusades* (New York: Macmillan Company, 1972), p. 54.

96   Yet 108,696 people . . .: Ibid.

96   to 129,076 who put . . .: Ibid.

97   So in California we had . . .: Rumbough, OHC.

98 to help change the Chicago anti-Ike . . .: Gray, OHC.
108 were changing to 19 for General . . .: Ibid., p. 53.
108 Ralph Cake, a thoroughgoing professional . . .: The Reminiscences of Ralph H. Cake (1977), 78 pp., in the Oral History Collection of Columbia University, hereafter Cake, OHC (Eisenhower Administration Project).
109 probably had had as much to do . . .: Ibid.

V. "I LIKE IKE"

112 physical fact symbolized . . .: Emmet John Hughes, *The Ordeal of Power: A Political Memoir of the Eisenhower Years* (New York: Atheneum Press, 1963), p. 20.
114 "They were called upon to do . . .": Cake, OHC.
114 a minority party and the Democrat . . .: Ibid.
115 "we had to get votes away . . .": Clay, OHC.
115 "and were for Ike . . .": Clay, OHC.
115 What we tried to do . . .: Rumbough, OHC.
116 "very emotional and rather difficult time.": The Reminiscences of Mary Pillsbury Lord (1980), 428 pp., in the Oral History Collection of Columbia University, hereafter Lord, OHC (Eisenhower Administration Project).
116 "We'll go our way and not bother . . .": Rumbough, OHC.
117 A discussion took place . . .: Dwight D. Eisenhower Library, Abilene, Kansas.
117 that the citizens for . . .: Ibid.
117 "From then on,": Rumbough, OHC.
119 "Well, if you were such a hot . . .": The Reminiscences of Dr. Charles Masterson and Howard K. Pyle, Jr. (1980), 134 pp., in the Oral History Collection of Columbia University, hereafter Masterson and Pyle, OHC (Eisenhower Administration Project).
119 under Citizens for Eisenhower . . .: Rumbough, OHC.
121 "on the basis that . . .": Willis, OHC.
123 With the parade, . . .: Gray, OHC.
123 "became a trademark of . . .": Willis, OHC.
123 "Ike said the first thing . . .": Gray, OHC.
125 "Many of his [Eisenhower's] . . .": Adams, p. 37.
125 "felt vastly more concerned . . .": Hughes, p. 39.
125 "probably one of the last . . .": Willis, OHC.
126 "went into a lot of areas . . .": Gray, OHC.
127 "we didn't use television. . . .": Gray, OHC.
127 "had a large television . . .": Willis, OHC.
128 all the people who came in . . .: Gray, OHC.
128 [Hauge] came into the Citizens office . . .: Ibid.
129 He is now president . . .: Ibid.
129 He just came in to help, . . .: Ibid.
129 The exciting part to me . . .: Willis, OHC.
130 "No, it was just one . . .": Ibid.

130 "After three days on the Campaign Train . . .": In Dwight D. Eisenhower Library, Abilene, Kansas.
130 "There are 5,104 Clubs . . .": Ibid.
130 "ELECTION OUTCOME HIGHLY UNCERTAIN, . . .": James A. Hagerty, "Election Outcome Highly Uncertain, Survey Indicates," *New York Times,* November 3, 1952, p. 1.
131 He received not only fifty-five percent . . .: Richard C. Bain, *Convention Decisions and Voting Records* (Washington, D.C.: The Brookings Institution, 1960), p. 292.
131 There was a vacuum created . . .: Gray, OHC.

VI. THE GOVERNOR

138 "It was a good speech, . . .": Davis, p. 123.
143 "Whatever the truth . . .": *Time,* January 26, 1952.
145 "I am still a candidate . . .": Walter Johnson, *How We Drafted Adlai Stevenson* (New York: Alfred A. Knopf, 1955), p. 6.
146 "Stevenson seems effectively . . .": *New York Times,* April 17, 1952.
146 I am told that I am here . . .: April 17, 1952.
147 "to draw the Governor . . .": "The Reluctant Candidate—An Inside Story," *Reporter,* November 24, 1953.
147 "If we give up, . . .": Walter Johnson, p. 33.
148 "Why don't you put that question . . .": *Chicago Sun-Times,* May 2, 1952.
149 Have just seen circular letter . . .: Walter Johnson, p. 54.
150 The movement to draft . . .: Joseph Alsop and Stewart Alsop, July 17, 1952.
152 "Oh! Well, keep in touch . . .": Walter Johnson, p. 76.
155 "There is a statement in . . .": Ibid.
160 "I prefer Stevenson. . . .": Ibid., p. 75.
161 "they were on the conservative side. . . .": Ibid., p. 89.
161 "no political coercive power" . . .: Ibid.
161 "no political tools.": Ibid.
161 "only one concrete reward: . . .": Ibid., p. 90.
162 *"How do we know . . .":* Ibid.
162 "Without funds, without traditional . . .": Ibid., pp. 93–94.
166 This is not the time for . . .: Walter Johnson, *The Papers of Adlai E. Stevenson,* vol. 4 (Boston: Little, Brown & Company, 1974), pp. 11–14.
167 "The 'reluctant candidate' . . .": James Reston, *New York Times,* July 22, 1952.
167 "Yes, I will. . . .": Johnson, *How We Drafted Adlai Stevenson,* p. 111.
168 "done an amazing piece of work . . .": Ibid., p. 113
168 a group of delegates representing . . .: Ibid., p. 114.
171 "we want to get on . . .": Johnson, *How We Drafted Adlai Stevenson,* p. 130.
171 "left at the post . . .": John Madigan, *Chicago Herald American,* July 22, 1952.

172 "We are not going to nominate . . .": Johnson, *How We Drafted Adlai Stevenson,* p. 134.

174 "It was then that the Convention . . .": Felix Belair, Jr., *New York Times,* July 25, 1952.

174 "easily the biggest, noisiest, . . .": Howard Norton, *Baltimore Sun,* July 25, 1952.

175 "I had hoped they would not . . .": Statement, Governor Adlai Stevenson, July 24, 1952.

175 "As the Convention struggled . . .": William S. White, *New York Times,* July 25, 1952.

175 "In no time at all . . .": "The Democrats Debate, Loud in Zeal and Anger," *Life,* August 4, 1952, p. 19.

176 "That's the trouble with dealing . . .": Johnson, *How We Drafted Adlai Stevenson,* p. 149.

177 Then, state after state swung . . .: *Official Report of the Proceedings of the Democratic National Convention* (Washington: Democratic National Committee, 1954), pp. 456, 484, 538.

180 Perhaps it can be concluded . . .: The American Political Science Association, *Presidential Nominating Politics in 1952: The National Story,* 5 vols.

VII. "MADLY FOR ADLAI"

182 "more than anyone . . .": James Q. Wilson, *The Amateur Democrat* (Chicago: University of Chicago Press, 1962), p. 22.

182 "Who can name . . . ?": Memorial Services for Mrs. Franklin Delano Roosevelt, Cathedral of St. John the Divine, New York City, November 17, 1962, cited in Johnson, *The Papers of Adlai E. Stevenson,* vol. 8.

183 "Adlai Stevenson . . . brought more . . .": Richard G. Walton, *New York Times Book Review,* February 18, 1973.

183 "gift of making life larger . . .": Edward P. Doyle, ed., *As We Knew Adlai: The Stevenson Story by Twenty-Two Friends,* with a Foreword by Adlai E. Stevenson, III, "Affection and Always Respect" (New York: Harper & Row, 1966), p. 212.

184 "I could not accept the nomination . . .": Kenneth S. Davis, *A Prophet in His Own Country: The Triumphs and Defeats of Adlai E. Stevenson* (New York: Doubleday & Company, 1957), p. 394.

191 All of them became convinced . . .: Davis, *The Politics of Honor: A Biography of Adlai E. Stevenson,* pp. 277–78.

195 "There is deep personal satisfaction . . .": Adlai E. Stevenson, *Major Campaign Speeches of Adlai E. Stevenson,* with an introduction by Adlai E. Stevenson (New York: Random House, 1952), p. 57.

199 When an American says . . .: Stevenson, *Major Campaign Speeches of Adlai E. Stevenson,* p. 21.

199 We have learned from the past . . .: Bessie R. James and Mary Waterstreet, comps., *Adlai's Almanac, the Wit and Wisdom of Stevenson of Illinois*

(New York: Henry Schuman, Inc., 1952), p. 70. The reference is to serious race riots in Cicero in July 1951.

200 "I have been much interested . . .": Ibid., p. 42.
205 "a convert is a Republican . . .": Ibid., p. 42.
215 Stevenson was essentially . . .: Edward Costikyan, *Behind Closed Doors* (New York: Harcourt Brace & World, 1966), pp. 18–19.
219 Someone asked me, . . .: Stevenson, *Major Campaign Speeches of Adlai E. Stevenson*, p. 319.
219 By a popular vote . . .: Bain, p. 292.
220 "The enthusiasm for Stevenson . . .": Wilson, p. 113.

VIII. THE ROLE OF VOLUNTEERS IN CAMPAIGNS SINCE 1952

225 The organizational secret . . .: David S. Broder, *The Party Is Over, the Failure of Politics in America* (New York: Harper & Row, 1971, 1972), pp. 18–19.
237 It's true that I have been . . .: Ibid.

Index